SSADM 4+ FOR RAPI DEV

DAVID HARGRAVE

McGRAW-HILL BOOK COMPANY

London · New York · St Louis · San Francisco · Auckland · Bogotá · Caracas · Lisbon
Madrid · Mexico · Milan · Montreal · New Delhi · Panama · Paris · San Juan
São Paulo · Singapore · Sydney · Tokyo · Toronto

Published by
McGRAW-HILL Book Company Europe
Shoppenhangers Road, Maidenhead, Berkshire, SL6 2QL, England
Telephone 01628 23432
Facsimile 01628 770224

British Library Cataloguing in Publication Data
Hargrave, David
  SSADM 4+ for Rapid Systems Development.–
(International Software Engineering
Series)
I. Title II. Series
658.40380285421

  ISBN 0-07-709082-9

Library of Congress Cataloging-in-publication Data
Hargrave, David.
    SSADM 4+ for rapid systems development / David Hargrave.
      p.   cm.
    Includes index.
    ISBN 0-07-709082-9 (pbk. : alk. paper)
    1. System design. 2. Electronic data processing–Structured
techniques.   I. Title.
QA76.9.S88H368
658.4′038′011–dc20   95-37896
                                                       CIP

McGraw-Hill

A Division of The **McGraw·Hill** *Companies*

1234 CUP 9876

Typeset by Keyword Typesetting Services Ltd, Wallington, Surrey
Printed and bound in Great Britain at the University Press, Cambridge.
Printed on permanent paper in compliance with ISO Standard 9706.

To my parents

CONTENTS

PREFACE

SSADM is one of the most widely used system development methods in the UK. Although it originated in the public sector it is now used by an increasing number of private sector organizations. In its time, SSADM has been through a number of changes, with Version 4 of the method being published in 1990.

Many things have changed in the Information Systems (IS) world since 1990. Relational databases, not hierarchical or CODASYL databases, now provide the standard development environment. Fourth generation languages, not COBOL, are often the preferred programming medium. Personal computers, which were often regarded as executive toys by 'serious' IT departments, are now viewed as a major hardware platform and can be linked together in client/server mode. Graphical user interfaces, which were restricted to a few specialist machines such as the Apple Macintosh, have now become common as Windows has become all-pervasive. Alongside this has come a growth in visual programming and development tools, which facilitate the construction of these interfaces. Prototypes used to be developed as throwaway products whose sole purpose was to validate user requirements. Increasingly they evolve into the final system. Finally, appearing from over the horizon is Object Orientation. There have been doubts about this approach, but in the author's opinion this will become the preferred development method in the near future.

These changes have not been limited to the information systems world. The whole business environment has been subject to increasing pressure. Activities have to be performed more quickly and cost-effectively. Gone are the days of the two-year project. Organizations have been flattened and downsized. Traditional IT departments, with their rigid demarcations between project managers, analysts and programmers, have not escaped these trends. More and more, systems people are changing into business-focused developers who have a smattering of all the necessary skills and who operate in small flexible teams rather than the cumbersome bureaucracies of the past. Finally, as more and more organizations retreat to their core activities, IS is often viewed as an activity ripe for outsourcing. This raises immediate issues of contracts, monitoring and control.

It is unlikely that SSADM Version 4 could have been designed to anticipate all these changes. This book emerged out of an attempt in 1993 to develop SSADM to meet some of these concerns. In particular, I was looking for a cut-down version of SSADM, 'Rapid SSADM', that would be of use in developing small systems for relational databases within a limited timescale. Most of these systems used 4GL techniques and involved prototyping. A secondary objective was to provide alternatives for those techniques that I and others had found time consuming and difficult. These were Entity Life Histories, Relational Data Analysis and Logicalization. Much of this work was used on a successful series of courses at the Civil Service College.

Shortly after the completion of the manuscript for this book SSADM Version 4.2 was announced. This was to be the first in a series of modifications to SSADM which are collectively known as SSADM 4+. Interestingly enough, many of the changes advocated in Version 4.2 were similar to those used in Rapid SSADM. Two which spring to mind were the early use of business analysis techniques and the attachment of processing to the Access Paths. There were differences in that, for example, Rapid SSADM placed Business Analysis in Logicalization, rather than at the start of the method. Such differences appear to be cosmetic rather than fundamental, and with this in mind Rapid SSADM has been altered slightly to bring it in line with Version 4.2.

This book has three parts. In Part One we set the scene for Rapid SSADM, discussing the environment in which it can be used and the impact of project management techniques and CASE tools. Part Two contains a detailed account of Rapid SSADM. 'Standard' SSADM techniques such as Dataflow Modelling are not discussed in great detail here as they are more than adequately covered elsewhere. Alternative techniques are suggested for Entity Life Histories and Relational Data Analysis. It is worth stressing that these are alternatives, not replacements. In Part Three of the book, the impact of Rapid Application Development, Evolutionary Development, Graphical User Interfaces and Object Orientation is considered.

ACKNOWLEDGEMENTS

I must first of all thank my employers, the Civil Service College, for giving me support and encouragement while writing this book. Thanks also go to my colleagues Chris Browne, my former colleague Stuart Macoustra and to Michael Collins of Weavers Business Solutions for ideas and advice. Janet Blowers O'Neil of the CCTA provides a technical review of the material. Roy Denness of the Civil Service College deserves particular thanks for his painstaking analysis and helpful comments made about the many drafts of this book. Finally I must thank my wife Margaret and my son Paul for their forbearance and understanding on the numerous occasions when I was immersed in this work.

I am grateful to the DSDM Consortium for permission to base Fig. 20.2 on the DSDM Framework Diagram which is their copyright.

SSADM is the registered tradesmark of CCTA.

LIST OF ABBREVIATIONS

BAM	Business Activity Model
BSO	Business System Option
CASE	Computer Aided Software Engineering
CID	Cycle Initiation Document
CLDD	Composite Logical Data Diagram
DBMS	Database Management System
DFD	Dataflow Diagram
DFM	Dataflow Model
DSDM	Dynamic Systems Development Method
EAP	Enquiry Access Path
ECD	Effect Correspondence Diagram
ELH	Entity Life History
EPD	Elementary Process Description
FCIM	Function Component Implementation Map
GUI	Graphical User Interface
HCI	Human–computer interface
IS	Information systems
LDM	Logical Data Model
LDS	Logical Data Structure
OO	Object Orientation
PBS	Product Breakdown Structure
PDI	Process Data Interface
PID	Project Initiation Document
RAD	Rapid Application Development
RDA	Relational Data Analysis
SSADM	Structured Systems Analysis and Design Method
TSO	Technical System Option

UPM	Update Process Model
WIMP	Windows, Icons, Menus and Pointing Devices

PART
ONE

SETTING THE SCENE

ONE

INTRODUCTION

1.1 THE CURRENT STATE OF SSADM

Go into any organization that uses or has used SSADM, the Structured Systems Analysis and Design Method, and ask for views about it and more than likely you will be assailed by comments such as:

'Too bureaucratic and long-winded'
'It seems like constant form filling'
'We don't have time to do all that sort of stuff'
'An old-fashioned dinosaur, a solution for the problems of yesterday'
'It can't really cope with modern technology and techniques'

Sometimes it seems that nobody has a good word to say for SSADM. The purpose of this chapter is to explain why this situation has arisen and to indicate a path that might be taken to improve the situation. In particular, we will see how the latest version of SSADM, Version 4.2, will change many of these negative attitudes, and will provide us with the basis for a simple development method relevant to the needs of the mid and late 1990s.

Before doing this it might be as well to ask whether it really is worth the effort. Perhaps SSADM has had its day, and ought to be jettisoned in favour of some more up-to-date and fashionable alternative methodology, which at the moment would be likely to have an Object Orientated (OO) or Graphical User Interface (GUI) flavour. There are two main reasons why I feel that this should not be done, and why therefore we should follow an evolutionary rather than a revolutionary path.

First, there is much that is good in SSADM. There are things in it that are difficult, things that are of less relevance today than in the past, but this should not disguise the fact that much of SSADM is still applicable to modern system development. After all, many of the techniques used were in existence well before the advent of SSADM, have stood the test of time and there is no reason to suppose that they are of any less relevance today. The negative comments might merely be indicative of the fact that when asked their opinion about anything, people often tend to complain about the bad and ignore the good. Ditching SSADM merely because of a few minor irritants is rather like throwing the baby out with the bath water.

The high level of investment in existing systems, staff skills and CASE tools provides a second reason for not abandoning SSADM. In the public sector, for example, the majority of existing systems have been designed using SSADM. These systems presumably need maintenance, both now and in the future. The task of re-engineering such systems to comply with another methodology should not be underestimated. So whatever our feelings, SSADM-designed systems are likely to be in existence for many years to come. Alongside this investment in systems is a comparable investment in people. Thousands of analysts have been trained in SSADM, many even holding formal qualifications in the subject. With the advent of new technology and new business procedures, such training might appear less relevant, but it does provide a bedrock of skills applicable to most types of systems development. Unless there were very real gains in efficiency or effectiveness, the cost of retraining these people in a completely different methodology does not make economic sense.

Financial considerations are even more important when considering CASE tools. Many organizations have bought multiple copies of such items of software. The cost of replacing all these copies would be enormous, even if the replacements were relatively cheap. This, however, is not likely to be the case, since the size of the SSADM market has led to an increasing number of such tools, which in turn has caused a sharp decline in their price. Any methodology which replaces SSADM is likely to be new and so will have the support of fewer and more expensive CASE tools.

If we do not abandon SSADM, then what can we do? We need to customize standard SSADM in order to make it easier to use for current developments. This will entail a slimming down of the method, offering alternatives for difficult techniques, and providing the flexibility to use SSADM for different lifecycles. That is the purpose of this book.

1.2 A HISTORICAL PERSPECTIVE

Before changing SSADM, it may be as well to explore the reasons for some of the negative attitudes. To do this, it is best to go back to the beginning, to consider the environment in which SSADM was developed, and to explore the extent to which SSADM has adapted to changing circumstances.

Prior to the arrival in 1981 of SSADM, systems were developed in a somewhat *ad hoc* manner. Many organizations had their own particular standards, but others quite often revelled in the lack of them. Many analysts of the era regarded systems analysis and design as just an overglorified form of programming. This is, however, to miss the point. Not only do systems involve a much closer liaison with users, but they are much larger than programs. Without proper product descriptions, resource allocations and some form of benchmarking, system development projects are liable to spiral out of control. As standards were not universally applied, some projects were abandoned, but even for those completed, the final products were often delivered late and over budget. Sometimes, problems even continued after implementation. Thus when a system was in place, the lack of any generally accepted documentation standards made enhancements or just plain day-to-day maintenance very difficult. This was by no means an insignificant problem, given that such maintenance tasks used to absorb up to 70 per cent of the resources of a typical IT department.

It should not be thought that the UK was alone in facing these problems. At the end of the 1970s, much research was concentrated on this area. A great deal of effort was expended in developing methods which all came to be classified as types of Structured Systems Analysis, a term first used by De Marco (1979). Other work influential at that time was that of Gane and Sarson (1977). SSADM was really CCTA's own version of this type of method. (CCTA is the UK government body responsible for IS matters.) It was not developed in isolation, but embraced many of the techniques introduced by others working in the field.

At that time, the major difficulties confronting system developers were of a technical rather than of a business nature. The majority of computer systems of that era were large batch systems running on mainframe computers. In many cases they were merely automated versions of existing clerical procedures. From the development point of view, this meant that projects were quite straightforward. The requirements were generally well understood, and design often consisted merely of transferring current documentation onto the computer. Any difficulties that did exist were the technical ones in actually making the transfer. After capture, data was generally held in a collection of semi-related files, or, at best, in a CODASYL database such as IDMS-X. Programs were usually written in a third generation language such as COBOL. Such programs were difficult to write and even more difficult to test. A large army of people was engaged on writing new programs, and a substantially greater army involved in their maintenance. From a management point of view, the major task was not so much in establishing what the new system should do but rather in ensuring that this army of programmers was well equipped to overcome any technical difficulties. Thus a major preoccupation of SSADM in the past was to help in *designing the system right*, rather than in *designing the right system*!

Since those days, SSADM has been developed, primarily in order to keep it abreast of the changing technological and business environment. Version 1 was released in 1981, with Version 2 following shortly after. Version 3, the first to become an open standard, was released in 1986, while Version 4 was released in 1990. The latest version, Version 4.2, was released in May 1995. Version 4, for example, was the first to include specification prototyping as one of its techniques. Despite these enhancements, SSADM still displays its ancestry in the world of big mainframe systems and unambiguous requirements. This is nowhere more evident than in its very structure. SSADM is an example of a system development method that conforms to what is now called the waterfall model of systems development.

Figure 1.1 illustrates where SSADM fits within such a model. From this, it is clear that the whole of the system development task can be divided up into a number of

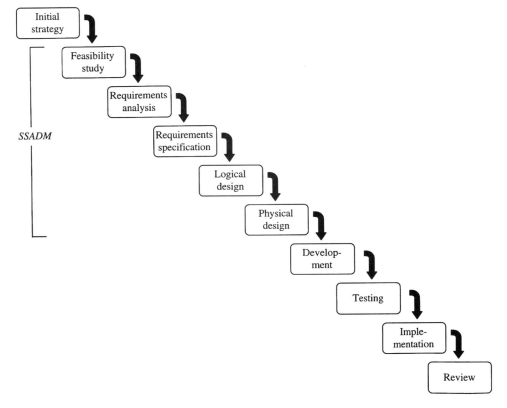

Fig. 1.1   The waterfall method

phases in which output from each phase will cascade down to form the input to the next. The phases are:

- *Initial Strategy*. Identification of a project that will support business objectives.
- *Feasibility Study*. Deciding if the project is technically and financially feasible.
- *Requirements Analysis*. Establishing requirements for the new system. (This may entail documenting any existing system.)
- *Requirements Specification*. Specifying the requirements in more detail.
- *Logical Design*. Designing the new system as far as possible without considering the effect of the target hardware and software.
- *Physical Design*. Designing the database/files and specifying the programs for the chosen hardware and software platform.
- *Development*. Traditionally known as programming, but now more usually referred to as system development, build or construction.
- *Testing*. May consist of unit, system and user acceptance testing.
- *Implementation*. Handing over the system. This might involve data capture, data conversion, user training and production of manuals.

- *Review.* A customer evaluation of the system some months after it has been operational. Has the system met the stated aims and objectives? Have the savings identified been realized?

Of these, SSADM covers those specifically concerned with system analysis and design.

The waterfall model is a very good for those projects in which requirements are well known and stable. Payroll is a case in point. The output is well defined, and there is clear agreement as to the rules that must be applied in the calculation of pay and tax. For any system like this in which the desired end-point is clear, a top-down approach, which divides the task into a number of well-defined sub-tasks, is bound to be logical, fast and efficient. Such an approach also gives the systems development team some idea of progress and, unlike some prototyping approaches say, does at least hold out the prospect of the project coming to a definite end. There are other advantages with the waterfall model. Given that the scope, objectives, inputs and outputs of each phase are usually clear, it provides a good template for those wishing to manage a project as a series of contracts.

To the system developer SSADM confers benefits over and above those it possesses by virtue of its adopting a waterfall approach. Most tools and techniques used in SSADM have a long and distinguished history, being used well before Version 1 of the method was developed. SSADM never was a new and revolutionary method, but was really a collection of existing best practices, repackaged into a standard format. Many of these techniques do cross-check each other, so adding to the confidence developers can place in any given product.

Next, SSADM recognizes that users are the ultimate owners of a system and so they are given a major role in any project. Not only do they actively review many of the products produced, they can also steer the project in the direction that they want by means of the substantial contribution they make in the choice of solutions. Finally, management can only be reassured by the existence of an extensive supporting infrastructure for SSADM. It is a standard method, it does have government support, and it does have a large user base in the UK. Thus there is a wide availability of training, consultancy and software support. Indeed, so extensive is this infrastructure that CCTA felt it beneficial to regulate the market. For the trainers they introduced accreditation, for the consultants and users of SSADM a Certificate of Proficiency and for CASE tools vendors a conformance scheme.*

All this sounds wonderful. So what went wrong? Why were there so many negative comments at the start of this chapter? Some of the problems are specific to SSADM, but many are to do with the waterfall method itself. Many of the latter are explored at length by Gilb (1979). The major ones are:

1. *Requirements have to be established in full at the outset.* This may have been fine in the past, when the requirements were reputedly clear and stable, but is less useful

---

*The schemes for trainers and consultants are run in tandem and are administered on behalf of CCTA by the Information Systems Examination Board (ISEB) Ltd. All consultants have to attend an accredited training course and also have to demonstrate competence by passing an exam in SSADM to obtain this Certificate. ISEB accredit the trainers and police the examination procedure. CASE tools are the subject of a Conformance Scheme. They are independently tested to ensure that they do in fact conform to SSADM.

today when systems are often completely new and the analysts are presented only with the vaguest of requirements. Even when there is clear agreement as to the requirements, today's precarious business environment means that they frequently change.

2. *The long delivery times.* The first time users get anything useful is after the development phase when the programs have been written. Often this can take years, and so leaves the user in the position of funding vast amounts of work that do not have immediate results. This breeds a sense of anxiety, often transformed into anger if the final product is not really suitable.

3. *Risk.* In any but the most stable of environments, the waterfall method is something of a gamble. Indeed, the vaguer the requirements, the worse the odds become! The major reason for this is that a great deal of time and money is invested in the first few phases of the project. If those in charge of the project do not drive it in the right direction, perhaps because the requirements are not fully understood, then the project is likely to fail and a great deal of money will be wasted. Both Gilb (1988) and Boehm (1988) suggest approaches that do not risk so much at such an early stage.

4. *The lack of feedback.* The waterfall method seems to be based on a paradigm based in the engineering world. Engineers building a bridge do not start from scratch, but build according to a well-developed theory and also use common practical experience gained in building countless similar bridges. With our present state of knowledge, systems development is not like this. There is no generally accepted theory, and every project develops something that is not merely new, but is often innovative. Innovation, whether it be in the form of a work of art or of a design for a new car, demands constant feedback and reworking, something that seems at odds with the rigidities of the waterfall approach.

5. *The lack of user involvement.* The waterfall approach in itself does not lead naturally to user involvement. Users state their requirements at the start, become involved with testing and implementation at the end, but have little formal input in the middle. With such an approach it is inevitable that the concerns of those developing the system are primarily directed towards the technology rather than the users. The first time they need to worry about the reaction of the users is at the end, when it might well be too late.

Although some of these shortcomings are addressed by the inclusion of additional techniques within the method, with, for example, the lack of user involvement being countered by user reviews and user options, SSADM does add a few problems of its own. At first, any SSADM project would appear to take too long and to consume a great deal of resources. There is far too much documentation, some of it merely repeating things found on other pieces of documentation. Practitioners often say that they find it inconceivable to complete an SSADM project without the use of a CASE tool. This surely is an admission of defeat. In the past large projects were completed with no more than pen and paper. An appropriate CASE tool might have made the delivery of the final product a little more efficient, but such a tool was not essential. Furthermore, despite assertions to the contrary, SSADM sometimes appears prescriptive and inflexible. Many of the steps in the method are tightly entwined. This is very much the case with those that relate to Entity Life Histories (ELHs), Effect Correspondence Diagrams

(ECDs) and Update Process Models. It is difficult to know what could be left out, and what would be the knock-on effect of doing so on the other steps. These difficulties are not made any easier by the baroque complications of some of the techniques. Entity Life Histories in particular now seem so esoteric as to be beyond the reach of the ordinary practitioner.* As it is hard enough to use them as intended, their customization merely adds another level of difficulty. This overall difficulty and lack of flexibility makes it hard to apply SSADM to lifecycles other than the waterfall model.

Much of SSADM is still influenced by the concerns of third generation programming languages. Thus is understandable to some extent, given its origins in the world of big government systems and COBOL. Thus large tracts of Version 4, and even of Version 4.2, are devoted to the concerns of programming. This is certainly the case with most of Logical Design, where the techniques of Jackson Structured Programming were imported directly into SSADM. This may have been something that would have been extremely useful in earlier versions of SSADM, which were targeted towards systems developed in COBOL or something similar, but it is hard to see its relevance to projects developed in the mid-1990s using modern 4GLs or even Object Orientated languages. Indeed, SSADM barely addresses the question of 4GLs at all, with world-wide standards such as SQL rating hardly a mention. Similar comments can be made about databases. Physical design seems targeted at CODASYL databases such as IDMS-X rather than relational databases. For example, the standard universal database design rules of step 620 in Version 4, with its groupings of entities, are not applicable to most relational databases.

Technology has, of course, moved on since 1990. Obviously, one would not expect SSADM to be right up to the minute and incorporate such recent developments as client/server, Graphical User Interfaces and Object Orientation. One would like, however, a fairly flexible method which would allow the easy incorporation of any new techniques. Although this proved far from easy with SSADM Version 4, the new version of SSADM, with its reliance on a three-schema architecture, has proved far more flexible.

1.3 THE SOLUTION

From the previous section it might appear that the most promising course of action would be to abandon SSADM and start again from the beginning. However, as argued earlier, this is far too drastic and would mean throwing away many valuable skills and resources. The solution is to construct a cut-down version of SSADM with easier steps and less documentation and with many of the difficulties and obscurities removed. This smaller version of SSADM should be cleaner, in the sense that the interfaces between the steps and the inputs and outputs to each technique should be readily apparent. This

---

*The addition of operations, in particular the Gain and Lose operations, make entity life histories much larger and so more difficult to draw. Death events are also more complicated in Version 4.2. With Controlled Deaths it is possible for an event to appear on an ELH affecting an entity after it has been deleted (e.g. see CCTA (1995) User Guide 3-75). This is not so much a life history, more an after-life history! Disciplined quits advocated by some, with or without posits and admits, also appear complicated.

is essential if the method is to be amenable to further tailoring. If a document is omitted or a step is passed over the impact of doing so on the rest of the method should be readily apparent.

In Part Two of the book, this-cut down version, 'Rapid SSADM', is presented. It is based on SSADM Version 4.2, but also tries to retain some of the best features present in earlier versions of SSADM. It is aimed primarily at those developing the smaller type of system which is to be implemented on a relational database. Also for those techniques often viewed as difficult, alternatives are suggested. In a little more detail, the main features of Rapid SSADM are as follows:

1. An alternative top-down technique for logicalization. This unifies Logicalization with Business Analysis, producing a functional decomposition which is far more useful than a Logical Dataflow Diagram in discussions with users.
2. A more accessible approach to functions. Functions, not events, will be the main vehicle for defining the processing. To do this successfully, we need to tighten up the definition of a function. We will also abandon I/O structures.
3. An alternative technique for Relational Data Analysis. This replaces the usual column approach with a pictorial one based upon dependency diagrams.
4. An alternative approach to Entity Life Histories. This is intended for those who find the construction of Jackson type structures difficult. The diagrammatic convention adopted is that of syntax diagrams which are formally equivalent to the Jackson structures.
5. A unified approach to Access Paths. Enquiry Access Paths and Effect Correspondence Diagrams are merely regarded as separate aspects of the same technique. One Access Path will be produced per function, and so will be the nearest we will get to describing its internal workings. The technique is extended to include volumetrics and processing detail. The processing is described not by operations but on Access Path Descriptions, which are akin to the LEPOs and LUPOs of Version 3. Although this might seem like more work, it does replace much of stage 5.
6. The introduction of a step dedicated to the identification of possible data errors.
7. The abandonment of stage 5 of Version 4.2 of SSADM. As mentioned earlier, the processing detail is recorded on the Access Paths. Dialogue design is relegated to Physical Design by which time the user interface software will be known.
8. The streamlining of Physical Design so that it is now more focused on relational databases.

It should be noted that the alternative techniques really are alternatives. The standard columnar approach to relational data analysis and the Jackson approach to Entity Life Histories are equally as valid as the techniques presented here. The new techniques should be viewed as extending the analyst's toolkit so that a choice of approaches is available for dealing with any particular problem.

Part Three of the book deals with further modifications and enhancements to the method. We first explore the extent to which Rapid SSADM is amenable to tailoring and examine which documents and which steps could be omitted. A number of different routemaps through the method are provided. The most radical of these is probably the routemap called 'Rapid Rapid SSADM'. This is about the minimum one can do and still be sure that one is doing SSADM. In it, stages 3 to 6 are telescoped into four steps.

In the opinion of the author, this tailoring is merely a palliative. By speeding up SSADM, all we will really do is to find out that we have gone wrong in months rather than in years. What is missing is some feedback mechanism, something that enables systems to grow in a more organic way. This we do next when we consider the way in which SSADM can be modified to deal with evolutionary development. It seems to me that more and more systems will be developed this way in the future. Finally we consider the effect on the method of recent developments in the area of Graphical User Interfaces and Object Orientation.

1.4 IS THIS SSADM?

Given that a number of changes have been made to standard SSADM, the question must arise as to whether the method presented here should still be called SSADM, or whether it should be called something completely different. This question is answered by the Version 4.2 manual (CCTA (1995) p. 1-23), which states that any SSADM variant must address the following three issues:

1. The three-schema architecture must be the basis for separating concerns. In Chapter 2 we will see how the techniques of SSADM are mapped onto the three-schema architecture.
2. The Logical Data Model (LDM) should play a central role. This should be very apparent in this book.
3. The event is significant in specifying processing. In Chapter 4 we will see how business events trigger business activities, in Chapter 13 we will see how system events can lead to the identification of system processing, and in Chapter 18 we will discuss their role in commit units.

With this in mind, I will continue with the name 'Rapid SSADM'.

CHAPTER TWO

THE STRUCTURE OF RAPID SSADM

2.1 INTRODUCTION

The purpose of this chapter is to introduce the structure of Rapid SSADM and to describe in broad terms what each part of Rapid SSADM is trying to do. As SSADM Version 4.2 is now the standard version of SSADM, as far as possible the concepts and structure have been adopted from this version. Thus Rapid SSADM appears to be a reduced-version of SSADM. As mentioned earlier, this is not the end of the story. Rapid SSADM is the base model, which can be reduced or modified further, or even moulded into different lifecycles.

2.2 MODULES

SSADM is divided into a number of modules (see Fig. 2.1):

- *The Feasibility Study Module*. The purpose of this module is to decide whether or not to proceed with the project. In SSADM terms, a Feasibility Study is rather like a condensed version of the Requirements Analysis and Requirements Specification modules. The study starts with a consideration of the Project Initiation Document and ends with a number of options for future development being presented to the Project Board. The Board's decision and documentation supporting its choice goes to make up the Feasibility Report, which is the main product of this module. It is worth noting that the Feasibility Study is not mandatory, often being omitted on small to medium-sized projects, on those that are time critical, or on those that are deemed essential to the business by top management.

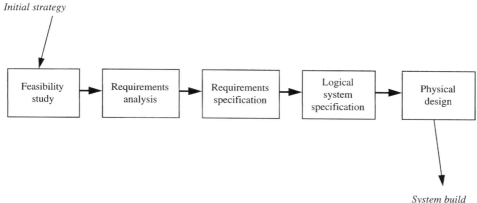

Fig. 2.1 The modules

- *The Requirements Analysis Module*. The purpose of this is to describe the current environment, to catalogue the user requirements, to list the proposed users of the new system and finally by means of Business System Options (BSOs) to decide which requirements are to be satisfied by the new system. The major products are:
  Requirements Catalogue
  Business Activity Model
  User Catalogue
  Current Data Flow Models
  Current Logical Data Model
  Selected Business System Option
- *The Requirements Specification Module*. Having decided in the previous module which requirements are to form the basis of the new system, the purpose here is to specify in greater detail what this might entail. The major products are:
  The Function Catalogue
  The Required Logical Data Model
- *Logical System Specification*. The purpose of this module is to complete the design of the system as far as is possible without considering the effects of the required physical environment such as the target hardware and software. This module is much reduced in the fast-track approach, the major product being a specified Technical Option.
- *Physical Design*. Here the design process is completed by considering the effects of the physical environment—in particular the hardware and the software. The major products are:
  Database design
  Program specifications
  It is worth mentioning that there is no 'standard' approach to this module laid down by SSADM. The major influence is the chosen database management system, and it is quite conceivable that what is done in this module might differ substantially for different products.

Modules were new to Version 4 of SSADM. Previously SSADM had been divided into stages, which were defined on a technical basis. Stages do still exist, but the modules represent the more business-orientated approach of both Version 4 and Version 4.2. A module is a unit of work that could be run as a single contract, and it is envisaged that each would be large enough to be commissioned at Project Board Level. In theory each of the modules could be completed by different organizations—for example, company A doing the Feasibility Study, the Requirements Analysis being done in-house, Company B doing the next module and so on. In practice, such a haphazard allocation of work is not really sensible, but the attempt to give SSADM this business orientation has had beneficial side-effects. First, the interfaces between the modules have to be clear and well defined, otherwise there would be the possibility of grave disagreements between contractors responsible for adjacent modules. Second, iteration of activities and reworking of products can only take place within a module. This is quite sensible, for if matters had deteriorated enough to entail the reworking of products from previous modules, which after all had been accepted by the Project Board, then something would be seriously wrong. The Project Board would have to be informed of these developments and of any extra expenditure that would have to be incurred in order to rectify the situation. Finally, most of the modules have a natural stop point at the end. For example, the Requirements Analysis Module ends with Business Systems Options, and one option is always to abandon the project.

Figure 2.2 shows the modules further split into stages. Note that the diagram is indeed correct, and the omission of Stage 5 is quite intentional. We will examine the stages in a little more detail below. When this is done, each stage will be accompanied by a diagram which shows the steps in the stage. It is worth stating immediately that the arrows on the diagrams merely show the sequencing of the various activities. They do *not* show the flows of products.

2.3 STAGE 0—THE FEASIBILITY STUDY

This is much the same as standard SSADM (Fig. 2.3). In summary, the steps in stage 0 are:

- *Step 020—Define the Problem*. Here the current environment is described in terms of business activity models, dataflow diagrams and logical data structures. Requirements for the new system are placed in the Requirements Catalogue and users of the system in the User Catalogue. A Problem Definition Statement summarizing the findings of this step is sent to the Project Board.
- *Step 030—Select Feasibility Options*. A number of options, each of which is a composite business and technical option, is prepared. The Project Board selects one of them.
- *Assemble the Feasibility Report*. In Version 4 this used to occupy a step on its own, but is now part of step 030. The document is to be produced in accordance with organizational standards. Typically such a report will contain
  Introduction and background
  Management Summary of findings
  Details of how the study was conducted

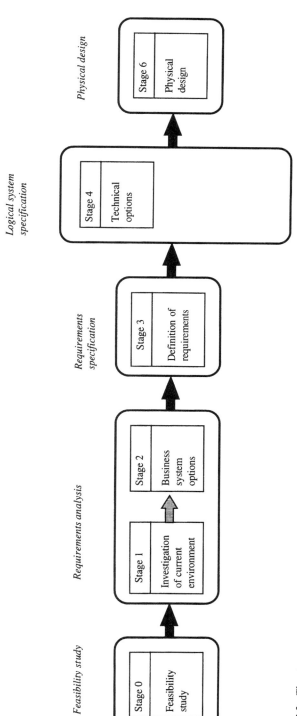

Fig. 2.2 The stages

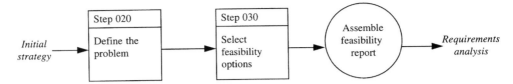

Fig. 2.3   Stage 0—The Feasibility Study

Existing IS support to the business
Future IS support required by the business
Details of the chosen option
Details of rejected options
Financial Assessment
Development Plan
Technical Annexes

The Feasibility Study is really like a high-level gallop through the first three stages of SSADM. It stands alone, separate from the rest of SSADM, and so is often the place where other techniques are used. In certain circumstances, for example, the Feasibility Study might involve the building of a prototype. This would certainly be the case where the *technical* feasibility of a system were in doubt. As the Feasibility Study module is treated more than adequately elsewhere (see, for example, CCTA (1990a), Ashworth and Slater (1993), Eva (1992), Skidmore *et al.* (1992), Weaver (1993), and Goodland and Slater (1995), we will not go into much more detail in this book.

2.4 STAGE 1—INVESTIGATION OF THE CURRENT ENVIRONMENT

With the exception of step 150, much of this is again the same as standard SSADM (Fig. 2.4). In summary, the steps are as follows:

- *Step 115—Develop Business Activity Model.* This is an attempt to model the system from a business perspective.
- *Step 120—Investigate and Define Requirements.* The main products from this step are the Requirements Catalogue and the User Catalogue.
- *Step 130—Investigate Current Processing.* Here the main processing activities of the system under investigation are documented by means of a Dataflow Model.
- *Step 140—Investigate Current Data.* In this step the data used by the current system is documented on the Logical Data Model.
- *Step 150—Define Logical View of Current Services.* The aim here is to describe the current system in terms of business functions rather than a physical organization. Traditionally this is done by means of a dataflow model, the much simpler technique of functional decomposition can be used instead.
- *Assemble Investigation Results.* Although not a named step in Version 4.2, this is an important end-of-stage activity. The major task is to review the products of the stage

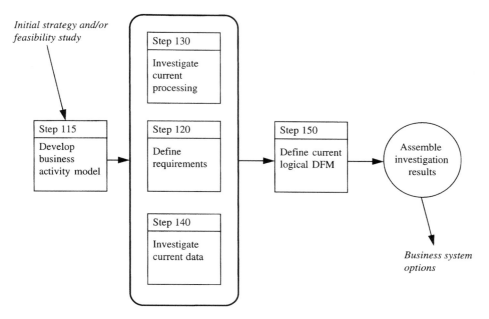

Fig. 2.4   Stage 1—Investigation of the Current Environment

and consolidate the Requirements Catalogue. The major products of the stage are collected together into a document called *The Current Services Description*.

Note that steps 120, 130 and 140 are bracketed together as they are usually done in parallel.

2.5 STAGE 2—BUSINESS SYSTEMS OPTIONS

Stage 2 is the same as in standard SSADM, and consists of only two steps (Fig. 2.5):

- *Step 210—Define Business Systems Options*. A menu of choices meeting the requirements of the system is developed.
- *Step 220—Select Business System Option*. The Project Board selects an option for the development of the future system.

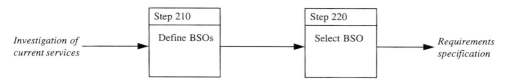

Fig. 2.5   Stage 2—Business System Options

2.6 STAGE 3—DEFINITION OF REQUIREMENTS

In this stage the consequences of the choice made in the previous stage are explored further. Each of the requirements addressed by the Business Systems Options are specified in much greater detail. It is in this stage where Rapid SSADM diverges in a significant way from standard SSADM. The major difference is in the choice of functions, rather than events, as being the main vehicle for defining the system processing. This is reflected in the steps which are as follows (Fig. 2.6):

- *Step 310—Define Required System Processing.* This is normally achieved by means of a Dataflow Model (or more likely a Functional Decomposition) for the required system.
- *Step 320—Define Required Data Model.* Here the Logical Data Model for the required system is produced.
- *Step 330—Develop System Functions.* This is the heart of Stage 3, where the processing is defined in terms of functions. To reflect their importance in Rapid SSADM, the Function Catalogue is reintroduced as the one place where all the system processing can be found. I/O structures are *not* produced.
- *Step 340—Perform Relational Data Analysis.* This is used to check the Logical Data Model. The traditional columnar approach can be used, but we will suggest an easier graphical alternative.
- *Step 350—Develop Specification Prototypes.* If prototypes are to be used to check that the system requirements have been correctly defined and to enhance the human–computer interface, this is the place for them. Prototyping can, however, assume a much more significant role in SSADM.
- *Step 360—Check System Processing.* The objective here is to plug any gaps in the Function Catalogue. This is done by producing Entity Life Histories. Although the more traditional Jackson approach can be used, a more user-friendly technique will be presented. As the purpose of this step is to check the processing, not to specify it, the choice of representation for Entity Life Histories really does not matter.
- *Step 365—Define Access Paths.* In this step, Access Paths and Access Path Descriptions are developed for each function, in order to further document the processing descriptions of the functions. In Rapid SSADM the concepts of Enquiry Access Paths and Effect Correspondence Diagrams found in Version 4 are unified and extended.
- *Step 367—Define Error Processing.* Here we consider what errors should be trapped by each function, and standard the messages via the Error Catalogue.
- *Step 370—Confirm System Objectives.* This is where we check that all the requirements have been covered and finalize Service Level Requirements.
- *Assemble Requirements Specification.* The Required System specification is produced.

2.7 STAGE 4—TECHNICAL SYSTEM OPTIONS

Stage 4 is the same as in standard SSADM, and just consists of two steps (Fig. 2.7):

- *Step 410—Define Technical Systems Options.* A menu of choices defining the target physical environment is developed.

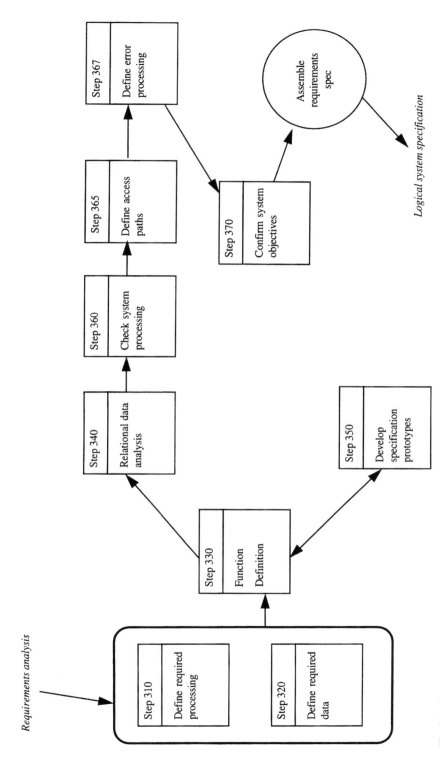

Requirements analysis

Step 310 | Define required processing

Step 320 | Define required data

Step 330 | Function Definition

Step 340 | Relational data analysis

Step 350 | Develop specification prototypes

Step 360 | Check system processing

Step 365 | Define access paths

Step 367 | Define error processing

Step 370 | Confirm system objectives

Assemble requirements spec

Logical system specification

Fig. 2.6   Stage 3—Definition of Requirements

19

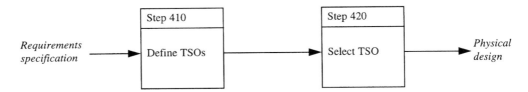

Fig. 2.7   Stage 4—Technical System Options

- *Step 420—Select Technical System Option.* The Project Board selects an option.

Most projects do not do as much as this, and the more usual strategies are covered in Chapter 17.

2.8 STAGE 6—PHYSICAL DESIGN

The major purpose of this step is to complete the design process by considering the effect of the chosen physical environment on the design (Fig. 2.8). The steps are:

- *Step 610—Prepare for Physical Design.* Here a decision is made as to how the database product can best be applied in an SSADM project.
- *Step 620—Create First Cut Database Design.* This is the first attempt to convert the Logical Data Model into a database design.
- *Step 630—Design the Dialogues.* These are produced for each user role and demonstrate how the on-line functions are to be packaged.

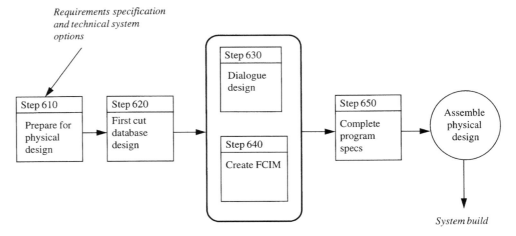

Fig. 2.8   Stage 6—Physical Design

- *Step 640—Create the Function Component Implementation Map (FCIM).* In this step a decision is made as to how the functions are to be physically implemented.
- *Step 650—Complete Program Specifications.* This is only done in those cases where the programs are likely to be substantial.
- *Assemble Physical Design.* A review of the final products.

Note that steps 630 and 640 need not be done in sequence, and it is quite possible that they would be done in the reverse order, or even in parallel. Much depends upon the nature of the physical environment. Although most of what is written in Chapter 18 on Physical Design makes reference to relational databases, the principles are, however, more widely applicable than this.

2.9 THE THREE-SCHEMA ARCHITECTURE

What has been presented so far in this chapter is the traditional Version 4 way of looking at the structure of SSADM, in which interest is focused on the activities taking place in the method. Of late, many in the SSADM community have come to believe that this view is somewhat old-fashioned and indeed is a positive handicap when attempting to customize the method. What has been proposed in Version 4.2 is the adoption of a Three-schema Architecture. Here the purpose of SSADM is considered to be the building of a model of the required system in which all the techniques of SSADM contribute towards the final product. Not all the techniques contribute in the same way, and the final system can be conceived as consisting of three aspects (sometimes called views or schemas) (Fig. 2.9):

- *The external design.* This is how the system appears to a user. It will be generally described in terms of screens and reports, and what in very broad terms the processes actually do.
- *The conceptual model.* This consists of the business rules which control the working of the system.
- *The internal design.* How the system is physically implemented.

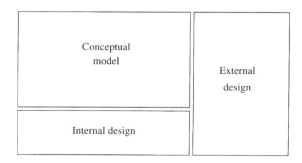

Fig. 2.9   The Three-schema Architecture

The Version 4.2 techniques map onto the three schemas as follows:

External design	**Conceptual model**	**Internal design**
Dataflow Model	Logical Data Model	First Cut Database Design
Function Definition	RDA	Process Data Interface
Dialogue Design	Entity Life Histories	
	ECDs and EAPs (Access Paths)	
	Process Models	

Most of these techniques, with the exception of Process Models and the Process Data Interface, will be discussed in subsequent chapters. The two missing techniques are not really appropriate to a Rapid Application of SSADM.

This way of viewing a system is not particularly new, but has its roots in the schema architecture first employed with CODASYL databases (see, for example, Date, 1990). It has resurfaced recently with the rise of client/server applications. Here the Three-schema Architecture is quite useful in separating what should be implemented on the client and what on the server.

The Three-schema Architecture demonstrates how the SSADM techniques can contribute to the final design. This, however, is only part of an SSADM project. To see how all the techniques work together, the System Development Template (Fig. 2.10), which includes the Three-schema Architecture, is needed.

The System Development Template gives an overview of how a complete systems development project fits together. It shows how the analysis and design activity relates

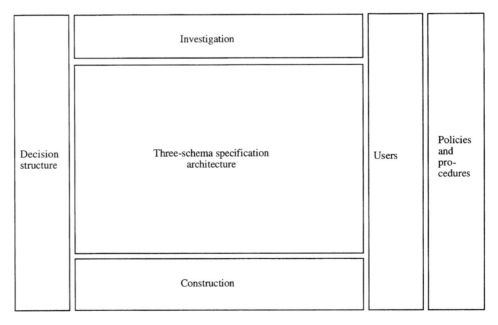

Fig. 2.10 The System Development Template

to the project as a whole and to the organizational environment. This template provides a structure for all types of projects:

- *Investigation*. This consists of those activities necessary to scope and establish baselines for the project. SSADM Documents produced are:
  Requirements catalogue
  Business Activity Model
  Current Dataflow Models
  Current Logical Data Model
- *Construction*. This entails the building of the physical database system. It is outside the scope of SSADM.
- *Decision Structure*. This is where management decisions are taken. The parts of SSADM that take place here are
  Business System Options
  Technical Systems Options
- *User Organization*. This is concerned with decisions about who is to use the system and how they are to use it. SSADM techniques used here are:
  User roles
  Work Practice Modelling
- *Policies and Procedures*. These are any that affect SSADM developments. One example is the existence of a style guide.

Rapid SSADM has been customized in accordance with the Three-schema Architecture. It concerns itself primarily with the external schema and parts of the conceptual schema, but not very much with those techniques more appropriate to the internal schema.

THREE

MANAGEMENT, CASE AND THE USER

3.1 INTRODUCTION

Although SSADM does play a key role in developing many systems, it cannot be used in isolation, but must be part of a larger framework of tools and techniques applied across the whole of the lifecycle. Among these are business analysis techniques applied at the start of the lifecycle, program design techniques used in the building of the system and testing strategies coming at the end. The huge range of such techniques is illustrated in surveys such as Pressman (1994). All have their part to play in the successful completion of a project, but it is important to stress that all must shelter under the umbrella of some appropriate project management method. Clearly, there is no point in having good analysis and design techniques or wonderful programming methods if the project management is faulty. Given this, it is not surprising that weak project management is often quoted as being one of the most common causes of project failure.

If a project management method can be said to give a project direction from the top throughout the lifecycle, CASE tools are equally important in providing the project with basement-level support. (CASE stands for Computer Aided Software Engineering. A good review of the scope and limitations of CASE tools is given in Pressman, 1994.) Some of these tools are useful throughout the whole of the lifecycle, others only part of it. The choice of tool can be vital as far as the success of a project is concerned. If the choice is bad, much of the energy of a project team will be directed towards overcoming the problems and frustrations of working with a second-rate piece of software, rather than being focused on the requirements of the customers.

Project management methods and CASE tools are usually directed towards standard SSADM. Given their importance to the success or failure of a project, it is essential that we consider the extent to which they might be affected by our customization of SSADM.

3.2 MANAGING THE PROJECT

SSADM is primarily concerned with the question of how a 'correct' system can be developed. It does not attempt to provide answers to such questions such as to how many people will be needed on the project, how the work should be scheduled, how much money it will cost or how long it will take. These and similar issues are really the concerns of project management, and are more properly addressed by an appropriate project management methodology. The one which is promoted by CCTA and which complements SSADM is PRINCE. (For a full description of PRINCE, see CCTA, 1990b.)

As PRINCE can be used during the systems analysis and design part of project development, it might be thought reasonable to combine it with SSADM and have an all-embracing systems development methodology. There are three reasons why this has not been done. First, it seems sensible to keep separate the activities of the IS practitioners from the activities of those that manage and control them. Even if the project is small, and one individual performs the two functions, it does seem sensible to keep the two roles distinct. Second, there is no reason why SSADM must always operate under the umbrella of PRINCE. It is marketed as a distinct product, and it is quite possible for SSADM to be used with an alternative project management methodology. Similar comments can also be applied to PRINCE and system development methodologies other than SSADM. Finally, PRINCE is applicable to areas such as programming and testing, and so does cover rather more of the system development cycle than SSADM.

Keeping the two methodologies distinct is all well and good on large projects, where the analysts and the project management do consist of separate groups of people, but there are dangers on the smaller type of project where the one individual performs both roles. There is always the temptation to concentrate on one rather than the other. In practice this is liable to be SSADM rather than the management, since the former tends to produce identifiable and useful products while the latter activity can all too often appear to be a hindrance to forward progress. This is, however, to court disaster, as experience demonstrates that weak or non-existent project management is a major cause of project failure. Much has been written about the importance of good project management practice. A recent survey by PA Consulting Group shows that over 50 per cent of projects still fail to meet their objectives (see Williams, 1994).

CCTA is a little ambivalent as to the applicability of PRINCE to smaller projects. In the main PRINCE manual it is explicitly stated that the methodology is not applicable to projects consisting of less than three people, and of less than three months' duration (see A.1 page 1 of the Management Guide of the main PRINCE manual (CCTA, 1990b)). On the other hand, CCTA have issued specific advice about small projects (CCTA, 1990c), in which they suggest drastically tailoring PRINCE for projects consisting of less than nine person-months. In this latter publication CCTA make the point that any omission of PRINCE controls does add to project risk, and therefore project managers should be aware of the full scope of PRINCE before embarking on such tailoring.

In summary PRINCE provides the following

- *A framework for development.* Each project is broken down into a number of stages. Exactly what comprises a stage is not tightly defined by PRINCE, but is decided on an individual basis for each project. A stage is a chunk of work that can be managed in a sensible way. For medium- to large-scale projects, the stages would probably be as shown in Fig. 1.1 of Chapter 1. Thus each module of SSADM would become a PRINCE stage,* and would be followed by other PRINCE stages corresponding to development, testing and implementation. This is very much the same with Rapid SSADM, but the more the method is customized, the more it is reduced, the less will this structure make sense. Indeed for our final customization, Rapid Rapid SSADM (see Chapter 18), it is quite likely that the whole of the analysis, design, building and testing phases would become a single stage.

- *A management organization.* Every project is ultimately the responsibility of a Project Board. The Project Board will contain representatives from three strands of the business—the users of the proposed system, the technical IT staff and those with responsibility for the business as a whole. As befits a body whose purpose is to control and direct the whole of the project, the Project Board is usually peopled by senior managers. Among their responsibilities are the decision as to what constitutes a stage and the appointment of Project and Stage Managers. The Project and Stage Managers, who are charged respectively with responsibility for the management of the project as a whole and of stages within a project, may be separate individuals or the same person playing different roles. Separate from this controlling structure is the Project Assurance Team whose responsibility is to quality assure all products produced by the development team. Again PRINCE demands that this latter body should have representatives from the three areas of the business. These are known as the User Assurance Coordinator, the Technical Assurance Coordinator and the Business Assurance Coordinator.

  How much of this is applicable to the smaller type of project envisaged by Rapid SSADM? Some form of overall control is obviously essential. The CCTA guide for the use of PRINCE on small IT projects cautions against reducing the project board to one individual. However, on the smallest of projects this might be inevitable and in this case it might be more relevant to think in terms of the *customer* rather than the Project Board. Furthermore, in such a small-scale development the Project and Stage Manager roles will usually be played by the one individual. Indeed, this individual would probably be doing some of the development work, and so it is even more important to separate the management and technical responsibilities. Finally there is the question of quality assurance. It is quite likely that a small project would not have sufficient resources to fund a full-time Project Assurance Team, and Quality Reviews are more likely to be *ad hoc* affairs with the participants being drawn from whoever is available. In this situation it is quite tempting to skimp this activity, but experience shows that a lack of any form of quality assurance merely stores up problems for later. Gilb (1979, p. 221) quotes an example where ICI, in abandoning formal quality assurance techniques for one year, found that maintenance costs increased tenfold.

- *A product framework.* PRINCE describes all products produced on a project in detailed Product Descriptions and classifies them by means of a Product Breakdown Structure (PBS). The Product Breakdown Structure contains three

---

*It is unfortunate that a PRINCE stage is *not* the same as an SSADM stage. The author understands that the terminology is as it is purely for historical reasons.

major categories. The first, Management Products, contains such things as plans, estimates and reports of development problems. The second, Technical Products, contains all the SSADM products as well as technical products from other PRINCE stages such as the Acceptance Test Strategy. The third category, Quality Products, contains all the documents produced by the quality review process. In this book we will concentrate upon the technical products emanating from SSADM. A full description of these is given in Appendix 1.

- *Planning and control procedures.* Plans are made at the start of the project and at the start of each PRINCE stage. There are two types of plans: technical and resource. Technical plans indicate which products are to be produced and often involve the production of a product flow diagram. As far as the Rapid SSADM portion of the lifecycle is concerned, the product flow diagrams are as shown in Chapter 19. Resource plans show how much time, money and staff are required to complete the stage, or indeed the project as a whole. Normally such plans will have an in-built tolerance. Control is effected mainly by means of End of Stage Assessments. At the end of each PRINCE stage, progress is reviewed against the initial plans. If the tolerances are exceeded a new plan, called an Exception Plan, is created to replace the existing plans. Often these new plans are approved at a Mid-Stage Assessment.

    As far as Rapid SSADM is concerned, it is important that all these planning and control mechanisms are retained. They need not have the formality accorded to them when full SSADM is used, but without them it is likely that the project will lack any form of direction.

Clearly we cannot give a full description of PRINCE here, but the above comments should indicate how it could be tailored to complement Rapid SSADM.

3.3 CASE TOOLS

Over the past decade, CASE has seemed to be the holy grail of system developers. Equipped with the perfect CASE tool, all our problems would be over. All we would have to do would be to feed in our requirements, push a few buttons and out would pop the final system. Unfortunately CASE tools have not quite fulfilled these expectations, or in the words of Tom Love (1995):

> We have wanted our tools to be more than they are, and have promised more than the tools can deliver. We have sometimes imagined that tools would replace hard work in designing and building systems . . . All tools are defective—in some important way.

Thus, often they have proved to be no more than an expensive drain on the project, and it is worth exploring why this has happened.

CASE tools provide some or all of the following features:

- *Drawing tools.* This is the ability to draw and to change technical documents such as dataflow diagrams. Obviously, the easier this can be done, the better. This is normally the sexy feature which sells a CASE tool!

- *Repository/data dictionary*. For those working on projects, some database capability which can keep track of data items, functions and requirements is as important as the capability of being able to draw the diagrams.
- *Report-producing facilities*. These might be built-in facilities, or may be a way of transferring data to other software packages such as word processors.
- *Automatic generation of code*. The more of this that can be done, the better. The case tool might have built-in screen painters and report generators, but at the very least, there should be a way of transferring information to the target database.
- *Multi-user facilities*. All but the very smallest of projects involve more than one individual. Maintaining separate copies of the project documentation has obvious drawbacks.
- *Version control*. This is vital if the project is developed in an evolutionary way, when there will in all likelihood be several versions of a particular document.
- *Support for a method*. Clearly, if we decide to use something like SSADM, a CASE tool supporting SSADM is of rather more value than one that does not. It is worth noting that some CASE tools are more focused on a particular method or a particular part of the lifecycle than others.
- *Consistency and error checking*. This is one of the great virtues of CASE tools. We need to be able to do such things as check that the different levels of a Dataflow Diagram are consistent. Obviously this type of checking can only be effective if the project is embedded in some form of methodology.
- *Impact analysis*. If some of the documentation is changed, what effect will this have on other documents? In SSADM, for example, if a relationship is changed on a Logical Data Structure (LDS), it might affect the Entity descriptions, the Entity Life Histories, the Relationship descriptions and the Function Catalogue. Obviously, the more this can be automated, the better.
- *Flexibility*. A CASE tool should be applicable to a wide variety of projects, each with different needs and timescales.

CASE tools are often categorized as being either upper CASE tools, concerned with the analysis and design phases of the lifecycle, or lower CASE tools, concerned with system building and implementation (the dividing line between a lower CASE tool and a 4GL is somewhat ambiguous). Different types of tools stress different features—automatic code generation, for instance, being very important to lower CASE tools. It is, however, the upper CASE tools that aid SSADM, and it is these we will concentrate upon.

One of the reasons upper CASE tools have not always delivered the anticipated benefits is that some of features mentioned above are in conflict. Much of this is to do with the embedding of a tool in a particular method. Many such tools do not give just method support, but rather impose a methodological straitjacket on the user. The project *must* be run according to the method and *must* deliver all required products. This is all very well if the method is ideally suited to the problem being tackled, but if not it can cause problems. The chief of these is the lack of flexibility. Tailoring a method and still hoping to use such a dogmatic case tool is well-nigh impossible.

As Rapid SSADM is already a customized version of a standard method and is itself amenable to further tailoring, flexibility must be a prime consideration in the choice of CASE tools. Given that the perfect CASE tool has yet to be built, the emphasis should be on aiding rather than replacing the analyst. Any technique should be easy enough to be used with pen and paper, and all a CASE tool should do is to make the process more efficient. From this point of view, there is no reason why a *variety* of tools could not be used within the lifecycle. This does have the disadvantage that information might need to be moved from tool to tool, and that consistency checks between different techniques might have to be done manually, but if the alternative is to use a poor CASE tool, in the author's opinion this is a small price to pay. In the final analysis, it is possible to mimic an upper CASE tool just using a general-purpose drawing package, a database and a word processor,* so unless a CASE tool confers benefits substantial enough to outweigh the considerable costs of its purchase and the subsequent training, it is best avoided.

The situation with regard to lower CASE tools is somewhat different. Code generation has been very successful in shortening the time needed for system delivery. Indeed, some Rapid Development methods are impossible without such a facility.

3.4 THE USER

By its very nature, this book concentrates upon the techniques of system development. There is not much here about users, their aspirations or their relationship with the development team. This should not be taken as an indication that the author feels that users are unimportant, but rather that the dynamics of the analyst/user relationship are outside the scope of this book. Without doubt, if potential users of a system are not involved with and consulted about the design of a system, that system will fail. Traditional SSADM tries to keep users on board by involving them in quality reviews and option choices. I feel that often this is not sufficient, and that the key users should be more directly involved in the development process. I will return to this point when discussing user workshops in Chapter 20.

Many of the difficulties would disappear if we substituted the word 'customer' for 'user'. This would change analysts' underlying attitudes to this group. These people would then be regarded not as passive consumers of the products of the development process but as active players who could withdraw their support, and more importantly their money, at will. Despite these reservations about the vocabulary, I have stuck with tradition and retained the word 'user' in what follows.

---

*Producing things like Dataflow Diagrams with a general-purpose drawing tool used to be quite difficult. The major problem was that the shapes were not connected and so moving one component, such as a process, entailed manually moving all the connecting items. In the past year a new product, VISIO, ® Shapeware Corporation, has altered this. This product allows the user to construct their own template of shapes, and to 'glue' connectors (dataflows, for example) to the basic shapes (processes, external entities, datastores), so that when the shapes move the connectors move with them. SSADM diagrams can be produced relatively easily by such a package.

Keeping track of functions, events and such like can easily be done with a PC relational database such as Access or Paradox. (A partial ERA model would be useful here.) The form and report-generating facilities could be used for things like Function Definitions.

Finally as all these products operate under Windows, it is not too difficult to cut and paste any information or diagram between the packages or indeed into any general word processor.

TWO

RAPID SSADM

THE BUSINESS ACTIVITY MODEL

4.1 MANAGEMENT PRELIMINARIES

Before embarking upon any systems development work, it is essential that the analysts understand the scope of the project and what in broad terms is required. If this is not done well, much of the subsequent work will be of little value. In Version 4 of SSADM, these activities took place in step 110. This, however, was more a management than a technical step, and so much of the activity there was not really the province of SSADM but more that of a project management methodology, such as PRINCE. For this reason step 110 has been removed from Version 4.2 of SSADM.

There is a danger in this change in that it sends the wrong messages to those developing the smaller, more rapid type of system. It does not give developers of such systems *carte blanche* to abandon all forms of planning and management controls. Despite its omission from Version 4.2, it's clear that *any* project should be preceded by the following management tasks:

- A review of any available documentation, in particular the Project Initiation Document and the Feasibility Report. The team need to decide whether these documents are still relevant or whether things have changed substantially since their production.
- An identification of key users of the proposed system. The team will need to discuss with them the degree of user involvement.
- Planning of the rest of the stage and project, in other words, to decide what needs to be produced, how it will be produced, who will produce it and how long it will take. Any plans and estimates should be agreed with the Project Board.

Only when these management tasks have been completed, can the team turn to the production of their first SSADM product, the Business Activity Model (BAM).

4.2 THE BUSINESS ACTIVITY MODEL

A frequently raised criticism of earlier versions of SSADM were that they were too 'techy'. The method was focused primarily on the needs of the IT department, only secondarily on the needs of the users, and hardly at all on the needs of the business as a whole. The three-way separation of interests, between users, the IT department and the business has always been part and parcel of PRINCE, but the only time it impinged upon SSADM was in those steps which had a high management content, such as the selection of Business Systems Options. For the most part, SSADM analysts were concerned with technical issues and the needs of the users, and probably in that order! Broader business issues were not a prime concern. Given the right choice of user, of course, such issues would be aired. Unfortunately such a choice is not easy. Most users are as narrowly focused as their technical counterparts, though in their case it is on part of the organization rather than the technology. Only the Business Assurance Coordinator and the Chair of the Project Board have a formal responsibility for representing the business as a whole, and their involvement is often part-time.

Much of this has changed with the introduction of Version 4.2 of SSADM. From the very start of a project, business issues take centre-stage. The first step in SSADM is now concerned with Business Analysis and here the area under investigation is described from a business perspective. To be more precise, the analysts develop what is called a Business Activity Model, in which the four of Kipling's 'six honest serving men' are described:

- *What* business activities take place
- *Why* they take place
- *When* they take place
- *How* they take place

The *who* and *where* of business activities are covered by other SSADM techniques, in particular the current physical Dataflow Model. In a full implementation of SSADM, they would also be addressed by the Work Practice Model.

Business Activity Modelling is the first step in the investigation of the system. Thus, the major inputs to the step are the Source Documents, in particular the Project Initiation Document and, if available, a Feasibility Report (Fig. 4.1). Although most of the information about a Business Activity Model is obtained from interviews with senior managers, other business related documentation in the shape of Business Strategies and Reports can also prove useful.

Fig. 4.1   Inputs and products

4.3 IMPLEMENTING A BUSINESS ACTIVITY MODEL

Any Business Activity Model must address the four following points:

- *Why.* This is a statement of the basic objective(s) of that part of the business under investigation. Eliciting such a statement is often quite difficult, and so other standard business analysis techniques might prove useful. For example, a discussion with user management of critical success factors should help in separating the essential from the inessential. The move from the question 'What is the purpose of your business?' to the 'What would cause your business to fail?' can often reveal fresh insights. Similarly, the identification of stakeholders, and a discussion of what they might require from the business might also provide a slightly different angle on the problem. Another approach is to name key performance indicators. After all, any such measures should be directly related to the aims and objectives of the business. All these different approaches should not be seen as an end in themselves, but merely as a device to establish a succinct statement of the business's objectives. Finally it has to be stated that any view as to the aims of a business is likely to be subjective. Thus in talking to several individuals, a variety of different perspectives might emerge and so compromises would have to be made in merging them into a single overall view.
- *What.* This involves the identification and documentation of essential business activities. Such activities can be categorized as:
  1. *'Doing' activities.* These are activities that contribute towards the accomplishment of the primary business objectives. Thus for an insurance company, 'sell policies' is fundamental.
  2. *Enabling activities.* These are of a secondary nature, and are often concerned with ensuring that the correct environment and sufficient resources are in place so that the doing activities can be accomplished. Thus for the insurance company, any advertising or marketing activity would fall into this category.
  3. *Planning activities.* These normally precede all the other activities.
  4. *Monitoring activities.* These activities are intimately concerned with measuring performance. Indeed, if no performance indicator is in place, one must question why monitoring is happening.
  5. *Controlling activities.* These are really the feedback mechanisms of the monitoring activities.
- *When.* Business events are those 'happenings' in the business world which can trigger business activities. They can be one of three types:
  1. *External inputs*—e.g. a customer sending in a booking form.
  2. *Internal business decisions*—e.g. a decision to raise the prices of products.
  3. *Scheduled points in time*—e.g. end of financial year. This might trigger several business activities—the production of accounts, the issue of a new prospectus, etc.

Business events are those that trigger any meaningful business activity. They should not be confused with system events which will be introduced when we discuss Entity Life Histories. System events lead to the updating of data, which is not necessarily the case with business events. Thus 'Customer request for information' is a business event, which leads to business activities, but does not necessarily involve updating any files or records.

- *How*. This is a statement of the business rules which govern how activities are performed. The rules come in two types:
  1. *Constraints*. The conditions under which activities may or may not be performed. For example, a customer with a credit rating of 'B' or below cannot be accepted for a booking without the authorization of a senior manager.
  2. *Operational guidance*. This covers how a business activity must be performed. An example is the calculation of tax. Such guidance need not be procedural.

No definitive guidance is given by SSADM Version 4.2 on the notation to be used for a Business Activity Model. This is explicitly stated to be outside the scope of SSADM. The examples in the manuals (CCTA, 1995) are developed in terms of the soft systems methodology. This is described more fully in Checkland (1981) and Wilson (1992). Soft systems methodology is perhaps most appropriate to those projects where there is considerable doubt as to the scope and requirements of the system and where a full application of SSADM is essential. Alternative methods suggested for constructing a Business Activity Model are Functional Decomposition and Resource Flow Diagrams. The former are most appropriate for those systems that have to be developed quickly and the latter for those where a large part of the system under consideration is manual. In essence, SSADM Version 4.2 allows any modelling notation provided that the following are covered:

- Objectives and purpose
- Connectivity—how the activities relate to each other
- Performance measures
- Monitoring and control mechanisms
- Decision-taking procedures
- The boundary of the system
- Resources—what is used by the system
- System hierarchy

Given that we are interested in developing systems rapidly, Functional Decomposition looks to be the most appropriate for our purposes and this is what we will use.

4.4 DEVELOPING A BUSINESS ACTIVITY MODEL

In our customization of SSADM, a Business Activity Model will consist of the following:

- A Statement of Business Objectives
- A Functional Decomposition
- A Context Diagram
- Business Activity Descriptions

The first to be produced is the Statement of Business Objectives. This should answer the *why* part of the preceding section. It should be a brief, succinct statement of one or two paragraphs which encapsulates the main aims and objectives of that part of the business under investigation. In the rest of this book we will be using the 'Happy

Camping' system as a case study. As its name suggests, this concerns a company whose primary business is in selling camping holidays to the general public. An example of a Statement of Business Objectives for the 'Happy Camping' system is given in Fig. 4.2. It might be thought that the main business objective of Happy Camping is to make a profit. While this is undoubtedly true, it is not of much use to those given the task of producing an information system. Better is the definition given which is more focused on the activities that take place within the business.

4.5 DEFINING THE FUNCTIONAL DECOMPOSITION

In defining the Functional Decomposition, we need to think very clearly about what the system is trying to achieve. The first thing to do is to decide on a reasonable number (up to seven or eight) of major business activities. Each will be described in terms of what it does, not in terms of how it is done, who does it or even where it is done. These major business activities should be viewed as pure units of work. Unfortunately, there is no certain method of identifying such activities. Obviously, during the course of interviewing people an analyst might have gained considerable detailed knowledge of the workings of the system. But now, analysts must divorce themselves from these considerations, stand back and try to concentrate upon the major aims of the system. In short, they need to think!

Consider a system based upon the work of an insurance company. The major business activities are probably something like:

- Selling new policies
- Collecting annual premiums
- Investigating claims
- Paying out on claims
- Calculating premiums for new types of policy
- Maintaining customer information

Obviously this is a somewhat simplistic view of the work of an insurance company, but it does give pointers as to the type of activity we are looking for. It is worth mentioning

The main purpose of Happy Camping is to sell camping holidays to the general public. These holidays take place in tents erected and maintained by Happy Camping both on their own sites and on other privately owned sites.

Fig. 4.2 The Happy Camping statement of business objectives

that some form of 'housekeeping' activity normally needs to be included on the decomposition. For the insurance company, 'Maintaining customer information' obviously fills this role. With the possible exception of this last activity, the activities listed are closely allied to the business aims of the company.

Returning to the Happy Camping system, the major business activities are

- Deal with Customer Bookings
- Produce Customer Joining details
- Receive Customer Payments
- Check yearly site invoices for payment
- Prepare next year's programme

Figure 4.3 shows these placed on the first level of a functional decomposition. The next step is to decompose each of these major business activities into a maximum of seven or eight sub-activities. For each of the major activities on the top level we ask what needs to be done to achieve the objectives of that activity. Thus the first, 'Deal with Customer Bookings', can be decomposed into six sub-activities:

- Check plot availability
- Enter or change customer details
- Check customer credit rating
- Make provisional booking
- Cancel Customer Booking
- Change Booking details

Figure 4.4 shows these and other sub-activities added to the functional decomposition. For the Happy Camping system this is as far as we will go, since each of the sub-activities corresponds to a well-defined task.

Obviously, a larger system would need further decomposition. Each second-level activity would be broken down into a maximum of seven or eight third-level activities. This could continue forever, but as with Dataflow Diagrams we normally impose a limit of three or four levels. In other words, the decomposition continues until such time as all activities can be captured fully within the confines of a Business Activity Description (see later).

The question often arises as to which activities should be included on the hierarchy. The simple answer is that all included activities should be meaningful to that part of the business under investigation. They might not be computerizable, but should be of some consequence to the workings of the information system under development. Every activity on the lowest level should be triggered by a Business Event and should

Fig. 4.3   The Happy Camping Functional Decomposition (top level)

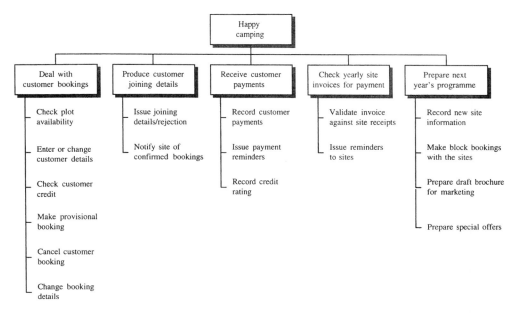

Fig. 4.4   The Happy Camping Functional Decomposition (all levels)

completely deal with the consequences of the event. Thus in the Happy Camping scenario, the activity 'Check Plot Availability' is triggered by and deals completely with the Business Event 'Customer Enquiry about Availability'. Related activities, such as 'Make Provisional Booking', are triggered by a different, if related, business event, in this case 'Customer decision to make Booking'. As we will see later, we do document all the Business Events, but if difficulties are encountered in identifying bottom-level activities, it might be useful to draw up a list of events. Finally it is worth noting that, in general, the size of a bottom-level activity should equate to the size of a bottom-level process on a Dataflow Diagram and both should be about the same size as a program.

A further issue that arises in connection with elementary activities concerns the question of repetition. In a stock control system, one could well imagine a sub-activity such as 'Check stock availability' appearing in several major business areas. As a consequence, this activity would appear several times on the decomposition. This is not a problem. Obviously one does not want to end up doing some things such as screen design several times over, and so eventually these activities need to be identified as being the same. The simplest way of doing this is to use italics, underlining or even a different colour when entering them.

Any functional decomposition consisting of one or two levels can be represented in a similar fashion to that on Fig. 4.4. Indeed, the whole system can be represented on one sheet of A4, or possibly A3, paper. Clearly, once the system expands to three or more levels, this representation is impossible. A three-level decomposition can best be represented by being split into a series of hierarchies as in Fig. 4.5. The first page will show the major business activities, subsequent pages will demonstrate the decomposition of these activities. Hierarchies consisting of four or more levels can be treated similarly.

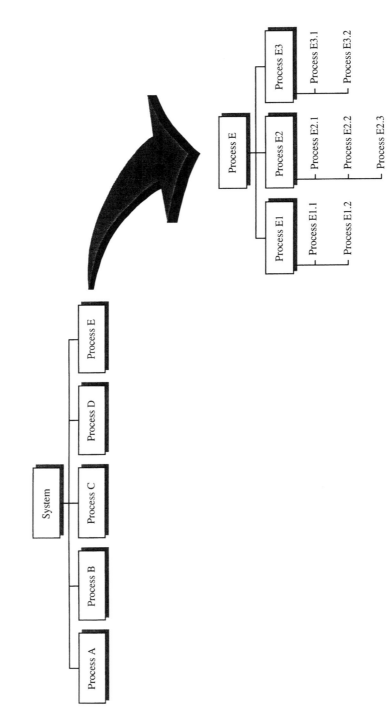

Fig. 4.5   Three levels of hierarchy

Before being formally presented to the user, a final check should be made of the completeness of the decomposition. Are all the types of activity mentioned under the *What* heading present? There is a natural tendency to concentrate on the 'doing' activities. The analyst must, therefore, ensure that all the enabling, planning, monitoring and controlling activities have also been covered.

An alternative way to represent a functional decomposition is by the use of outliners. Here the decomposition is represented as text with the levels indicated by different amounts of indentation. Thus the Happy Camping decomposition would be shown as

- Deal with Customer Booking
    Check site availability
    Enter or change customer details
    Check customer credit rating
    Make provisional booking
    Cancel Customer Booking
    Change Booking details
- Produce Customer Joining details
    Issue joining details/rejection
    Notify site of confirmed bookings
    etc.

Obviously different sized types, different styles such as italics or underlining and the use of varied bullets would make such a representation clearer. Whichever representation is used for the decompositions is a matter of personal choice. The author finds the diagrams far more helpful and so will continue to use them.

4.6 COMPLETING THE BUSINESS ACTIVITY MODEL

The major drawback to a functional decomposition is that it represents only the internal activities of the organization. What is missing is some description of the interaction between the system and the external world. Such a description is best provided by a Context Diagram, which shows the external entities, those organizations, individuals and groups outside the scope of the system who interact with the system, and the major inputs to and outputs from the system. The context diagram for the Happy Camping system is shown in Fig. 4.6. While Customer is obviously external to the system, the context diagram has the virtue of showing very clearly that the Site, Marketing and Accounts are also outside the scope of the system. The construction of a context diagram will not be described in detail here, as this is done more than adequately in most standard SSADM texts, such as Ashworth and Slater (1993), Eva (1992), Weaver (1993), and Goodland and Slater (1995).

In many cases, the Functional Decomposition and the Context Diagram are more than sufficient documentation this early in the project. They do not, however, cover the *when* and *how* issues that SSADM requires of a business model. To complete our description of the business, we need to consider each of the bottom-level activities, that is, those at bottom of the decomposition, and identify what triggers the activity,

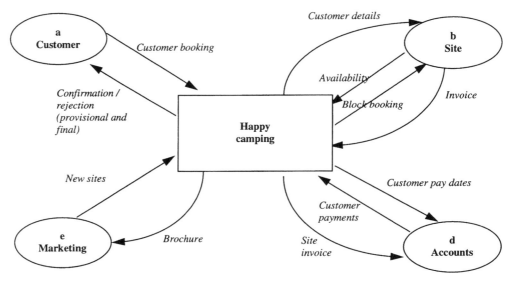

Fig. 4.6   The Happy Camping Context Diagram

what rules govern the activity, and what are the major inputs and outputs to the activity. To do this systematically, a form, called a Business Activity Description, should be completed for each of the bottom-level activities. An example of such a form, taken from the Happy Camping system, is given in Fig. 4.7.

Business Activity Description				
System Happy Camping	**Current** X	**Required**	**Date** 31/5/93	

Act ID 1.4	*Activity Name* Make Provisional Booking

Description

This is the initial activity that takes place when a customer wishes to book a holiday. A booking will be for a plot on a specified site for a specified period of time. Bookings can arrive via a booking form or via the telephone. If a deposit does not arrive within 10 days the provisional booking is cancelled.

Associated Activities	*Business Events*
Check plot availability	Receipt of Customer Booking

Inputs	*Outputs*	*Constraints/Guidance*
Booking details from Customer Plot/site availability Past Customer records (if any)	Confirm/rejection letter Payment dates to Accounts Dates of holiday to site	Previous customers with credit ratings of B will only be accepted on the authority of the Office Manager

Fig. 4.7   Business Activity Description

The final task in step 115 is to obtain the user's agreement to the model. As the model details the scope and the major business activities of the system under investigation, any disagreements now would lead to disaster. As this is a high-level business view of the system, senior user managers would be the best people to be involved with any validation of the model.

FIVE

REQUIREMENTS DEFINITION

The purpose of step 120 is to identify who are likely to be the users of the new system and to establish what their requirements might be. Although much of the discussion may revolve around the problems of this group of users, we cannot ignore the needs of the business as a whole. How well these requirements are analysed will influence the extent to which subsequent work on the project is successful.

The main outputs from this step are the Requirements Catalogue and the User Catalogue. The starting point for the work is the source documents, in particular the Project Initiation Document (PID). This contains the main objectives of the system, which in a sense are the requirements expressed in the broadest of terms. Clearly any preliminary versions of the Requirements Catalogue produced in the Feasibility Study will also be of interest. It is doubtful whether any form of Business Analysis could take place without some consideration as to the requirements for the new system. Indeed, it is likely that in the course of interviews with senior management, the Business Activity Model would be developed in parallel with the Requirements Catalogue.

In SSADM Version 4.2, requirements are classified as being functional or non-functional. The first of these, the *Functional Requirements*, describe what the system is supposed to do. This is usually defined in terms of the reports and enquiries, but should

Fig. 5.1   Inputs and products

also be extended so as to cover controls and monitoring processes. At some stage consideration should also be made of what data is held and how it can be changed. Strictly speaking, the decision about which data is to be held is not recorded in the Requirements Catalogue, but rather on the Logical Data Model. Updates, however, are functional requirements which should be placed in the Catalogue. It seems impossible to envisage what these might be without some consideration of the data to be held. Finally, very few systems now operate in isolation, and any requirements for interaction between the target system and other systems needs documenting. The identification of functional requirements might seem fairly straightforward, but does give rise to a number of problems.

The first of these is one of detail. It appears as if every single required enquiry and update should be documented in full. But this seems to be like proposing a solution in advance of the investigation. In other words, it implies doing the design before the analysis. Furthermore, if this level of detail is included, the Requirements Catalogue will duplicate much that is recorded in other documents such as the current physical Dataflow Model, and indeed will start to resemble the Function Catalogue. On the other hand, vague requirements are of little use especially to those preparing costings for Business System Options. Obviously some degree of compromise is needed.

One solution to the problem is to develop a hierarchy of requirements. Figure 5.2 shows an initial requirement obtained from the Project Initiation Document for a system called 'Happy Camping'. This might be quite sufficient, a more detailed description of the Customer Booking procedures being documented on the Dataflow Model. However if more detail is required, the requirement can be expanded as in Fig. 5.3. SSADM Version 4.2 does not do this but tends to treat every requirement as being on the same level.

A second problem with functional requirements was touched upon in Chapter 1. Often the prospective users are not really clear about what they do want. This might be because the proposed system is not replacing well-understood existing procedures but is completely new, or it may be because the users do not appreciate the capabilities of a computerized system. In such cases, it is only when the system has been delivered and the users begin to use it on a day-to-day basis that they perceive the limitations of what has been done and begin to formulate their real requirements. There appears to be no easy solution to this problem. SSADM Version 4.2 suggests using prototyping, but this is just a step in the right direction, being no substitute for daily contact with a real system. The only plausible stratagem seems to be to adopt an evolutionary approach, and we will return to this later.

Even when requirements are reasonably clear, disagreements between the users can still occur. These conflicts can be of either a vertical or a horizontal nature. Vertical conflicts occur when the user management disagree with the operatives as to the procedures or needs of a particular area. If it is impossible to obtain agreement, the analysts normally accede to the view of the major stakeholders, that is, the management. Horizontal conflicts arise when a number of similar users disagree about common areas of work. An example of this might occur when an organization has a number of regional offices. Each should be doing exactly the same things and have exactly the same requirements, but often they do not. In such cases, an individual or group have to be nominated as representatives of the whole of the user community. The correct choice can greatly influence the outcome of such a project.

Requirements Catalogue (Functional)

| System | Happy Camping | Date | 31/5/93 | Version | 1 |

Requirement	Source	Prty.
1. Automate Customer Booking System	PID	H

Resolution

Fig. 5.2   Happy Camping High-level Requirement

The second type of requirement introduced by SSADM are the *Non-functional Requirements*. These are a little more complicated than functional requirements and are categorized as follows:

- *Service Level Requirements*. These attempt to establish such things as the hours during which the system should be available, the number of transactions it should cope with in a given time period, the speed of response of the system and the overall reliability of the system.
- *Access restrictions*. These concern which items of data need protection, who is allowed to update, how they are allowed to update and what level of protection is required. Usually this involves such things as passwords, physical security devices and encryption for very sensitive systems.
- *Security*. These refer to security against loss and are concerned with such questions as back-up and recovery of data.
- *Monitoring*. This covers what reports or statistics should be produced about the levels of use and overall efficiency of the system.

Requirements Catalogue (Functional)			
System Happy Camping	**Date** 31/5/93		**Version** 1

Requirement	Source	Prty.
1. Automate Customer Booking System	PID	H
1.1 Check site availability		H
1.2 Make provisional booking		H
1.3 Change booking details		H
1.4 Cancel Booking		H
1.5 Produce site booking history	Office Clerk	M
1.6 Check Customer Credit Rating	Accounts	M

Resolution

Fig. 5.3   Requirement Decomposition

- *Audit and control*. Requirements in this area cover both financial audit and system audit.
- *Constraints*. These are not development constraints such as costs and timescales, but rather required constraints. Examples quoted concern such things as conversion from current system, interfaces with other systems and archiving.

Clearly many of these are the province of the expert. To guard against loss or damage to data, the analyst is well advised to call on the services of a professional security adviser or, at the very least, use an appropriate risk analysis methodology such as CRAMM. Again, if the system is subject to some form of financial control, advice obtained from someone with professional accounting expertise is essential.

Although useful as a checklist, the reasoning as to why these requirements should be non-functional looks somewhat confused. The Audit and control category merely indicates those extra functions that should be provided by the design team. As such they are really functional requirements. Similarly remarks apply to the Access, Security and Monitoring categories, except that in this case the extra functionality would probably be provided by system software such as the operating system, database management system or a special utility. The one category that is different is that of 'Service Level

Requirements'. These do not indicate the existence of extra functions, but rather specify how well the other functions should perform, and so are truly non-functional.

This point is clarified in Gilb (1988). He defines a functional requirement as something that is done or is not done, while a non-functional requirement refers to how well something is done and so needs to be measured on some form of scale (Gilb calls non-functional requirements 'Attribute Goals'). Thus the question 'Has the requirement "Display Customer Details" been satisfied?' admits only two possible answers—Yes or No. However, putting a response rate onto this requirement is a little more difficult. We might, for example, state that 2 seconds is our target response time, but find that in only 90 per cent of cases is this target met. It is not clear whether this is satisfactory, and so we have to be a little more sophisticated in framing such requirements and aim for something like 85 per cent of responses in under 2 seconds, 95 per cent in under 10 seconds and 99 per cent in under 20 seconds. Whenever this is done it is useful to have any existing figures for comparison purposes.

Service Level Requirements used to be the only example quoted of non-functional requirements. Of late it has come to be recognized that there are other aspects of a systems performance that ought to be measured. The driving force behind this recognition has been the advent of the Graphical User Interface. As Graphical User Interfaces are sold on the basis of user friendliness, this aspect can hardly be ignored in the requirements. The SSADM User Group (SSUG, 1994) suggests the following non-functional requirements:

- *Productivity*. How many tasks a user can complete in a given time.
- *Learnability*. How long it will take a novice to use the system.
- *User satisfaction*. How happy the user is with the system.
- *Memorability*. If a user does not use the system for long periods, how long it takes him or her to get back to full productivity.
- *Error rates*. How many errors are made by a proficient operator in a given period.

Other non-functional requirements might be *maintainability* and *portability*.

In the past such requirements were often dismissed as being too vague. Functional requirements did, after all, ask for something concrete and so had far greater appeal. But this is to miss the point. From the point of view of the user the success or failure of a system in large measure depends upon these vaguer requirements. What is the point of a system doing everything it is supposed to do, if it does it in such an unfriendly way that user satisfaction is zero? What is required is a way of measuring this type of requirement. In detail, we need to specify:

1. To which functions or group of functions the requirements apply
2. How the requirement is to be measured
3. Target ranges and how these targets are to be tested.

The testing is sometimes a problem, and quite often involves some form of questionnaire or statistical survey. Such is obviously the case with user satisfaction. Figure 5.4 shows a typical non-functional requirement for the Happy Camping system.

The Requirements Catalogue has replaced what in earlier versions of SSADM was known as the 'Problem Requirements List'. Problems are, therefore, no longer explicitly mentioned. The reasoning behind this is that every problem is merely an opportunity for a corresponding requirement. If a user has a problem with part of an existing system, there is obviously a requirement to improve it. However, this translation of problems into immediate requirements does seem a trifle hasty. During the course of her or his investigations, an analyst will hear of many problems, some being no more than the habitual grumbles and gripes of the dissatisfied, but others revealing major flaws in the system. To immediately elevate all such problems into requirements for entry into the Catalogue is premature. The analyst is best advised to maintain an informal *Problems List*, and to discuss this with the appropriate user representative when the Requirements Catalogue is finalized in step 160.

The final task of step 120 is to initiate the User Catalogue. This is a list of the prospective users of the system, their responsibilities and activities. Figure 5.5 shows a portion of this Catalogue taken from the Happy Camping system.

Requirements Catalogue (Non-Functional)				
System Happy Camping	**Date** 31/5/93		**Version**	1

Requirement	*Source*	*Prty.*
47. Reduce the number of errors when making a provisional booking	PID	H

Measure	Number of errors made per 100 bookings
	Target Range 0–4
	Present Value 8

Testing	Each booking clerk will be tested once every three months– preferably monitored by software otherwise observed.

Resolution	

Fig. 5.4   Happy Camping Non-functional Requirement

	User Catalogue			
System	Happy Camping	**Date**	31/5/93	**Version** 1

Job Title	*Job Activities*
27. Customer Clerk	Deal with Customer queries, check site availability and make provisional bookings. Keep track of changes to Bookings.
28. Customer Manager	Supervise customer clerks and cover for them in times of emergency. Authorize bookings from customers with dodgy credit ratings.
29. Site Liaison Clerk	In general responsible for dealing with campsites. Keeping track of bookings made for each site. For each year procure a block of plots for the use of Happy Camping

Fig. 5.5   Happy Camping User Catalogue

DESCRIBING THE CURRENT SYSTEM

6.1 INTRODUCTION

One of the major aims of the Requirements Analysis module is to describe the current environment. This is done primarily by means of the Current Physical Dataflow Model (step 130), the Logical Data Model (step 140) and the Current Logical Dataflow Model (step 150). As much of this is the same as standard SSADM and is more than adequately covered elsewhere (see, for example, CCTA, 1995; Ashworth and Slater, 1993; Eva, 1992; Skidmore *et al.*, 1992; Weaver, 1993; and Goodland and Slater, 1995), this chapter will present the material only in an overview form. The one exception to all this is step 150, in which an alternative technique is introduced for logicalization. This will be covered in full in the next chapter.

Besides acting as a reminder of well-established techniques, this chapter serves to expand upon the case study 'Happy Camping' that runs throughout the rest of the book.

6.2 STEP 130—INVESTIGATE CURRENT PROCESSING

The purpose of this step is to document the processing that takes place in the existing system and by doing so to establish the scope of the system under investigation. A Dataflow Diagram is the main device used for recording these details. Dataflow Diagrams are among the most accessible diagrams in SSADM, and as such are an excellent vehicle for communication with the user.

Dataflow Diagrams have a long and distinguished history being present in some form in nearly every structured analysis methodology (every concept used in the production of DFDs was present in the early work of De Marco, 1979 and Gane and

Sarson, 1977). From the very beginning it was recognized that they were very useful for communicating with users. Indeed, De Marco (1979, p. 48) pointed out that in the early days Dataflow Diagrams were more acceptable to the users than to IT departments! So successful were the diagrams that early versions of SSADM used them throughout the analysis and design process. This was a little too much of a good thing, since they are not really the best tool for program design. Version 4.2 has placed Dataflow Diagrams back in their rightful place, at the start of the analysis phase where they are used for documenting the existing system in a form that most users can understand.

The major product from step 130 is the Current Physical Dataflow Model, which is a set of Dataflow Diagrams describing the existing system plus some accompanying documentation. An updated Requirements Catalogue is also an output, since the very process of documenting detailed processing is liable to uncover further requirements. The starting point for this step is the PID or a feasibility study and the Business Activity Model produced in step 115. These are the Source Documents of Fig. 6.1.

The basic symbols used in a Dataflow Diagram are shown in Fig. 6.2. The external entities are those individuals, organizations or 'things' that are outside the scope of the system under investigation, but which pass information to or receive information from it. A process box is used to describe operations that can take place on data. It contains space for a brief description of the activity and the name of whoever performs the activity. A datastore is where data is stored. Finally, dataflows show the routing of data around the system.

Standard SSADM also includes symbols to model resource flows. We have not done so, as they are of less importance to analysts and if employed are normally replaced by dataflows at a very early stage.

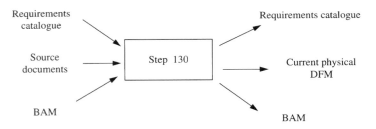

Fig. 6.1   Inputs and products (step 130)

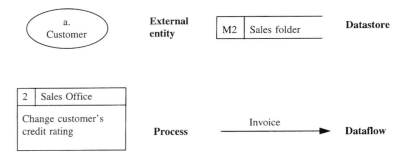

Fig. 6.2   Dataflow Diagram symbols

A typical Dataflow Diagram is shown in Fig. 6.10 at the end of this chapter. Although such a top-level Dataflow Diagram gives a very good summary of the processing that takes place in a system, it is all too easy to miss the wood because of the trees. If this should happen, it is quite useful to refer back to the Context Diagram. This describes more clearly the system boundary with the key inputs and outputs highlighted. Indeed, the Context Diagram is quite often a good starting point for the production of the Dataflow Diagram.

One of the chief virtues of the Dataflow Diagram technique is the way in which it can be used to model the system in a varied level of detail. This is achieved by exploding a process on a top-level Dataflow Diagram into a lower- or second-level diagram. Each process on a second-level Dataflow Diagram can itself be expanded into a third-level diagram and so on. In theory this process can continue indefinitely, but in practice a maximum of three levels are usually sufficient. Processes at the bottom level are described in full by means of an Elementary Process Description (EPD). Usually these descriptions consist of one or two paragraphs of text, but could include alternative techniques such as decision tables or even flowcharts.

The final output from this step is a Dataflow Model (DFM) of the Current System. A Dataflow Model consists of the following:*

- (Context Diagram)
- Dataflow Diagrams (all levels)
- Elementary Process Descriptions
- External entity list
- I/O descriptions
- Datastore description

The external entity list is exactly what it says, just a list. It is easy to produce and is useful if only as an index. An I/O description describes the content of a dataflow crossing the system boundary (i.e. between an external entity and a process). These are adequately described by a copy of a form, a screen dump or something similar. On very few occasions should there be the need to complete extra pieces of documentation to describe all the flows. The Datastore description is just a brief statement of the purpose of the datastore plus a list of its contents. Again copies of existing documentation will usually suffice. Obviously, there is little point in doing this for transient datastores such as in-trays.

How much of this should be done in Rapid SSADM? If there is an existing system, much of this documentation is very sensible, especially in view of its relevance to most users. There is, however, little point in taking things to an extreme by recording every facet and small idiosyncrasy of the existing system. After all, it is likely to be replaced.

---

*This list differs in two respects from that given in the official manuals. There, there is no attempt made to describe the datastores until the logical Dataflow Diagrams are produced in step 150. Given that Dataflow Diagrams are the major point for user agreement, it seems sensible to include more detailed descriptions here. A second point concerns the Context Diagram. Strictly speaking, this is part of the Business Activity Model. It is, however, produced in the same way as a Dataflow Diagram, and so in some sense it is part of the whole dataflow model. This was certainly the view in the earliest days (cf. De Marco, 1979).

The Current Physical Dataflow Model should only be developed to the extent where it remains useful to the analyst or the user in helping to clarify either's understanding as to what may be required in the future system.

6.3 STEP 140—INVESTIGATE CURRENT DATA

The purpose of this step is to develop a rigorous model of the information requirements of the system called the Logical Data Model. The Logical Data Model consists of a diagram called the Logical Data Structure and various items of accompanying documentation. Essentially it is an attempt to describe all the items of data held by the system and explore the relationships between them.

Logical data modelling has some claims to being the single most important technique within SSADM. Indeed, the Logical Data Model plays a variety of roles throughout the method. It first appears in stage 1 where we attempt to define the structure of data within the existing system, next in stage 3 where the structure of data required for the new system is modelled and finally in stage 6 where the model forms the basis for the database or file design. Even in the smallest of systems, implemented with the most restricted of timescales, it is liable to be the one technique that is used in full.

Like Dataflow Diagrams, Logical Data Modelling also has a long and distinguished history. It was first introduced by Chen (1976) and has been refined considerably since. Similar diagrams were introduced by Bachman (1969) for CODASYL type databases. It was developed and used successfully well before the appearance of SSADM. Indeed, so successful is the technique that all system development methodologies include it or something very similar. As is usual with such widespread techniques, it appears in many different guises and under a number of different names.

In order to produce a Logical Data Model effectively, an analyst would need to be aware of the scope of the system, and so would need to refer to the usual source documents, such as the Project Initiation Document. Clearly, the main output from step 140 is a full Logical Data Model (Fig. 6.3). In addition, however, the Requirements Catalogue is usually updated as the whole investigative process often uncovers fresh requirements.

Logical Data Models are first and foremost concerned with *entities and attributes*. In SSADM these are defined as follows:

- An *entity* is a thing or concept of interest to an organization about which information is stored.
- An *attribute* of an entity is an item of information stored about the entity.

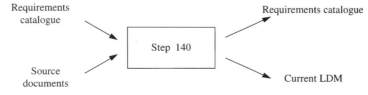

Fig. 6.3   Inputs and products (step 140)

An important distinction has to be made between an *entity* and an *entity occurrence*. Entity occurrences are the individual instances of an entity, while an entity really refers to the whole class of instances. Thus in a library system, the entity Book refers to the whole collection of books, while the individual occurrences of this entity are such things as *Oliver Twist* and *Jane Eyre*. For this reason, the name of an entity is always given in the singular, and so one talks of the entity Book, *not* the entity Books. Moreover, in this text the name of an entity will always start with a capital letter, while occurrences and any real-life objects referenced by the entity will start with a small letter. To confuse matters somewhat, methodologies other than SSADM use the terminology in a slightly different way. Sometimes what we understand as an entity is called an entity type, while the word 'entity' refers to the individual instances of an entity type!

For any 'candidate' entity, if it proves difficult to think of attributes, doubts must be cast as to whether it is indeed an entity. In a library system, for example, we might initially have thought that Title was an entity. After all, a library does store information about titles and so it seems to satisfy all the conditions of the original definition. It is when we attempt to define the attributes of a Title that we encounter problems. There is nothing we would want to record about a Title other than its actual value. To most people, a Title is really no more than a string of characters such as *Oliver Twist*.* There is nothing other than this we would like to record about a title. In other words, a Title doesn't really have attributes, but instead is itself an attribute of another entity such as a Book.

It might appear that entities spontaneously emerge from the mists of the current system merely by the use of an analyst's SSADM skills. Unfortunately, life is rarely quite as simple as this. Some entities are easily identifiable, but others are not. There is no guaranteed method that can be used to find these elusive entities, only a number of possibilities. The first of these is to search through the existing documentation looking for possible keys. Such a data item usually indicates the presence of a corresponding entity. Thus a Customer Number leads to a Customer entity. A second way of identifying entities is to obtain a textual description of the system and underline all the nouns. This is a something of a blunt instrument. If used on a library system, say, it would uncover genuine entities such as Book and Borrower, but might also identify things such as File (too vague), Title (an attribute), and Registration (an operation creating occurrences of a Borrower). This approach is one used quite frequently in the world of object orientation, but does tend to rely on the existence of a well written piece of text (for a much more detailed description of this technique, see, for example, Rumbaugh *et al.* 1991). A third and perhaps the most useful approach is to use the technique of Relational Data Analysis on existing documentation. This will be covered later.

It is important not to be too dogmatic about recording an entity's attributes. In theory, these should be precisely those items of data recorded about an entity in the current system. It is important, however, not to lose sight of the purpose of the work in

---

*There is an interesting philosophical point as to whether an object can really be equated with its contents. An amusing illustration of such arguments occurs in Chapter 8 of Lewis Carroll's *Through the Looking-Glass* when the White Knight discusses the naming of his song. For a full discussion of the ramifications of this, see Gardner (1970). Notwithstanding such matters, we will take a commonsense view that the title of Charles Dickens's third book and *Oliver Twist* are one and the same thing.

this step. It is to provide not a perfectly correct picture of the current system but rather a springboard for the design of the database or files in the new one. Thus if an item of data is logically necessary for the functioning of the current system, it should be included as an attribute even if not revealed by a thorough trawl through the documentation.

Another point to note about attributes is that they must be atomic, that is, single-valued. So for any occurrence of a Patient, say, there should be one and only one Name, one and only one Address, and so on. The statement that attributes should be atomic and single-valued can pose problems. Is, for example, an attribute called 'Address' a single-valued data item or is it a composite data item consisting of 'Road', 'Town' and 'County' or even of 'Line 1', 'Line 2' and 'Line 3'? Whether we regard this as a single data item or as three separate data items doesn't really matter, as long as we are consistent. What we cannot do is to define an address as consisting of a variable number of lines. Again this is something that is further clarified by Relational Data Analysis (for a full discussion of the problems of atomicity, see, for example, Date, 1990, p. 378).

After identifying the entities, we next establish the *relationships* between them. A relationship between two entities cross-references occurrences of the first entity to occurrences of the second. Thus in a medical system there could well be a relationship between a Doctor entity and a Patient entity, which is shown diagrammatically as in Fig. 6.4.

In general, there can only be a relationship between the two entities if they can be connected together in some simple sentence which makes sense within the context of the system. Thus we can say 'A patient is allocated to a doctor'. SSADM Version 4.2 achieves this more formally by the use of link phrases, in which both ends of the relationship are annotated. Each link phrase describes the relationship from the point of view of the nearest entity. The syntax used is quite strictly defined. The entity names and link phrases are used to complete the following sentence:

Each . . . [must be/may be] . . . [one and only one/one or more] . . .

The dotted spaces should be completed by the names of the subject entity, the link phrase and the object entity respectively, while the square brackets indicate a choice. Thus in Fig. 6.4, reading the relationship from top to bottom we would obtain: 'Each

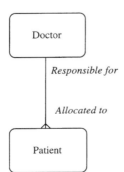

Fig. 6.4   Doctor/Patient relationship (with link phrases)

doctor must be responsible for one or more patients'. Choosing meaningful phrases can be extremely difficult, and quite often the phrase at one end of a relationship is merely a rephrasing of that at the other end. Moreover, a diagram full of link phrases is somewhat difficult to read. For this reason, Rapid SSADM recommends only using link phrases when trying to dispel any possible confusion, and in this case only one per relationship. Note, however, that many CASE tools do enforce the full syntax.

In Version 4.2 of SSADM, each relationship line can be considered to be in two halves, each of which can be either dashed or solid. A solid line indicates that the relationship is mandatory, a dashed line that it is optional, both from the point of view of the nearest entity. Figure 6.5 illustrates the four possible types of optionality in a relationship.

(i)   A doctor has zero or more patients, but a patient must be allocated to a single doctor. This caters for the possibility of doctors without patients.
(ii) A doctor has one or more patients, and a patient is allocated a doctor. No unallocated doctors or patients here!
(iii) A doctor has one or more patients, but a patient is allocated one or zero doctors. This copes with the case of a patient whom no one wants to see.
(iv) A doctor has zero or more patients, and a patient is allocated one or zero doctors. This is the loosest situation, allowing the possibility of freewheeling doctors and patients.

Which of these is correct depends upon the system being modelled. Deciding whether or not a relationship is optional is sometimes very difficult, especially from a master's point of view. Sometimes it even brings up discussions about the life of the entity. (For example, when a hospital first takes on doctors do they immediately become responsible for a group of patients?) For this reason, it is not too bothersome if optionality from the master's end is missed. (Version 3 of SSADM survived quite well for several years on a much restricted view of optionality.)

There are really three different degrees of relationship: one-to-many, one-to-one and many-to-many. These are depicted between the entities Doctor and Patient in Fig. 6.6. Which of these is correct depends upon the precise nature of the relationship that is

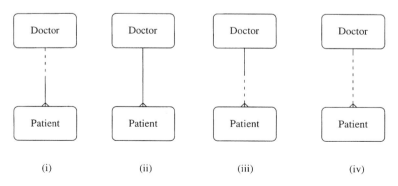

Fig. 6.5   Optionality

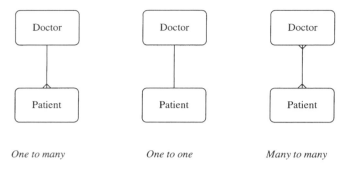

One to many   One to one   Many to many

Fig. 6.6   Degrees of relationships

being modelled. The relationship on the left-hand side depicts the usual situation with regard to GPs. The many-to-many relationship might model a hospital situation where a patient can be seen by many consultants. The one-to-one situation only really applies to Roman emperors, princes of the royal blood, etc. who have their own personal physician. Normally we do not allow a many-to-many relationship on a Logical Data Structure, replacing the original one with two one-to-many relationships and a link entity. Figure 6.7 shows how this might occur with a Doctor/Patient relationship. Similarly, a one-to-one relationship is usually removed by merging one of the participating entities with the other. These guidelines should not be followed slavishly, as quite often many-to-many and one-to-one relationships can be maintained until physical design. Ultimately, it is the comprehensibility of the model which is important.

The presence or absence of keys is another hotly debated topic. Although every entity in the Logical Data Model for the new required system produced in step 320 will require a key, they are not essential for the current system Logical Data Model. If, for example, employees are identified by their name rather than a unique number, as far as the current Logical Data Model is concerned this is fine. Where keys are included there is often further debate as to whether the key of a master should be included in a detail and vice versa. Thus for the two entities of Fig. 6.4 should a Patient list among its attributes a reference to the Doctor, and should a Doctor list the patients allocated to him or her? The answer to the second of these questions is no. Attributes should be single-valued, and there is no limit to the number of patients a particular doctor could be allocated. The connection between these two is really the responsibility of the relationship. The situation with regard to the Patient entity is not quite so straightforward.

Fig. 6.7   Many-to-many relationships

Doctor could certainly be recorded as a single-valued attribute of it. On the other hand, it could be argued that this merely duplicates information carried by the relationship. Despite this argument, it is often included as an attribute, since this conforms with the results of Relational Data Analysis.

A particular entity can have any number of masters. If we wish to put some choice into a Logical Data Structure, an exclusive arc has to be used. In Fig. 6.8 only one of the relationships is active. In other words, a site must be represented by a Rep or be privately owned. Exclusive arcs applied to an entity's masters are quite common and can be applied to any number of relationships. If an arc crosses three relationships, only one of these can apply to any given occurrence. Exclusive arcs can also be applied to an entity's details.

Version 4 of SSADM introduced the concept of sub-types. Loosely speaking, these are used where two entities share many attributes but also have significant differences. In a hospital system, for example, we might wish to differentiate between in-patients and out-patients. Obviously, for each type of patient there is much that is common, but there are important differences. Figure 6.9 shows how this might be modelled.* The attributes of the 'superentity' Patient are those that are common to both types of patient, while the attributes of each 'subentity' are those that are individual to it. Thus the attributes of each might be

Patient	*In-patient*	*Out-patient*
Name	Ward number	Treatment centre
Address	Bed number	Number of visits
Date of birth	Days in hospital	Date of next visit
. . .	. . .	. . .

In some sense, each of the sub-types inherits attributes from the super-type.† Note also that each of these entities can participate in a relationship. Of course, it is possible to ignore subtypes completely. We could have two separate entities, but this would

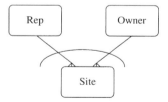

Fig. 6.8   Exclusivity

---

*There is an alternative notation, used by ORACLE CASE for example, and now introduced into SSADM Version 4.2, where a sub-type is contained within a super-type. Although this appears more intuitive, it does not agree with the conventions usually used in the Object Orientated literature and cannot cope very well with sub-types of sub-types.

†Sub-types have their origin in the world of object orientation. There sub-types inherit operations (methods) as well as attributes. Indeed it is possible for a sub-type to have no attributes, but just to have inheritable methods. For a full discussion of these concepts see, for example, Rumbaugh *et al.* (1991) or Henderson-Sellers (1992).

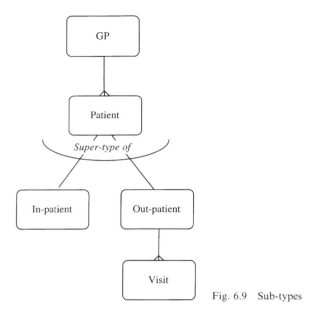

Fig. 6.9   Sub-types

mean that every operation involving patients as a whole would have to reference the two entities, or we could have one giant entity, but this would cause a proliferation of null attributes.

A logical data model consists of the following items of documentation:

- Logical Data Structure
- Entity descriptions
- Attribute descriptions
- Grouped domain descriptions
- Relationship descriptions

The entity descriptions are just a list of the attributes of an entity. A more detailed description of each attribute, its length and format for example, are contained in the attribute descriptions. This is quite a sensible approach for those using CASE tools, but if pen and paper are all that are available, a combined Entity/Attribute description is of more use. Grouped Domain Descriptions are only really useful to those using a data dictionary as part of a CASE tool, and their use therefore should be governed by the facilities available in the tool. Since such CASE tools are often used, standard SSADM groups Attribute and Grouped Domain descriptions together as part of the Data Catalogue rather than the Logical Data Model. Finally, it is worth noting that relationships are well described by means of the Logical Data Structure. The only thing that is really missing is volumetric information, and it is doubtful whether this merits the extensive documentation of full Relationship Descriptions.

Despite these last comments, it is worth emphasizing that the Logical Data Model is an essential document in the system development process, and as such should always be developed in full.

6.4 STEP 150—DEFINE LOGICAL VIEW OF CURRENT SERVICES

So far we have concentrated on *how* the current system works, rather than attempting to describe *what* it does. The Current Physical Dataflow Model in particular is an attempt to represent things as they are done, not as how they should be done. It's as if we painted a portrait of the workings of the current system which detailed every little wart in glowing technicolour. Obviously matters cannot be left like this, for then all our knowledge would be about the detailed technical procedures of the existing system, and we would have little comprehension as to what the system is trying to achieve or as to why it works in the way it does. If a future system was built upon the inadequate foundations of Current Physical Dataflow Model, it would merely computerize existing processes, and so perpetuate many of the problems and constraints present in the current system. In step 150 the Current Logical Dataflow Model is developed to surmount these concerns. Exactly how this is done is detailed in the next chapter.

6.5 ASSEMBLE INVESTIGATION RESULTS

The last task in stage 1 is to assemble the Investigation Results and to finalize the Requirements Catalogue. The major documents emerging from the investigative phase of Rapid SSADM are:

- Business Activity Model
- Current Logical Data Model
- Current Physical Dataflow Model
- Current Logical Dataflow Model

Although this is a full list of the SSADM products from the stage, it is incomplete. PRINCE, for example, suggests extending this list by including such things as hardware usage, current costs and limitations of the current system. In a manual system, organizational hierarchies might also prove useful. All in all, when publishing this summary document, the analyst should be guided by the standards of the organization.

Requirements are also finalized here. There may be discussion as to what is and is not a requirement, especially if conflicts have arisen between users. Whatever the result of these discussions, the final task is to prioritize any requirements. Whether they are divided into mandatories and desirables, or scored on a scale from 1 to 10 doesn't really matter. What is important is that some form of ranking exists.

6.6 THE HAPPY CAMPING CASE STUDY

This is for the Happy Camping Holiday Booking System which forms the basis of the case study in this book. Happy Camping is a company that owns a number of camping sites and also runs a camping holiday business. The work of Happy Camping is based upon three branches—the Customer Office, Site Liaison and Finance. In more detail the system operates as follows.

Customers send in booking forms to reserve a plot on one of a number of sites (Fig. 6.10). These may be one of Happy Camping's own or one of a small number of

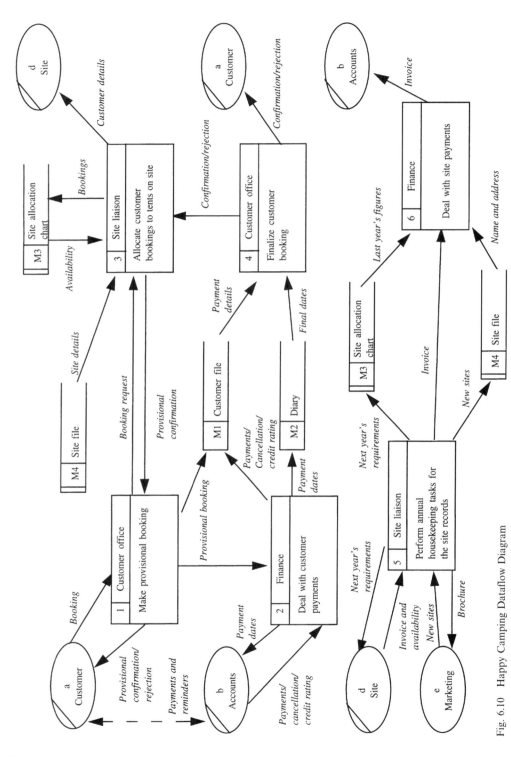

Fig. 6.10 Happy Camping Dataflow Diagram

privately owned sites used by the company. Bookings are initially dealt with by the Customer Office. Details of the dates and sites required by the customer are sent to Site Liaison who inform them whether or not a plot is free. If not, the Customer is sent a rejection letter. Usually, however, the plot is free in which case the Customer is sent a provisional confirmation, the provisional booking is placed on the Customer File, and details of the booking are sent to Finance. Payments normally have to be made one month before the start of the holiday. This date is entered by Finance into the Diary. Finance also send the payment due dates to the Accounts Department of Happy Camping.

When any payments are received or the Customer cancels, Accounts notify Finance, who enter details in the Customer File against the appropriate provisional booking. Accounts also notify Finance of any changes in customer credit ratings. The Customer Office are also responsible for checking that a booking has been paid in time. This they do by looking in the diary to determine which holidays are due to start in a month's time. From the Customer file the payment situation is checked. If the holiday has been paid for, a final confirmation letter is sent to the Customer, and their details are passed to Site Liaison, who in turn pass them on to the actual site. Otherwise, the booking is cancelled, a rejection letter issued and the plot released.

At the end of each year, the site sends an invoice to Happy Camping. Site Liaison pass this on to Finance, who check the figures against the Site Allocation Chart before passing it on to Accounts. At the same time as the invoice arrives, the site informs Happy Camping about availability for the next year. Site Liaison then book a block of plots for that year. Finally, Marketing sends details of any new sites to Site Liaison, who in turn prepare next year's brochure which is passed back to Marketing for publication and distribution.

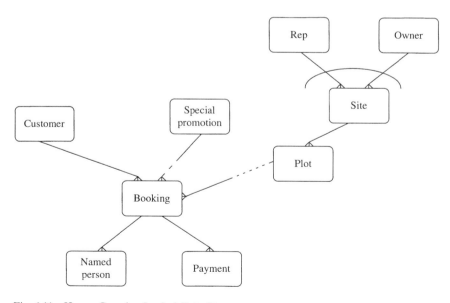

Fig. 6.11   Happy Camping Logical Data Structure

The Logical Data Structure for the Happy Camping System is as shown in Fig. 6.11. From this it is clear that customers make holiday bookings, and that each booking is for a tent on a plot on a site. The bookings can be for a party of several people and may be made under special promotional schemes (for example, a 10 per cent reduction might apply to bookings made in February). Each booking is subject to a number of payments, usually consisting of a deposit and a final payment.

THE LOGICAL DATAFLOW MODEL

7.1 PURPOSE

Even in the best ordered of systems there are problems and physical constraints. These constraints arise for a variety of reasons. Sometimes they are purely procedural. For example, a specific item of work, filing orders say, may in a manual system be done more efficiently upon a whole batch of input. On the Current Physical Dataflow Diagram this necessitates the existence of a temporary holding store. There is no logical reason why each order could not be processed immediately upon arrival, and so the batching procedure would not be present on any logical model. Other constraints may be geographical. This type of constraint often leads to duplication and redundancy. For example, a company might own two sites, one in Exeter and one in Glasgow. It might be in the best interests of the company to split the work functionally between the two sites, but such compartmentalization might not always be possible. Thus Exeter and Glasgow could end up doing the same sort of things. This implies some duplication of processes, and hence some redundancy on the Current Physical Dataflow Diagrams. Political and managerial decisions can often lead to similar problems.

Oddities in a system can often have historical origins. For example, some time ago a particular individual in team A may have found an aspect of the work to be difficult, and as a result, part of this work may have been transferred to team B. The individual concerned might long since have departed, but the work remains with team B, even though it should logically reside with team A. All these idiosyncrasies should not to be allowed to linger into the new system, and so should be removed as soon as possible. There is, however, one type of constraint that should remain. These are legal constraints. There are usually pressing reasons for these and so they will have to be reproduced on the final model.

The Current Logical Dataflow Model is produced in step 150. This model excludes the physical constraints, duplication and redundancy so often present in the Current Physical Dataflow Model. It is an attempt to provide a picture of what the system does, rather than of how it does it. As such, it illustrates, to both analysts and users alike, a clearer picture of the system and so provides a much better springboard for the design of the required system.

The Logical Dataflow Model is also useful in unifying the two representations of data. Previously in stage 1 two separate views of the data were developed, one as the datastores on the Dataflow Diagrams and one as the entities on the Logical Data Model. There is no guaranteed connection between these two. After all, when constructing the Logical Data Model, it's as if we deliberately went out of our way to strip all the individual data items from the datastores and rearrange them into nice logical piles called entities. To reunite these two opposing views, the Logical Dataflow Diagrams contain new logical datastores designed explicitly from the Logical Data Model.

The Current Physical Dataflow Model and the Logical Data Model are the major inputs to step 150 (Fig. 7.1). During logicalization, new requirements are often uncovered and so the Requirements Catalogue could well be updated.

There is obviously a close relationship between a Current Logical Dataflow Model and a Business Activity Model. The former documents what processes the system should perform, while the latter concentrates upon essential business activities. Trying to draw a distinction between what constitutes a process and what constitutes an activity seems rather like semantic nitpicking, and so in this book the view will be that processes on the Logical Dataflow Model should not differ from activities on the functional decomposition.

7.2 STEPS

There are two ways of constructing a Logical Dataflow Model: the 'top-down' approach and the 'bottom-up' approach. The first approach involves looking at the system as a whole, and deciding what needs to be done in terms of seven or eight major business activities. Each of these business activities is decomposed into increasingly

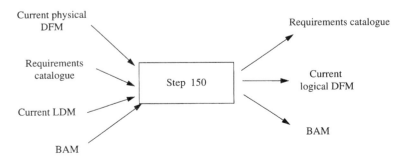

Fig. 7.1   Inputs and products

finer detail. This approach is quick and easy for experienced analysts, but could risk missing out essential detail documented on the Current Physical Dataflow Model. The 'bottom-up' approach avoids this problem by attempting to rearrange the Current Physical Dataflow Model in a more 'logical' way. This approach is safer in that existing procedures are unlikely to be overlooked, but it is long and cumbersome. Given that we are developing a faster version of SSADM, and already have a functional decomposition, the 'top-down' approach seems preferable. (Standard SSADM uses the 'bottom-up' approach. For a full description of this technique, see one of the standard SSADM texts, for example Ashworth and Slater, 1993; Eva, 1992; or Weaver, 1992.) Moreover, in those situations where there is no existing system, the 'top-down' approach is the only one that is viable.

There is a step-by-step approach to the production of Logical Dataflow Diagrams:

1. Revisit the Business Activity Model. The objective here is to ensure that all activities on the functional decomposition are still relevant.
2. Define Logical Datastores. These are the datastores that will be placed on the new Logical Dataflow Diagrams. They are derived directly from the Logical Data Model.
3. Produce a Logical Dataflow Model. This is drawn directly in a top-down way, taking the processes from the decomposition.
4. Check against Physical Dataflow Model. Has anything been missed?
5. Validate with the user.

7.3 REVISIT THE BUSINESS ACTIVITY MODEL

The Business Activity Model was an initial attempt to describe what the business does. In the functional decomposition the system was split into a maximum of seven or eight major business activities, with each of these being decomposed into sub-activities and so on. This view of the system was based primarily upon interviews with senior managers in the user area. Since then, the development team would have investigated the system in greater detail, spoken to those working in more operational areas, and so obtained fresh insights into the workings of the system. While the overall structure of the Business Activity Model and the higher levels of the Functional Decomposition should stay the same, it is quite likely that changes have to be made to the lowest-level activities on the hierarchy.

The question then arises as to which basic processes or activities should be included on the lowest levels of the decomposition. Again, the simple answer is that all included processes should be meaningful, and so should be of some consequence to the workings of the system. Trivial processes or those purely concerned with the physical organization should be omitted. In this latter category come processes that merely send data from one location to another, processes that batch data for later processing and processes that merely reorganize data (i.e. sorts). On the whole, the important processes included usually mean those that change data. For this reason, pure retrievals such as screen displays and printed reports are usually omitted from the hierarchy. Details of such retrievals are not lost, but are copied into the Requirements Catalogue.

Nonetheless, an analyst should not regard the last statement as giving her or him *carte blanche* to remove *all* retrievals from the functional decomposition. In statistics systems, for example, the retrievals are often the most important part of the processing. Removing all retrievals would probably leave nothing other than one process that takes on data and one that deletes data. For such systems, the important retrievals, such as the production of monthly figures and annual reports, are left on the decomposition, while *ad hoc* reports tend to be removed.

Payroll systems provide another example where retrievals often remain on the hierarchy. In this type of system, printing the payslips is often a pure retrieval. Removing this from the model would, I imagine, cause some concern. As a general rule, if a retrieval is important in the day-to-day working of a system, or if it is needed to make other processes function correctly, it should remain. For this reason, the process 'Check Plot availability' is still included on the Happy Camping decomposition in Fig. 4.4, as it is really a part of the whole booking process.

7.4 CONVERSION TO LOGICAL DATAFLOW DIAGRAM

The next step involves changing the functional decomposition into a Logical Dataflow Diagram. Activities on the first level of the decomposition become processes on the top-level Dataflow Diagram. Similarly, activities on lower levels of the hierarchy become processes on lower-level Dataflow Diagrams. Figure 7.2 illustrates this for the Happy Camping system. Note that as who does the process is no longer of any interest, the location part of the process box is not completed. Clearly though, before we can draw a Dataflow Diagram there are other components to identify and it is to the datastores we turn our attention next.

7.5 LOGICAL DATASTORES

Datastores on the Current Physical Dataflow Diagram are representations of actual physical stores of data. They can be manual files, filing cabinets, wallcharts, record cards, computer files, databases or many other things. Unfortunately, data in physical datastores is often not kept in the most efficient manner. A common problem, especially in regard to manual datastores, is one of data duplication and redundancy. We often record items of information in two or more different forms. Sometimes this is because different groups of people require access to the data and so need their own files. On other occasions it is because the data has to be accessed in different ways, and so the same data is held in two files ordered differently. Another problem with physical datastores is that the data often refers to a large number of entities. Thus a Customer Order File may contain information about customers, orders, products and suppliers. It is unlikely that it would contain full information about any of these entities. There is, therefore, no obvious correspondence between the datastores and the logical data model.

Logical Datastores overcome all these problems by the simple expedient of basing them directly on the Logical Data Model. Each Logical Datastore contains one or more entities. At first, the best approach would seem to be to make each Logical Datastore

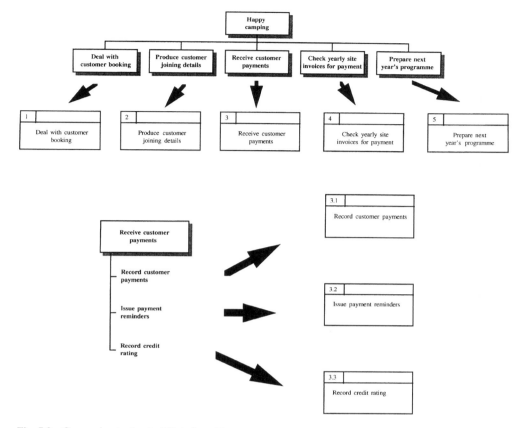

Fig. 7.2   Conversion to Logical Dataflow Diagram

equivalent to a single entity. Unfortunately, for a number of reasons, the rule 'one Logical Datastore equals one entity' is unsatisfactory. First, there are probably far too many entities. A medium-sized Logical Data Model might contain sixty to eighty entities, and a similar number of datastores would swamp any dataflow diagram. Second, link entities, especially those tersely named 'A/B link' or something similar, are often of little relevance to users. This is unacceptable given that dataflow diagrams are intended to be the most user-friendly diagram in SSADM. For these reasons, each Logical Datastore can contain more than one entity.

How are these groupings to be made? Logical Datastores are intended to be understandable to the user, thus the primary aim must be to partition the Logical Datastores in a 'user-friendly' way. Each grouping on the Logical Datastore should be capable of being described by a single name meaningful to the user. Thus a grouping of entities A, B and C into the 'A–B–C datastore' is unlikely to be successful. Another consideration is that the entities in any grouping should be connected. Clearly we shouldn't bring together entities appearing on opposite sides of the Logical Datastore. Finally it would be useful if entities grouped together were processed together. Not only are such entities likely to be closely related, but from a practical viewpoint if two entities are always processed together, then placing them in the same logical datastore cuts down the number of arrows on the dataflow diagram. Figure 7.3 shows possible groupings on the Happy Camping system Logical Data Structure.

There is a certain degree of subjectivity about the way in which the groupings are done. Some entities will always go together. For example, the Named Person entity represents the people who appear on the booking. Whatever happens to the Booking entity is quite likely to happen also to the Named Person entity. Moreover, the user is unlikely to recognize this entity as distinct, but rather would regard it as something that is entered on a booking form. Thus these two entities will always be grouped together. Other groupings are a little more problematic. In Fig. 7.3 Payments have been separated from the Bookings. It could be argued that this entity should be grouped with Booking and Named Person, as there are a fixed number of payments per booking. This is perfectly acceptable, but would lead to different groupings, and hence to different dataflows on the final Dataflow Diagrams.

The groupings made are formally recorded upon a document called the 'Logical Datastore/Entity Cross-Reference'. A copy of this document for the Happy Camping system is shown in Fig. 7.4. From this document it is clear that although a single datastore may group several entities, each entity is contained in one and only one Logical Datastore.

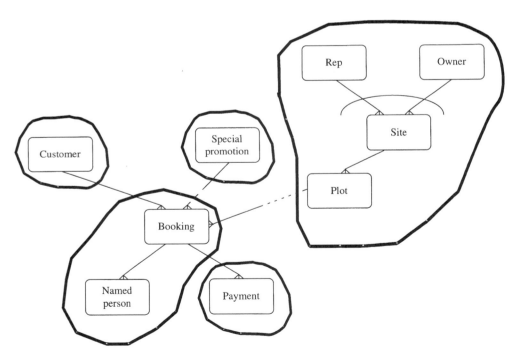

Fig. 7.3   Happy Camping Logical Data Structure groupings

Logical Datastore / Entity Cross Reference		
Current **X** Required ☐		
System Happy Camping	**Date**	31/5/93

DataSt ID	Logical Datastore	Entities
D1	Customers	Customer
D2	Bookings	Booking Named Person
D3	Payments	Payment
D4	Discounts	Special Promotion
D5	Campsites	Site Plot Owner Rep

Fig. 7.4   Logical Datastore/Entity Cross-Reference

7.6 COMPLETION OF LOGICAL DATAFLOW MODEL

So far, we have reviewed the functional decomposition and produced a complete set of logical datastores. Our next task is to put them all together and produce a complete set of Dataflow Diagrams. Obviously to complete the diagrams dataflows and external entities must be added. Hence for each process we need to ask the following questions:

1. What data does this process require as input and what does it produce as output?
2. Is the input data held internally or is it provided by an external entity?
3. If the input data is held internally, which datastore does it come from? This is akin to asking which entity stores the information, and then using the Datastore/Entity Cross-Reference to find the appropriate datastore.
4. Does the process update datastores (entities)?
5. Which external entity, if any, receives the output?

By answering these questions, the dataflows, logical datastores and external entities can be attached to a process. Figure 7.5 illustrates this being done for the first process on the decomposition.

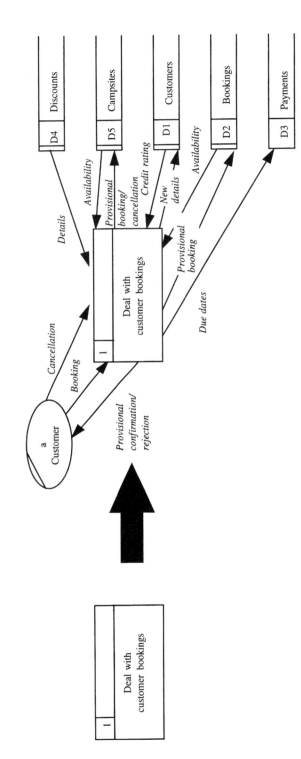

Fig. 7.5 Completion of Logical Dataflow Diagrams

Each level of the functional decomposition forms the basis for a Dataflow Diagram. Figure 7.6 illustrates the first level of the Happy Camping functional decomposition transformed into a top-level Dataflow Diagram. To construct a full Dataflow Model we need to produce Dataflow Diagrams for every level of the decomposition and to complete Elementary Process Descriptions for each of the bottom-level processes, I/O descriptions for each dataflow that crosses the system boundary and a list of external entities.

7.7 GUIDELINES FOR PROCESSES APPEARING ON THE LOGICAL DATAFLOW DIAGRAMS

There are a number of guidelines which govern the appearance and form of processes that appear on Logical Dataflow Diagrams. First, since we are no longer interested in how a job is done or who does it, all references to physical locations and physical media must be removed. Figure 7.7 illustrates this point. On the Physical Dataflow Diagram, the *Office Clerk* is the person who checks an application *form*. The name of the person and the medium of the customer booking do not survive in the Logical Dataflow Diagram.

Sometimes it is important that a particular task is done by a particular individual. An example of this appears in Fig. 7.8. The process on the left-hand side is taken from the current *physical* Dataflow Diagram, and shows the Personnel Manager selecting candidates for promotion. If it is important that the Personnel Manager is always involved in such decisions, then this process cannot remain on the Logical Dataflow Model, since to leave it would assume that the process could be done by anyone, or even that it could be automated. The solution is to take the work done by the named individual outside the system, and make that individual into an external entity. This is illustrated on the right-hand side of Fig. 7.8. The task of selection, as performed by the Personnel Manager, is now outside the system. Obviously, the Personnel Manager still needs to obtain information from the Employees datastore and to record his or her decision on it. Thus processes 4.3 and 4.4 are needed in order that the Personnel Manager can communicate with the system. Generally, all elements of subjective decision making must be taken outside the system. Ultimately, all processes on the Logical Dataflow Model must be capable of being automated.

All processes on the logical Dataflow Diagram should be as compact as possible. Tasks on the Current Physical Dataflow Diagram are often split into many processes since they have to be done by different people. Figure 7.9 illustrates such a case. In the manual system, responsibility for the collection of pay is spread between three individuals. In the logical system there is little need for such a split, and a single process will suffice. In earlier versions of SSADM, this point was made by the memorable phrase 'remove logically redundant inter-process dataflows'!

The Logical Dataflow Diagrams should give a clean picture of what the current system is trying to achieve. Figure 7.10 illustrates the ideal situation. At the top level we aim for 'one trigger/one process'. In other words, a single event should trigger one process, not a series of processes. Thus the situation on the right-hand side of Fig. 7.10 is acceptable, but that on the left-hand side is unacceptable. It should be

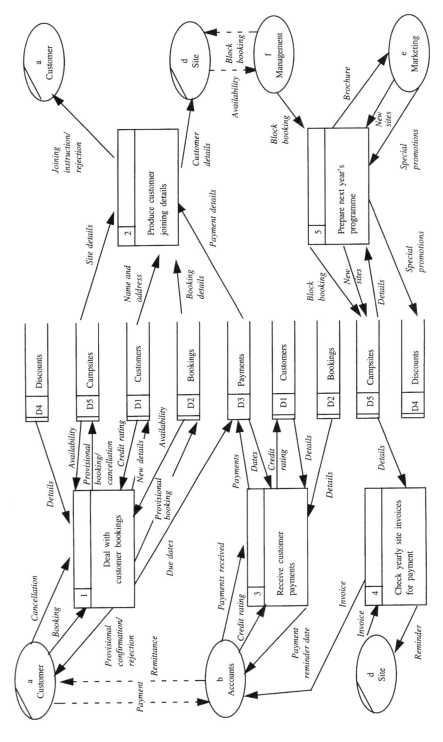

Fig. 7.6 Happy Camping Logical Dataflow Diagram

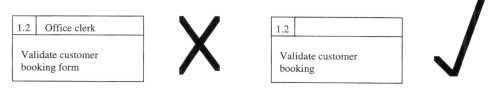

Fig. 7.7   Removal of physical attributes

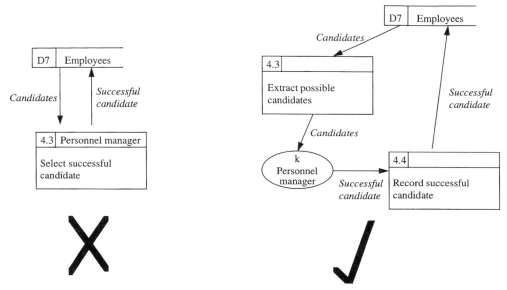

Fig. 7.8   Subjective decision making

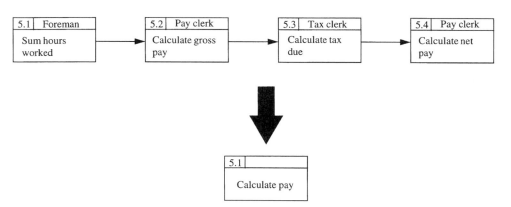

Fig. 7.9   Series of processes

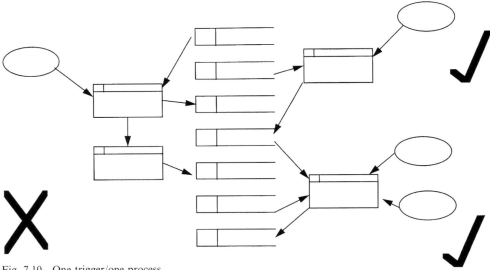

Fig. 7.10   One trigger/one process

emphasized that this is only an ideal, more likely to be realized on the upper levels of the Dataflow Diagrams.

7.8 TRANSIENT DATASTORES

A transient datastore is a short-lived datastore on the current system. Unlike the main datastores on a Dataflow Diagram, transient datastores are not used for the permanent storage of data, but rather for the temporary storage of data 'in transit'. Typical examples are in-trays and pigeonholes. Their major purpose is to handle physical constraints in the existing system and in particular to delay processing.

Because transient datastores only exist to overcome the physical constraints of the existing system, *they should NOT appear on the Logical Dataflow Diagrams*. In our 'top-down' approach to logicalization, we have no way of generating transient datastores, and so this will only be a problem when checking the Logical Dataflow Diagrams against the Physical Dataflow Diagrams. Transient datastores are more of a problem in standard SSADM which employs a 'bottom-up' method. In this approach they have actually to be removed from the diagrams. For this reason, standard SSADM denotes transient datastores by a T, and so an in-tray might be identified as T1/2(M). (The M in brackets signifies that it is manual.)

7.9 VALIDATION OF THE LOGICAL DATAFLOW MODEL

The final task in step 150 is to validate the Logical Dataflow Model. First, the Logical Dataflow Model is checked against the Physical Dataflow Model. This is absolutely essential in our 'top-down' approach since the logical model has been developed without any reference to existing dataflow diagrams. There are two things to check:

1. Are all the essential processes on the Current Physical Dataflow Model catered for on the logical model? To do this we can list all meaningful processes from the Physical Dataflow Model and tick them off against those on the Logical Dataflow Model. Obviously, trivial processes such as sorts and those producing minor reports should be ignored. We also need to ensure that each dataflow to and from a physical process is replicated for the corresponding logical process.
2. Are all the non-transient datastores on the Current Physical Dataflow Model covered by the Logical Datastores? We need to check that all flows to and from physical datastores are covered by the logical model.

The second aspect of validation involves the checking of the Logical Dataflow Model with the user. Here the pertinent question concerns the extent to which the Logical Dataflow Model represents the user's view as to what the business is trying to achieve. There is a problem here with Logical Dataflow Diagrams. Physical Dataflow Diagrams were excellent for eliciting a response from users actually doing the work. Each could see themselves, together with all the files they used and all the outside people they spoke to, right there on the picture. However, on the Logical Dataflow Diagram not only have they themselves disappeared, but so have their familiar day-to-day tasks and the files they use. These two latter items are replaced by abstract processes and logical datastores. All this is a little disconcerting to people intimately involved with the work of the existing system. They are more likely to be worried about how the job is done now, and from this perspective are likely to object to the Logical Dataflow Diagram.

It could be argued that by concentrating on what is being achieved, a Logical Dataflow Model really represents a management view of the system. Perhaps user management should validate the Logical Dataflow Model. This is all very well in theory, but in practice one finds that managers are often unwilling to expend time and effort in coming to grips with any technical document. Indeed, the more senior the management, the more likely it is that they would demand a simpler presentation of information. Even if they did agree to rigorously check the dataflow model, one should ask if any point is served in demanding that a user checks the content of a dataflow from a logical datastore to a logical process. It is far better to present senior user management with a copy of the functional decomposition, and ask them if this is a true and accurate breakdown of the business. Senior managers would have few problems in understanding this document. In fact most probably think in such terms already! How the information has been transferred from the decomposition onto the Dataflow Model is a technical issue which need not trouble the users.

7.10 LOGICAL DATAFLOW MODEL

A full Logical Dataflow Model consists of the following:

- Dataflow Diagrams (all levels)
- Elementary process descriptions, one for each of the lowest-level processes on the Dataflow Diagrams

- I/O descriptions. These describe the content of all dataflows that cross the system boundary (i.e. for those flows between an external entity and a process)
- External entity list
- Logical Datastore/Entity Cross-Reference

Is all this documentation really necessary? Following our discussions in the previous section, there must be doubts raised as to the usefulness of the diagrams. They are not as good as the functional decomposition in illustrating what the system does in terms of processing, so why bother expending time and effort in producing them? The only extra things they add are external entities, logical datastores and the accompanying dataflows. It might be argued that at least a Dataflow Diagram shows the interfaces between the existing system and the external world, but this is done equally well on the current physical one. It is unlikely that there would be much change to the external entities (other than the addition of those expelled for subjective decision making). There seems to be even less reason to develop logical datastores. After all, Logical Datastores are only a contrived device used to describe the interplay between the processes on the Logical Dataflow Diagram and the entities on the Logical Data Model. They have very little use until new system design, and even there this interplay is far better described by the Access Paths. However if the Dataflow Diagrams go, then so do the I/O descriptions, the External Entity List and the Datastore/Entity Cross-Reference. The only things that are left are the Elementary Process Descriptions and these are no more than the Business Activity Descriptions under a different name.

The relationship between the various models is shown in Fig. 7.11. The full Business Activity Model consists of

- Context Diagram
- Functional Decomposition
- Business Activity Descriptions (lowest level)

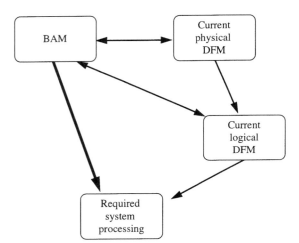

Fig. 7.11   Relationship between the Business Activity Model and Dataflow Models

which is quite sufficient for input to the design of the required system. In the author's opinion, the only reason for ever producing Logical Dataflow Diagrams is if one is mandated to do so by the customer.

The final question we need to answer concerns the viability of the Current Physical Dataflow Model. Since all future development is based upon the logical model, can we ignore the physical model, either completely or in part? Given that we are in the market for a rapid version of SSADM, such an approach has its attractions. If the physical model is completely abandoned, and only the functional decomposition is produced for the logical model, then no dataflow diagram will be produced at all. The major drawback to this is that no picture, other than the Context Diagram, will be produced showing the (vital) connections between the system and the external world. A top-level Dataflow Diagram, whether physical or logical, should perhaps be produced. Accepting this argument, the question still remains as to whether there is a need to produce a complete *set* of Dataflow Diagrams for the current physical system. It must be said that experienced analysts could produce a functional decomposition immediately from discussions with the user. Such an approach is, however, somewhat risky. It's all very fast and hectic, and doesn't give the analyst time to explore the workings of the system and to come to some reasoned judgement about its purpose. Moreover, without a formal recording of how things happen, it is quite likely that some perhaps vital processing detail would be missed. In the best of all possible worlds, the extent to which the current physical system is documented should be governed by its relevance to the future system, not by the amount of time available, or lacking, to the development team.

EIGHT

BUSINESS SYSTEM OPTIONS

8.1 THE GENERAL APPROACH

A Business System Option (BSO) describes what the future system is supposed to do. A number of possible approaches is developed in step 210 and the Project Board selects one of them in step 220 (Fig. 8.1).

Such options will, of course, be based primarily upon the Requirements Catalogue. Moreover, as the new system often emerges from the ashes of an existing one, another major input is a description of the Current Environment, in particular the Business Activity Model and the Logical Data Model. Although it is possible to directly construct options from these products, the analyst seldom has such a free hand. He or she is frequently constrained by earlier work documented in the Project Initiation Document or the Feasibility Report. These will contain relevant information about project

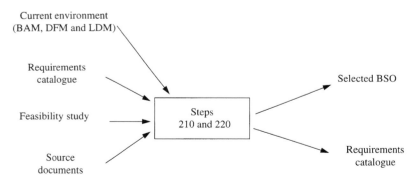

Fig. 8.1   Inputs and products

objectives, the major proposed products of the new system, anticipated benefits and costs, relationships with other systems/projects and IT security risks, all of which must influence the analyst. The only *required* output from this stage is the Selected Business System Option. This does not mean that any rejected options should be thrown away. They are important for historical reasons, not least for allocating blame if the project should go horribly wrong! With this in mind they are retained as management products in the PRINCE product classification.

The general approach to Business Systems Options is illustrated in Fig. 8.2. Each option consists of a group of requirements that could be satisfied by the required system. Obviously, each should address the mandatory requirements, though often a 'no-change' or 'do-nothing' option is included for the sake of comparison. A bare list of requirements is clearly insufficient for the Project Board to make a meaningful choice and so each of the options will contain details on the following:

- *Functionality.* Which requirements are included in the option? An option should not only consider the priority of the requirements addressed, it should also discuss the extent to which the functional areas integrate and in general justify the practicality of any choice.
- *Cost/benefit analysis.* This should be done according to the standards of the organization. In the public sector, it normally involves some form of discounted cash flow. This can be difficult especially if the technical solution has yet to be specified.
- *Development plan.* This should not only address system design and development, but should also look at issues such as testing, user training and procurement. Resource and technical plans should be available, if PRINCE is being used.
- *Impact analysis.* What are the consequences to the business as a whole of selecting this option? Special consideration should be given to staffing levels, staff working practices and training needs.
- *Risk.* An analysis of the overall business risk of the option to the project should be made. There are various checklists in existence.
- *Technical considerations.* Although Business System Options are primarily concerned with business issues rather than technical ones, it is impossible to provide reasonably firm costings without consideration of items such as hardware and software.

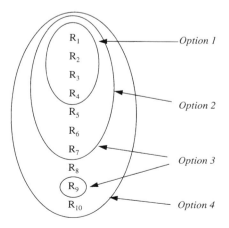

Fig. 8.2   Requirements choice

In step 210 the development team are supposed to prepare up to six options, including a minimal and a maximal solution. Creating a full Business System Option is a burdensome task, and so most teams initially produce only outline options. These are reduced to two or three after discussions with the user, and only the remaining options are developed in full. Clearly in the construction of any options, the team should be aware of constraints in terms of development time, resources, and prescribed hardware or software. The choice of option is made by the Project Board in step 220, usually after a formal presentation made by members of the development team. The Project Board can do one of three things. They can choose an option, in which case development proceeds to stage 3, they can reject all possible options thus stopping the project, or they can demand further options, which is in effect a reworking of step 210. In the latter case, the Project Board would have to meet again, this time hopefully either to go ahead or to abandon the project.

8.2 BUSINESS SYSTEM OPTIONS AND RAPID SSADM

How much of this is applicable to Rapid SSADM? In many cases the extent of the project is often determined when the business case is being examined, in which case there is little room for later manoeuvre. Nonetheless, it is important that Business System Options are not omitted, since this is one of the few opportunities for the users to influence formally the direction taken by the project. Obviously, the extent to which they are done must be governed by the urgency of the project. For the smaller and faster projects, a presentation to the Project Board is usually not necessary. The choices can be described in a paper which can be considered by the Board (or the Customer) more informally.

A final word must be said about those systems which are to be implemented by means of a package. These range from standard business systems, such as Personnel, to those of a more specialized nature which have a large number of potential users, such as patient records systems targeted at GPs. If the use of a package is mandatory, there being no desire to produce any form of bespoke software, steps 210 and 220 then become a 'Package Evaluation and Selection' step. The way in which the preceding stage of SSADM is changed is explored in Chapter 19.

THE REQUIRED SYSTEM

9.1 PURPOSE

The purpose of the Requirements Specification module is to specify in full what the new system is to do. The first two activities are those to develop a model of the required processing and a model of the required data. Although this takes place in two distinct steps of SSADM, in reality they are done together.

The major inputs to steps 310 and 320 are the selected Business Activity Model, the selected Business System Option and the Requirements Catalogue (Fig. 9.1). From these it should be clear what the new system is supposed to do. If any parts of the existing system are still relevant, the Current Dataflow Model and the Current Logical Data Model will be used as a basis for the corresponding models in the required system. The major outputs are, of course, a model of the required processing (a functional

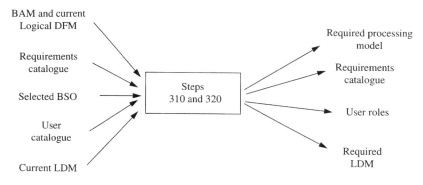

Fig. 9.1   Inputs and products

decomposition and/or Dataflow Model) from step 310 and the Required Logical Data Model from step 320. Finally, the User Catalogue is transformed into another document, the User Roles, and the Requirements Catalogue is updated with the solutions.

9.2 STEPS 310 AND 320

As it does not really matter which step is done first, we will start somewhat perversely with step 320. There is some sense in this, given that the Logical Data Model is the one document that is always produced in full. The Required Logical Data Model describes the data required for the functioning of the new system, and is usually based upon the Current Logical Data Model. Bearing in mind the requirements in the Catalogue, the analyst can add, delete or change entities, attributes and relationships on the existing model. Entity descriptions should be more detailed than for the Current Logical Data Model. In particular, each entity should be identified by a key, while relationships should be established by means of foreign keys. Although some might feel that this is strictly the province of Relational Data Analysis, the sooner it is done, the better.

In a similar way, the required processing model is generated from the Business Activity Model and the Current Logical Dataflow Model after a consideration of any extra requirements. It is worth noting that the required Dataflow Model is a Logical Dataflow Model, and so its construction is again a top-down process achieved by means of a functional decomposition. As the functional decomposition should reflect the underlying business, it should still be broken down into major business activities. An alternative approach is to envisage the system broken down into sub-systems rather in the manner of Fig. 9.2. The design of the decomposition is vital. If sufficient

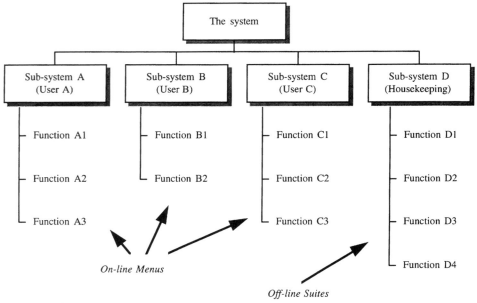

Fig. 9.2   Sub-systems

foresight is exercised, much of the subsequent work of stage 3 can be avoided. Eventually the bottom-level processes on the decomposition are to be transformed into functions, and so it seems sensible that these processes should be exactly the same as functions. (For details of functions see the next chapter.) The level above would then consist of a collection of functions probably later implemented as a menu available to a user or group of users or as a suite of off-line functions. A preliminary attempt to construct a User Role/Function matrix (see next chapter) might make the groupings easier. If the decomposition consists of three or more levels, the sub-systems themselves would need to be grouped. (In full SSADM Version 4.2 the mapping of the functions onto the decomposition is achieved more formally by means of a Work Practice Model.)

As with the current system, the functional decomposition can be expanded into a full Dataflow Model. Again if developing a system rapidly, it is worth questioning whether all the documentation is needed. The following is probably sufficient:

- A Context Diagram or top-level Dataflow Diagram
- A full processing hierarchy (or functional decomposition)
- Selected Elementary Processing/Business Activity Descriptions

The purpose of the Context Diagram or top-level Dataflow Diagram is to show the interfaces between the system and the external world. Sometimes a Context Diagram is sufficient, but at other times a more detailed description is required. The Functional Decomposition is the major vehicle for describing the processing and is useful for user communication. As the entries on it consist of, at most, a single sentence, Elementary Process Descriptions will sometimes be needed for clarification. However, it is worth noting that Elementary Process Descriptions do tend to duplicate what later appears on the Function Definitions.

There is little point in developing a full set of Dataflow Diagrams, since the information contained on them is far better conveyed by alternative techniques. Thus the dataflows between processes and external entities are described more succinctly as part of the Function Definitions, while those between processes and datastores are depicted on the Access Paths. As with the Current Logical System, the only reason to produce the extra documentation is if forced to do so by the Customer's standards. If this unfortunate set of circumstances should arise, it is easy, if tedious, to derive the full set of Dataflow Diagrams from the Functional Decomposition. The other documents, the External Entity List, the Datastore/Entity Cross-Reference and the I/O Descriptions, are easily compiled.

Two further tasks remain. The first is to annotate the Requirements Catalogue with the 'solutions'. This amounts to stating whether each of the requirements has been included on the selected Business System Option. The second task is to produce what are called the User Roles. A page from the User Roles document for the Happy Camping system is shown in Fig. 9.3. A User Role represents in some sense the way the computer system views a user. Every user will take one of these roles when interacting with the system, although some individuals will have more than just the one. The second column on the document, Job Title(s), refers to the actual or prospective jobs of those using the system, and so cross-references the people to the roles. These jobs should have been documented on the User Catalogue. Each role will,

User Roles			
System Happy Camping	**Date** 31/5/93		**Page** 3
User Role	**Job Title(s)**	**Func Id**	**Function**
Customer Clerk	Customer Liaison Clerk Customer Manager		
Office Manager	Customer Manager Tent Manager		

Fig. 9.3   Happy Camping User Roles

moreover, be allocated a package of functions. Thus from Fig. 9.3, the Customer Manager will have access both to the Customer Clerk and to the Office Manager system facilities. The appropriate columns on the form will be completed in step 330. (In standard SSADM the User Roles are allocated activities. These are translated into functions later.)

9.3 THE HAPPY CAMPING CASE STUDY

All the procedures in the current system are to be automated, and extra processes to keep track of the company's tents are to be included. The tents move between sites from season to season. The functional decomposition for the required system is shown in Fig. 9.4 and the top-level Dataflow Diagram in Fig. 9.5.

The major difference change to the Logical Data Structure for the required system is the addition of an entity for a Tent. As a tent can move around, there is an obvious many-to-many relationship between a Tent and a Plot. This is resolved by the link box Pitch which is rather like a booking for a particular tent on a particular plot (Fig. 9.6).

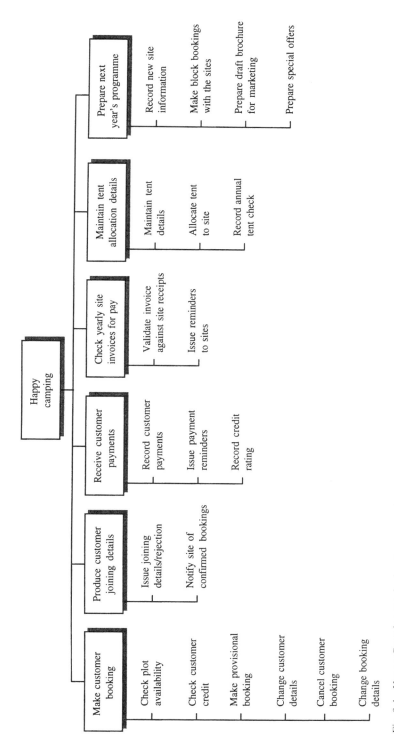

Fig. 9.4 Happy Camping required system processing

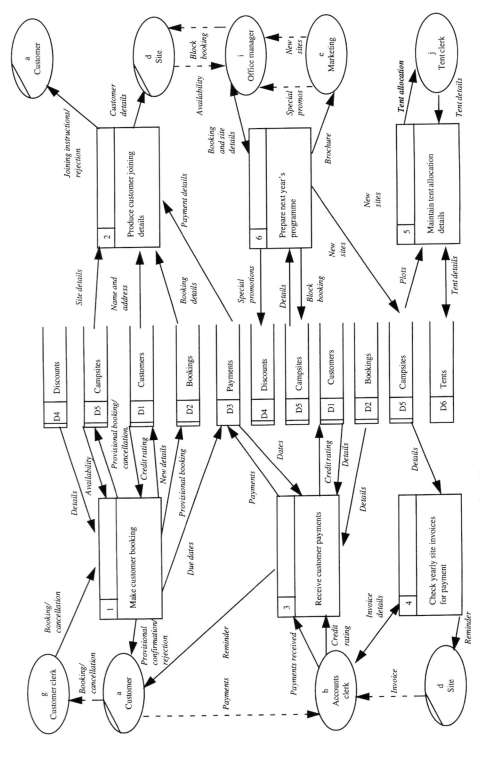

Fig. 9.5 Happy Camping required top-level Dataflow Diagram

88

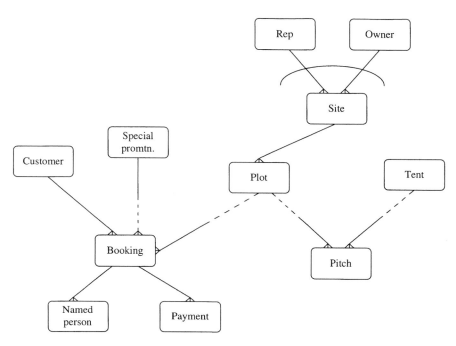

Fig. 9.6 Happy Camping required Logical Data Structure

TEN

FUNCTIONS

10.1 PURPOSE

In step 330 we construct the functions for the required system. These will represent the processing in a form that can be used easily as an input to stage 6. Earlier versions of SSADM used Dataflow Diagrams for this purpose. Indeed, it could be said that Dataflow modelling used to be *the* SSADM technique, being present at the start in stage 1 and at the end in stage 6. Unfortunately, Dataflow Diagrams do not really possess enough flexibility to embrace such a demanding role. They are fine for documenting existing systems, and for serving as a basis for communication with the user, but are far too subjective to be successfully employed in design. They tend to fall between two stools, being focused neither on the needs of the user nor on the processing requirements of a typical computer system. For this reason, in Version 4.2 of SSADM Dataflow Diagrams are abandoned soon after the start of stage 3 in the method, there to be replaced by the functions.

So what are functions? They are primarily defined as jobs the system will do for a user. There are two things we should note about this definition. First, a function is a 'job that the system will do', and as such is not far removed from a program. This contrasts with the situation with regard to DFDs, where the transformation from process to program is far from clear. Second, it is clearly an attempt to organize the system from a user's point of view, and so is much more likely to be successful in helping to achieve a system that will fully satisfy user requirements.

Although the functions replace the Dataflow Model, they can be generated from it and so tend to incorporate much previously documented material. Sometimes, functions will be based directly upon the Functional Decomposition supplemented by the Requirements Catalogue and the Logical Data Model. The collection of all the required system's functions is known as the Function Catalogue in Rapid SSADM. This is the main output from the step. Additionally, the packaging of the functions from a user perspective involves the updating of the User Roles. Finally, the Installation Style Guide may be needed for the production of first-cut screens (Fig. 10.1).

10.2 WHAT IS A FUNCTION?

In the preceding section we stated, somewhat loosely, that a function is 'a job that the system will do for a user'. Before going much further, we need to tighten this definition, and so will define a function by the following:

> A function is a distinct piece of the new system's processing as viewed by a user, which can be used independently by the user.

There are two parts to this definition. The first part states that a function must be a specific job that the system will do for a user. The second part states that a function must be able to be run as a whole by a user. Moreover, he or she should have the ability to choose whether or not to run a function independently of any other functions that might be running.* All this seems a little vague, so we will consider a few examples in the hope that this might render our definition a little clearer.

Most people will have had experience of a cash point machine. To use one, the customer is required to enter his or her cash card, and then to enter their personal identification number (PIN) via some form of keyboard or numeric keypad. The number entered is checked against that encoded on a magnetic strip on the back of the card. If the two numbers disagree, the machine will usually prompt the customer to re-enter the number via the keyboard. In the event of repeated failures, the machine will

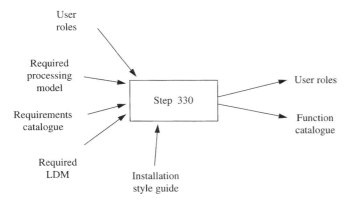

Fig. 10.1   Inputs and products

---

*SSADM Version 4.2 uses a weaker definition of a function, defining a function as a user-perceived piece of processing, ignoring any questions of independence. The main problem in doing this is that much then depends upon the level of user with which one is dealing. A technically knowledgable user might be able to identify parts of processes and programs, all of which exist at a level below that of a function.

normally swallow the card. Usually, however, the numbers do agree, in which case the customer will then be confronted with the main menu, perhaps something like

A	Cash	D	Statement request
B	Cash with receipt	E	Transfer between accounts
C	Balance	Q	Quit

After performing any of the tasks A to E, the system will normally return to this screen until such time as choice Q is selected.

So what are the functions here? Going back to our original definition, that a function is a job that the system does for a user, there are self-evidently five functions, namely:

- To provide cash
- To provide cash with a receipt
- To display the balance of an account
- To send a statement
- To transfer money between different accounts

Note that a function, rather like a process, is defined in terms of the system doing something. There are, however, a number of points to make in connection with this example.

First, on-line functions are often implemented as the bottom elements on a menu, or as the responses to a function or command key. When a choice is made and the function is entered, control passes from the user to the system. It is as if the user has moved from a car to a railway train, from a situation of having freedom of direction to one of having to follow predetermined lines as chosen by the system. Thus when a customer presses a button to ask for a balance, the system takes over, delivers the information, and returns control at the end of the function. Obviously a customer is not always quite as passive as this. When asking for cash, for example, he or she has to enter an amount. But even in this case the input is made under control of the system. It will be checked, and if the amount demanded exceeds a predefined limit the cash will be refused.

Second, emphasizing the above point, users usually make choices between functions, rather than within functions. If the first thing a function does is to ask a user whether he or she wishes to do task A or task B, then one must seriously ask whether this should be split into two separate functions. Usually the only choice a user has in determining the direction a function might take is between quitting or continuing with the function.

Finally, a function is not the same as a process on a Dataflow Diagram. There is a connection between the two concepts which we will examine later, but it is rarely straightforward. Neither will each function necessarily be transformed into a single program. Although this is a desirable state of affairs, there are instances when this might not happen. If we return to our example, it is quite likely that a single on-line program would handle much of the activity performed at the cash machine end. The function 'Provide balance', for example, would be implemented as part of this program. The situation with regard to the function 'Send statement' is, however, a little more complicated. It is unlikely that when a statement was requested the system would immediately print and despatch details. What is more likely is that all such requests would be logged, and at the end of the day a batch of statements produced. Thus the function should be implemented in two parts—an on-line component which handles the customer screen and logs the statement request and an off-line component which produces a batch of statements.

Lumping these two together probably goes against the grain for most IS professionals. They would tend to regard the on- and off-line parts as two distinct tasks which should be kept completely separate. However, the customer is not really interested where and when the statements are produced. All that concerns him or her is that when the button is pressed, a statement will appear in the post in the course of the next few days. Thus from the user's point of view, it is just the one function.

As a second example, let us turn to a typical payroll system. Here there may be many functions such as 'Provide pay analysis' or 'Alter annual salaries', but undoubtedly the major function would probably be something like 'Perform monthly payroll'. This is quite a large function, which could well be implemented as many programs. But again from the user point of view it is a single task that the system does, and hence is a single function. On the other hand, if a user perceives the payroll as consisting of a number of different tasks, each of which could be performed independently, then these would be defined as different functions. It is more likely, however, that any tasks identified by our knowledgable user would be things like 'Calculate employee pay' and 'Print payslips' which are not run independently but are automatically triggered by other parts of the Payroll function. In this case they would not be separate functions.

A payroll system may perform many housekeeping tasks, such as 'Remove defunct data from system', 'Archive inactive information' or 'Run weekly validation audit'. It might be argued that such tasks are the concern of the IS department, are not readily apparent to the user, and so cannot really be classified as (user-defined) functions. This, however, is a somewhat dangerous argument. Every housekeeping function will have some impact upon the user, even if only to the extent of costing more money to fund the writing of the programs. In the majority of cases, however, the impact on the user will be far greater than this. For example, no one in the development team should ever consider removing data from the system without consulting the user. On the other hand, it might be argued that the second of our tasks, the archiving one, is all to do with the physical performance of the database, and hence is far too technical for the user. But this is to miss the point. Archiving will tend to degrade performance and so will have an effect on the conduct of the business. Where and when data is archived is something which should be discussed with the user. Thus all housekeeping jobs, even if not initially recognized as user requirements, should end up as such, and so be defined as functions.

As a final example, let us consider a typical wordprocessor.* It is tempting to consider this as just a single function, after all it does perform the one task, wordprocessing, and even comes neatly packaged in the one box. However, when a wordprocessor is run, a writer is confronted with a vast array of choices. He or she can edit text, save text, retrieve text, run the spell checker, import graphics, get help, and so on. Each of these is a well-defined task, readily understandable to a user, and can be run

---

*Producing a wordprocessor is not a typical SSADM task! I have chosen this example because I wanted to talk about the role of functions in Windows-based applications and a wordprocessor is an example of such an application familiar to many readers.

independently. From our definition, each of these must therefore be a function. Hence, the wordprocessor is really a wordprocessing system consisting of a number of functions. If the wordprocessor operates under Windows, it is quite likely that all these functions are represented as choices on a pull-down menu. This is quite typical of a Windows-based product, with most of the choices on pull-down or pop-up menus quite likely turning out to be functions.

A word of warning! In all the above examples, we have tended to talk about functions in terms of their final implementations. We have done this in an attempt to provide a feel for what a function might be. In practice, functions are defined in stage 3, well before physical implementation. Functions are units of logical processing, and, after all, we should not be too concerned about questions of physical implementation at this point in time.

10.3 FUNCTION COMPONENTS AND CATEGORIES

Every function can be considered to consist of two parts, one concerned with its external appearance and one with its internal workings. The external appearance part governs how the function appears to a user. The user will be interested what the function does in broad terms and what it will look like, particularly in terms of screens and printed reports. All this will be fully defined in this step. The internal workings part details how the function will work, what data it will access and the order in which things are done. The degree to which one needs to consider such matters for any particular function depends to a large extent on how the function is to be implemented. Less detail is required for something that is to be implemented in SQL or any other fourth generation language than for something requiring thousands of lines of C coding. SSADM Version 4 took the view that most people will be taking a 3GL approach perhaps using something like COBOL. Thus the whole of stage 5 was devoted to detailed program design. In Rapid SSADM, we have embraced a minimalist approach in assuming that the majority of people will be using a 4GL. Thus the only step where we will be concerned with the internal workings of a function is step 365 where we construct Access Paths. This is also the approach of Version 4.2 (Fig. 10.2).

Functions can also be categorized in three different ways:

1. *Update or enquiry.* A function that changes data, in however small a way, is an update function. In all other cases, a function is merely retrieving data and so is an enquiry.
2. *On- or off-line (batch).* We differentiate between those jobs that are run from a terminal (keyboard and screen) and those run as background jobs. Note that some functions, such as the 'Provide statement details' example discussed above, do have both on- and off-line components.
3. *User or system initiated.* User-initiated functions are just what they say they are, functions started by users. In the majority of cases, an initiating user would be sat at a keyboard, and so such functions tend to be on-line. Nowadays most functions one encounters are of this type. A system-initiated function is one that is started by the system or the operators. Usually it is time triggered and often it is batch. An example of such a function would be 'End of day stock update'.

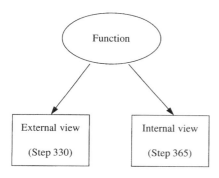

Fig. 10.2   Components of a function

10.4 IDENTIFYING FUNCTIONS

The question now arises as to how we might identify possible functions. There are five starting points for this:

1. The Required System Dataflow Model
2. The Required System Functional Decomposition
3. The Requirements Catalogue
4. Groupings on the Logical Data Model
5. System knowledge

SSADM Version 4.2 suggests that the majority of functions can be generated from the DFM and we will consider this approach first. Rather than describing how to do this in the abstract we will illustrate the process by reference to our Happy Camping case study. As functions represent a detailed view of the processing it is fairly evident that we must start from the lowest levels of DFD, and Fig. 10.3 depicts one such diagram from the case study.

This process illustrates the main tasks that take place in connection with customer bookings for holidays on one of the company's sites. Recalling that basically a function is an 'independent job that the system does for a user', what functions emerge from this diagram? Obviously process 1.1 represents one such function. This function 'Check campsite availability' is clearly an on-line user-initiated enquiry. Other functions are not, however, quite so easily identified.

Processes 1.2, 1.3 and 1.4 are connected by dataflows. This indicates that process 1.2 triggers process 1.3 which in turn triggers process 1.4. Since a function is something that can be run independently as a whole by a user, it must be the case that all three processes constitute a single function 'Make provisional booking'. In other words, from the user point of view, the three processes will be run as a single job. Nevertheless, it might emerge in discussions with the users that although in the vast majority of cases all three processes should be run together, they would also like occasionally to run process 1.3 'Check customer credit rating' independently. If this were the case, then this would become a further function. Such 'overlapping functions' do share much common processing, and might be implemented by common programs, but for the moment they are treated as logically separate functions.

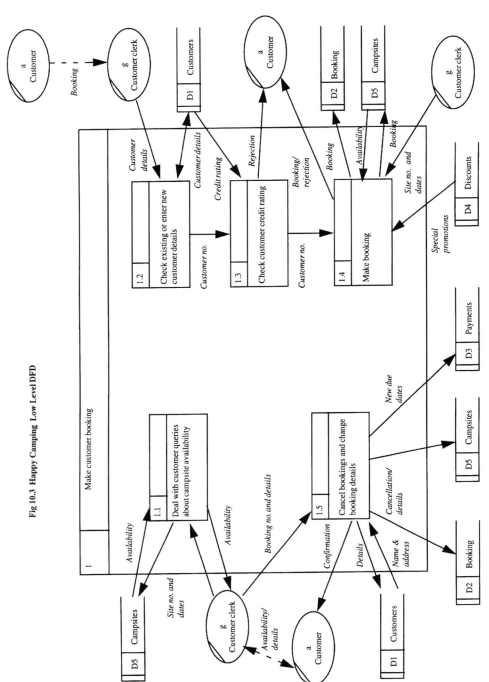

Fig 10.3 Happy Camping Low Level DFD

Fig. 10.3   Happy Camping low-level Dataflow Diagram

96

Process 1.5 represents a different type of correspondence between processes and functions. Here the process description 'Cancel bookings and change booking details' would seem to indicate the presence of two separate functions. If there is any doubt about the matter, consider how the process might operate as a single function. The first question the system would ask would be 'Do you wish to cancel a booking or just to change one?' As mentioned earlier, such a question does indicate the presence of two functions. Moreover, unless there are compelling business reasons to the contrary, it is as well to separate functions that create, delete and amend occurrences of an entity. After all, they do different things, and may well be allocated to different groups of users.

From the preceding discussion, it is clear that there is no simple correspondence between the processes on the Dataflow Diagram and the functions. Sometimes many processes form a function and at other times one process generates many functions. It might be argued that this only occurs because the Dataflow Diagrams have not been 'properly drawn'. Such arguments do, however, tend to fly in the face of practice. Dataflow Diagrams are subjective documents, being constructed primarily for the purpose of user communication. One can well understand how such a Dataflow Diagram as that of Fig. 10.3 came to be drawn. The analyst concerned would be aware that the work was primarily about customer bookings, and so decided to concentrate on what he or she perceived as the most important tasks. As a result, the processing which deals with the initial booking (1.2 to 1.4) appears in a great deal of detail. Moreover, customers need to know about campsite availability before they can book, and hence process 1.1 is also quite detailed. Finally, the analyst would be left with a list of minor tasks that were concerned with bookings and so had to be placed somewhere on the diagram. As they appeared less important, they were stuffed into a remaining process, that is, 1.5. Perhaps this is not the best way of constructing Dataflow Diagrams, but it is as well to be aware that it is quite often done this way in practice.

In the preceding chapter, we stated that it was possible to construct a Functional Decomposition and not to bother with Dataflow Diagrams except perhaps a top-level one. In this case the entries at the lowest level of the hierarchy have to be functions. To produce a successful decomposition, the analyst needs to have a feel for the scope and type of function to be included. Indeed, function definition then commences at a much earlier point in stage 3. Going from a functional decomposition to functions through Dataflow Diagrams is much safer, in that decisions as to what constitutes a function can be left until later, but, of course, this approach does take far longer.

Even the most fulsome and best constructed of Dataflow Diagrams or functional decompositions will not contain all the required system processing. These documents tend to concentrate upon the major tasks, especially the updates. This begs the question as to where we can find details of the minor jobs, the occasional reports and the *ad hoc* enquiries. For these our first port of call must be the Requirements Catalogue. Functional details are often placed there, especially for areas that are new and so have not been covered in the documentation of the existing system. How useful this is depends to a large extent on the level of detail in the Requirements Catalogue. A requirement such as 'Provide annual sales analysis by month and customer within region' is obviously quite useful, something more vague such as 'Automate new grants system' less so.

Another approach to function identification is via the Logical Data Structure. Here one can look at entities and groups of entities and ask what one needs to do with them. For example, consider a portion of the Happy Camping Logical Data Structure as shown in Fig. 10.4. The first question to ask is which entities will be processed together and which will be treated separately. In our example, the Booking and Named Person entities should be grouped together. The Named Persons are merely those people whose names appear on a Booking. From the user's point of view, they are part of a booking and so will always be processed along with the booking. On the other hand, customer information is often treated separately from booking information, and so should be left distinct. Having decided on groupings, we need to consider what functions or methods could be applied to them. At the very least we need to be sure that we can create, amend and delete all items of information. From the point of view of our Named Person entity, the questions we should ask are whether it is possible to add people to a booking, remove them from a booking or to change their personal details. If the answer to any of these questions is no, then an appropriate function should be designed for this purpose. Much of this work anticipates that done later in connection with the Entity Life Histories but there is not much harm in bringing it forward to this step.

The final way of identifying functions is the most obvious one of all, that of talking to the users! Even if functions were to be approached via Dataflow Diagrams, it is quite likely that an analyst would still need to discuss any putative ones with a user, as they will probably finally emerge in a slightly different form from those suggested initially by the diagram. Experienced analysts, who have a feel for what constitutes a function, should have little difficulty in constructing them directly from these discussions.

These two latter approaches, that is, those via the Logical Data Model and via discussions with the user, are liable to uncover fresh requirements which are additional to those included in the Catalogue. It could be argued that this would invalidate the Business System Option. In stage 2 we did after all agree a list of requirements, and even went to the bother of putting costs and timescales to them. Yet here we are now producing fresh requirements! All this is correct, and it is certainly true that *major* new requirements uncovered at this stage will negate the chosen Business System Option, forcing a fresh one to be negotiated. (The allocation of blame for such a sorry state of affairs is, of

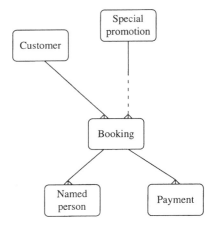

Fig. 10.4   Portion of Happy Camping required Logical Data Structure

course, the province of PRINCE!) Minor changes should cause few problems, and allowances should have been made for such contingencies in the Business System Option. After all, systems development is about giving the users the system they require.

When all the functions have been identified, they should be listed somewhere. Figure 10.5 shows a page from such a document. The column headed 'Ref' refers to the document that defines the need for the function, and is usually a process or reference to the Requirements Catalogue. This document is not essential, as it will soon be replaced by the full Function Catalogue, but is quite useful as an index.

10.5 FUNCTION DEFINITION

Having identified what they are, the next task is to complete the external definition of the functions. We will completely document how the function will appear to a user, what it does, what screens will be displayed and what reports will be produced.

To help us in this we need to complete a function definition form. This contains a great deal of information and comes in two parts.* The appropriate form(s) for the

		Function Index		
System	Happy Camping	**Date**	31/5/93	**Page** 1

Func Id	Ref	Function	Type	Comments
40	1.1	Check campsite availability	O/L Enquiry	Used mainly in response to telephone enquiries
41	1.2 1.3 1.4	Make Provisional Booking	O/L Update	This is the normal way of registering a booking
42	1.2	Change Customer Details	O/L Update	
43	1.5	Cancel Booking	O/L Update	Request from Customer
44	1.5	Change booking details	O/L Update	Site and/or dates
45	req	Find Customer details by name	O/L Enquiry	
46	req	Display credit rating	O/L Enquiry	Office manager only
47	LDM	Change people details on booking	O/L Update	Same number, same type

Fig. 10.5   Happy Camping Function Index

---

*Problems with layout are the only reasons the form has been split into two. With a CASE tool this would be presented as a single document. The discerning reader would have noticed a subtle distinction between a logical and a physical view!

function 'Make provisional booking' in the Happy Camping system are shown in Figs. 10.6 and 10.7.

Let us consider each of the individual entries on these forms:

1. *Function Id.* This is a unique number allocated to every function in the system.
2. *Function name.*
3. *Type.* This shows how the function is categorized in terms of update/enquiry and on-/off-line.
4. *Function description.* This is a high-level description of what the function does. It should be done in a language that is understandable to users and so technical terms should be avoided.
5. *Errors.* This space is reserved for recording what data input errors might be recognized by the function. At the moment we are not really concerned with identifying every single error, tending to ignore such things as syntax and integrity errors. Syntax errors are basically errors in the format of data (e.g. a part number must consist of an alphabetic letter followed by five digits). Integrity errors are usually caused by trying to reference non-existent items of data (e.g. using a syntactically correct Customer Number for which no Customer exists). These types of error are

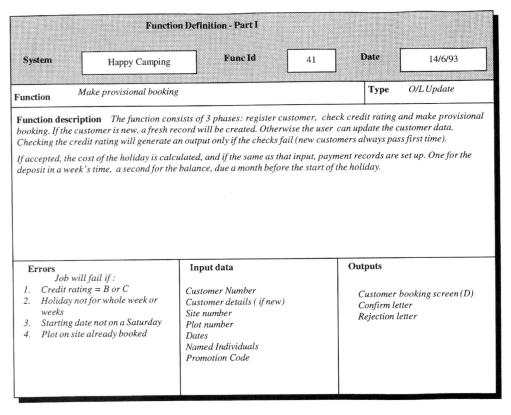

Fig. 10.6 Function Definition—Part I

Function Definition - Part II					
System	Happy Camping	**Func Id**	41	**Date**	14/6/93

Function	*Make provisional booking*
User Roles	*Customer Clerk*
Req. reference	*Requirement No 1—fully documented as processes 1.2, 1.3 and 1.4 on DFM*
Events	*Receipt of Booking*
Related Functions	*40 – Check campsite availability* *45 – Find Customer details by name*
Common Processing	
Processing Considerations	
Frequency	*35 per day*
SLRs	*Each record should take no more than 3 seconds to retrieve*

Fig. 10.7   Function Definition—Part II

usually easy to identify, and are documented in full in step 367 'Error Identification'. What concerns us here are the Business Rule Errors. These occur when acceptance of data would imply a function doing something that is contrary to the rules of the business. An example of this is given in Fig. 10.6, where the first of the errors will occur if a customer with an inappropriate credit rating books a holiday. Such errors are difficult to identify without a thorough knowledge of the business, and so should be jotted down in the space provided as soon as they are recognized. Thus an entry on the form is more in the nature of an *aide-mémoire*, rather than a formal entry in a catalogue.

6. *Input data.* What items of data are demanded by the function from the user?
7. *Outputs.* This is a listing of all the output formats, that is, screen and print layouts, for the function. They will be attached to the function definition, and we will discuss later in this chapter how they are created.
8. *User roles.* Basically the users who are allowed to use this function. Again there will be a more detailed definition of user roles later in this chapter.
9. *Requirements reference.* This is where the need for the function is documented. Usually this will refer to an entry in the Requirements Catalogue. Reference might also have to be made to other documents such as the Dataflow Model, if the requirement is not sufficiently detailed.

10. *Events*. What events can trigger this function? This is used only for update functions. A full discussion of events is contained in Chapter 13.

11. *Related Functions*. What other functions will be used alongside this function? In our example, the function 'Make provisional booking' requires a customer number, a site number and a plot number as inputs. It does assume that the user of this particular function, the Customer Clerk, actually knows what these data items are. In practice, the Customer Clerk will have a booking form containing a customer name, a campsite name and some dates. So in order to be able to use this function, the clerk will need to find the customer number from the name and check if the site has any plots available for the appropriate dates. Hence the need for the related functions. (There is an argument that these search routines should be part of the original function. We will return to this question later in Section 10.8.)

12. *Common Processing*. This space is used to record details of any special routines that might be used in several processes.

13. *Processing considerations*. This is used to record details of those functions that split into two logically distinct parts. The only example of this that we have encountered concerns the sending of statements by a cash machine, where an on-line component of the function handled the user interface while an off-line part sent the statements.

14. *Frequency*. How often is the function used?

15. *SLRs* (Service Level Requirements). Here we record target response times in the case of on-line functions and target elapsed times in the case of batch functions. Obviously there is an element of wishful thinking in this, as we have yet to obtain detailed information as to whether a particular function could actually achieve these targets. This question is explored further in steps 365 and 370.

10.6 INPUT AND OUTPUT FORMATS

To complete our description of the external appearance of a function we need to design input and output formats. Standard SSADM uses I/O structures for this purpose. These are Jackson diagrams which depict the flow of data across the system boundary. Their major drawback is that they represent data 'in the abstract' and give little indication as to what a screen or report might actually look like. For this reason they are not useful for user communication, and so I do not advocate the use of I/O structures in Rapid SSADM.*

---

*I/O structures are very good at depicting the sequencing of data items in the dataflows. They do unfortunately have a number of drawbacks. First, they are not very good in depicting less structured data, such as that often used in Windows applications where the user can roam at will through a screenful of information with the aid of a mouse. Second, they do not illustrate what screens or printed forms will actually look like. The stated reason why this should be so is that screens or printed forms are dependent upon the technical environment which has yet to be decided but will be chosen in stage 4. In stage 3, we are dealing with a logical system and therefore should not consider anything that depends upon such a physical choice. This argument seems to me a little spurious given that fact that screens and printed reports vary little from one environment to another. Moreover, most practitioners need to sketch a screen or print layout anyway before they can begin to construct the I/O structures. Finally, users find I/O structures, like most Jackson diagrams, difficult to understand. Given the fact that we are designing a function from their point of view, this is a major drawback.

I would not wish to be too prescriptive here. Report design and especially screen design is very subjective, often being influenced by installation standards as well as personal taste. The target technical environment is also an important factor, especially in the last few years which have seen major advances in Graphical User Interfaces. No doubt the way in which we design the user interface has changed radically and will continue to do so for the foreseeable future. What follows is, therefore, more in the nature of suggestions as to how one could design a user interface, rather than prescriptive guidelines as to how it should be done.

From the Function definition form in Fig. 10.6, it is clear that the function 'Make provisional booking' has three input/output formats, one for a screen, one for a confirmation letter and one for a rejection letter. The screen layout is shown in Fig. 10.8 and the print layout for the confirmation letter in Fig. 10.9. The layout for the rejection letter would be similar. These diagrams should be self-explanatory (PC on the screen means 'Promotion Code'). Again it is worth repeating, they are only suggestions, perhaps useful for only one type of environment.

Many on-line functions will only require a single screen. Some, however, might require more than this. If this is the case, some form of screen navigation needs to be developed. An example of how this might be done is shown in Fig. 10.10. This uses a sequencing technique which will be fully described in Chapter 13. In Fig. 10.10 it is assumed that the function 'Make provisional booking' uses four different screens. First, the function displays the Existing Customer or New Customer screen. Whichever is

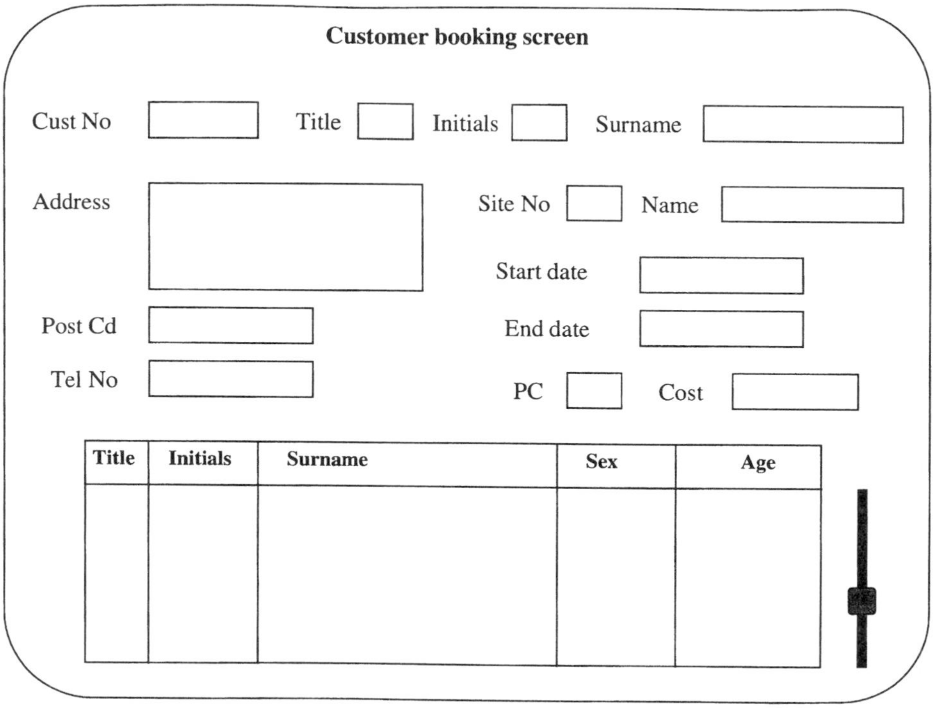

Fig. 10.8   Customer Booking Screen

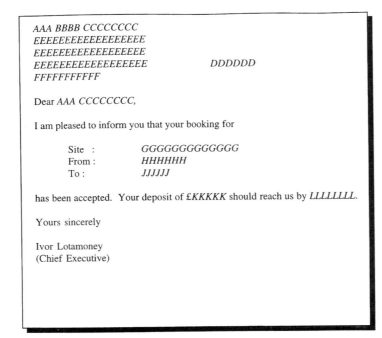

Fig. 10.9   Happy Camping confirmation letter

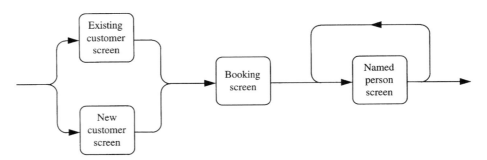

Fig. 10.10   Screen navigation

chosen, the Booking Screen comes next. This is presumably where site details are entered. Finally, we have a repetition of Named Person Screen. In other words, a fresh screen would be started for every individual in the party. Each of these screens would be described by means of a separate screen layout. Note that we are concerned here solely with data screens, the means or prompts by which a user can choose between one screen and another are a matter for later discussion.

A final word of warning about what we have been doing. We have tended to talk very loosely about *screen* design. This might give the impression that a screen layout for a single function is intended to occupy the whole of a physical screen. This might not be the case. In a Windows environment, for example, each function should be constrained to run within its own window. (Here we are using the term 'window' as an area of the screen under the control of a specific application. A function might appear as several 'frames', each of these being something that can be mapped onto the window.) This provides maximum flexibility, allowing one function to be run in parallel with another. On the other hand, a function should not really have more than one window, since this would imply parts of the function operating separately, and therefore suggests more than one function. With this in mind, perhaps we really should rename much of the activity in this step as *logical* screen design, the logical screen being implementable as a whole screen or as a window within a screen.

10.7 USER ROLES

The final task in this step is to complete User Roles. From the very start of SSADM prospective users of the new system have been recorded in the User Catalogue. We now need to decide what functions should be made available to these users. This is not quite as simple as it sounds, since different users might wish to use the same bundle of functions, and conversely an individual might work in a very compartmentalized way and wish to be presented with different functions when working in different roles.

To help us in this task, we will update the User Roles. Recall that a User Role is really how the system perceives a user, and in Dataflow Diagram terms a User Role equates to an external entity. In some senses it is no more than a menu of functions that will be made available to a user. The second column on the document in Fig. 10.11, 'Job Title(s)', refers to either actual or prospective real jobs. This contrasts with the User Role, which is really quite an abstract concept. The final column is a cross-referencing of the functions to the User Roles. If a function is used by more than one User Role, it should be entered once for each of the User Roles.

SSADM Version 4.2 shows the allocation of functions to User Roles by means of the User Role/Function matrix. An example for the Happy Camping system is shown in Fig. 10.12. As a concept, this is fine, for it shows very clearly the interaction between the functions and the User Roles. However, like most matrixes it has its limitations. On the scale of that shown in Fig. 10.12 it works very well, but for a system with forty User Roles and 300 functions, the picture is not quite so clear. One point that often worries people, when confronted with the matrix, is the existence of functions, such as numbers 50 and 51, which appear to be used by no one. The reason for such functions is fairly obvious, since they are system initiated. If one were really worried about blank entries for these functions, all that needs doing is to invent another User Role called 'the system' or something similar. SSADM Version 4.2 also suggests that a more detailed approach to Job Design might be taken after the User Roles have been identified. As much of this is outside the scope of SSADM, it has not been included here.

10.8 FUNCTION GRANULARITY

The final question that arises concerns the size of a function. Should a function be a large all-inclusive process or a series of small ones? For example, consider the Happy Camping function 'Make provisional booking' from earlier in this chapter. To use this

User Roles			
System Happy Camping	**Date** 31/5/93	**Page** 3	

User Role	Job Title(s)	Func Id	Function
Customer Clerk	*Customer Liaison Clerk*	*40*	*Check campsite availability*
	Customer Manager	*41*	*Make Provisional Booking*
		44	*Transfer dates of booking*
		45	*Find Customer details by name*
		47	*Change people details on booking*
		48	*Add person to booking*
		49	*Delete person from booking*
Office Manager	*Customer Manager*	*40*	*Check campsite availability*
	Tent Manager	*42*	*Change Customer details*
		43	*Cancel Booking*
		45	*Find Customer details by name*
		46	*Display credit rating*

Fig. 10.11   Happy Camping User Roles

Func Id	Function	Customer clerk	Accounts clerk	Tent clerk	Office manager
40	Check campsite availability	X	X	X	X
41	Make provisional booking	X			
42	Change customer details				X
43	Cancel booking				X
44	Transfer dates of booking	X			
45	Find customer details by name	X	X		X
46	Display credit rating		X		X
47	Change people details on booking	X			
48	Add person to booking	X			
49	Delete person from booking	X			
50	Issue joining instructions/rejection				
51	Notify site of confirmed bookings				
52	Record customer payments		X		

Fig. 10.12   User Role/Function matrix

function, the user needs to know the customer number, the site number and a plot number as well as the dates for the holiday. The actual booking form probably contains only the name of the customer, the required holiday dates and the name of the site. A clerk making the booking will probably need to use the system to search through existing Customers for the number and to find a vacant plot on the site for the required dates. With this in mind, the temptation is to enlarge the function by tacking two search procedures onto the start. This is probably a mistake, as it tends to make the function large and unmanageable. There will, moreover, probably be a need to find customers and to find vacant plots without making any form of booking. In other words, both searches also are needed as independent functions.

When designing functions it is probably best to adopt the maxim 'small is beautiful'. It is easier to design, test and implement small functions and they do fit in far better with a 4GL type of environment. Functions should really be regarded as components in a larger system, and so should be on the small side. How they are packaged together is really the business of physical design. Such an approach certainly fits in with the more modern Windows type of environments.

The main problem with the 'small' approach is that of communication between functions. If, as suggested, the functions 'Find customer by name' and 'Make provisional booking' are kept separate, then there has to be a way of transferring a Customer number from the first function to the second. It would be ludicrous for the clerk to have to write down a number found by the first function, merely to re-enter it on the second. It should be realized, however, that this is merely a problem of physical design. Increasingly, physical environments provide some form of 'cut and paste' technique which gets round this problem. If the worst comes to the worst, all the functions can be combined into a large program at Physical Design.

ELEVEN

RELATIONAL DATA ANALYSIS

11.1 PURPOSE

In SSADM, the major purpose of Relational Data Analysis is to provide a cross-checking mechanism for the Logical Data Model. Recall that the Logical Data Model was originally defined in quite a subjective way. Entities were recorded as entities if in the opinion of the analyst they were things of interest to the business, and about which information was held. To the uninitiated, it can appear as if the analyst is conjuring these things from thin air. Nevertheless, experienced analysts can produce good and accurate Logical Data Models very quickly using this approach. Unfortunately, it is easy to make mistakes, to omit entities, to record attributes incorrectly or to get the relationships wrong. The great virtue of Relational Data Analysis is that it is a much more objective technique which uses the data in the system to build up a model that can be compared directly with the Logical Data Model.

User-defined data, such as forms, screen or print layouts and record descriptions, are the basic raw materials for Relational Data Analysis, which is a somewhat mechanical process, with the analyst following clear step-by-step rules converting this raw data into a Relational Data Analysis structure. This structure looks very similar to a Logical Data Structure and forms a basis for comparison with the required Logical Data Model. Thus Relational Data Analysis is essentially a 'bottom-up method', which complements nicely the 'top-down' style of the Logical Data Model.

By taking its starting points as the user-defined outputs, the Relational Data Analysis structure will ensure that the data is fully defined (Fig. 11.1). In other words, the structure contains sufficient data to actually produce the output. However, Relational Data Analysis does more than this. By following its rules in a fairly mechanistic way, it allows us to identify relationships between entities and to

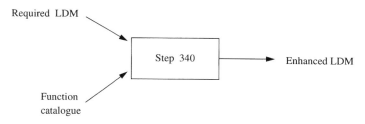

Fig. 11.1   Inputs and products

remove data duplication. On an intuitive level, Relational Data Analysis can sometimes be seen as an attempt to place or file data items in the logically most sensible place.

Step 340 is the usual place where Relational Data Analysis makes an appearance within SSADM. Here the basic raw material for the technique is provided by the input and output documents, usually in the form of screen and print layouts as contained in the Function Catalogue.* From these we construct a 'partial data model' which is used to check and possibly enhance the required Logical Data Model. The technique can, however, be usefully employed at other points within the method. One such place is step 140, when the analyst is attempting to construct a Logical Data Model for the current system. If difficulties are encountered in initially identifying entities, applying Relational Data Analysis to existing system documents is often found helpful.

11.2 BACKGROUND

Relational Data Analysis stems from the work of Dr Edgar F. Codd of IBM. Codd was the person who did much of the early work that led ultimately to the introduction of relational databases. Codd realized that for databases to function effectively, the data had to be nicely structured. Raw data, or unnormalized data as Codd called it, was unsuitable for large databases. In his paper of 1970, Codd proposed refining, or normalizing, this data by employing a three-stage process. Unnormalized data would be transformed to data in first normal form, then to second normal form and finally to third normal form.

At the time third normal form was regarded as the ultimate in data organization. Subsequent work has improved upon this. What we now use when we refer to third normal form is an extension of Codd's work, due to Boyce, called Boyce–Codd normal form. Things did not stop here, however. In the late 1970s, further research uncovered fourth and fifth normal forms. These are very theoretical and of limited practical interest and so neither is used in SSADM.

*As a technique Relational Data Analysis can be applied to any collection of data items. In SSADM Version 4.2, for example, the technique is applied to I/O structures, something we do not use in our approach.

11.3 RELATIONS

Most of Codd's work was theoretical, mainly using the branch of mathematics known as set theory. In it all data is structured into *relations*. This is a mathematical term for what is really nothing more or less than a well-defined table. In simple terms one can envisage a relation as a file, and a row of the table as a record. An example of a relation is shown in Fig. 11.2. This shows a list of employees in a company.

Given its background, Relational Data Analysis abounds in mathematical terms such as

- *Tuple (or n-tuple)*. Row of a table
- *Domain*. Set of values that the entries in a column can assume
- *Cardinality*. Number of rows in the table
- *Degree*. Number of columns in the table

We will not use them here.

Obviously, depicting a relation in full, as in Fig. 11.2, can become a little tedious. So when talking about relations we will use a short-hand representation in which we just write the column headings or data items. For the table in Fig. 11.2 this would be

<u>Pay No</u>
Name
Branch
Division

In each table we can select a column or combination of columns which serves to uniquely identify rows in the relation. This is called the *key* of the relation. In the above example we have chosen Pay Number as the key. In other words, once we know the Pay Number, we know which row we are talking about. In our short-hand version we indicate a key by underlining the data item or data items. Other data items in a relation are often called dependent data items.

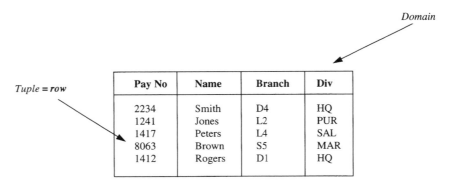

Fig. 11.2 Example of relation

Earlier, we stated that a relation was a well-defined table. Well defined in this case means that

1. No two rows are identical. In other words, no duplicate records.
2. The order of rows is insignificant. If the order were to be significant, then Codd would argue that some information is missing. In our previous example, suppose that the order in which these individuals appear is important. In other words, it is significant that Smith comes before Jones, who comes before Peters, etc. The obvious question to ask is why the rows are ordered in this way. If the ordering is one of employee seniority, say, then there is a missing data item which should determine seniority—Date of Joining, for example.
3. The order of columns is insignificant. Although it is conventional to put the keys at the start of a table, and although this might now be required by certain relational database products, this was not necessary as far as Codd was concerned.
4. Column names are unique. This means unique to a table. Thus we cannot have duplicate column headings. Note that column names are not necessarily unique across the whole of a system, since common column names are one way of cross-referencing one table against another.
5. Data items are single valued. This means that the following table showing a company's Orders

<u>Order number</u>
Customer
Customer Address
Product

cannot be a well-defined relation. This is because each row, as identified by a unique order number, refers to a single order. Although each order will refer to one Customer, one Customer address, it might contain many products. (There are a number of ways of getting around this difficulty. The usual approach is to have another relation called order line, which is in a one-to-many relation with order. Another approach is to determine the maximum number of products that can be allowed on any one order, and have a number of product data items indexed up to this figure. So if the maximum number of products appearing on any one order were to be ten, we would establish ten separate dependent data items called Product-1, . . . , Product-10. Obviously the majority of orders would probably contain less than ten products and so their entries in the relation would be full of blank or null entries.)

11.4 KEYS

As mentioned earlier, a key is a data item or combination of data items that can uniquely identify a row in a relation. Keys can be classified in several ways:

- *Primary key*. This is the data item or data items that have been chosen as the key of a relation.

- *Simple key*. This is a key consisting of a single data item. The employee relation given above has a simple key—Employee Number.
- *Compound key*. This is a key consisting of more than one data item, each of which can be a key in its own right. An example is given in Fig. 11.3. This shows the amount of time individuals work on particular projects. Clearly no one column can serve as a key for this relation. Therefore we have to choose a combination of columns. Given that the relation is all about employees working on projects, an obvious choice of key would be Project Code and Employee Number. In the short-hand notation the relation would be expressed as

  Project Code
  Employee Number
  Employee Name
  Elapsed Time (on project)

  Note that both parts of this key are unique in their own right. In other words, there may well be two other tables, the one about projects and the other about employees, that have Project Code and Employee Number respectively as their keys. Also note that in writing out the column headings we do so in full. On tables and on forms, space is at a premium and so we are often forced to write such things as 'Empl' Numb' rather than 'Employee Number'.
- *Composite key* (sometimes called a hierarchical key). This is a key consisting of more than one data item, in which part of the key is only defined with reference to other parts of the key. For example, consider the relation in Fig. 11.4 which is about lecture rooms on a campus. Obviously the key to this relation is a combination of Building and Room. At first, this might appear to be a compound key. However, in a compound key, each part of the key must be able to stand by itself, and be able to serve as the key for another table. Here the rooms are numbered 1, 2, 3 . . . and any

Project code	Empl' numb'	Name	Elapsed time
PD023	20445	Chung	3
PD023	20552	Browne	2
PD023	20881	Patel	1
PW112	20012	Arne	12
PW112	20552	Browne	3

Fig. 11.3   Compound key

Building	Room	Capacity
Drake	1	23
Drake	2	45
Drake	3	21
Nelson	1	21
Nelson	2	112

Fig. 11.4   Composite key

particular room number only makes sense once the building is known. This is an example of a composite key and in the short-hand notation, we use brackets to denote this.

(Building)
(Room number)
Capacity

- *Candidate key.* This is a data item which could become a key, but is not necessarily chosen. In our employee table of Fig. 11.2, Employee Name is a candidate key, in that it could serve as a key, but obviously it would not be chosen as the primary key. It is worth noting that the addition of more employees to the table could serve to eliminate Employee Name as a candidate key if there were a repetition of names.
- *Foreign key.* A dependent data item in one relation which is the key of another relation. Consider the two relations in Fig. 11.5. Here Pay Number is the key to the first relation, Division to the second. Division is then called a foreign key in the first relation. In some senses Division could be regarded as a key adrift in a foreign land.

11.5 THIRD NORMAL FORM

Now for our formal definition of third normal form. A relation is in third normal form if

1. Given a value for the key there is one and only one value for each attribute.
2. Each data item depends directly upon the key.

In other approaches to Relational Data Analysis, these two conditions are sometimes called the TNF tests, and are used as a final check that the data is indeed in third normal form.

In most traditional approaches to Relational Data Analysis, the data is transformed into third normal form by going through first and second normal form. One such is the standard SSADM approach which uses columns. In our quick approach to Relational Data Analysis, however, we will leap over first and second normal form, and attempt to place relations directly into third normal form. We will use a step-by-step approach to Relational Data Analysis:

1. *Collect data in unnormalized form.* As mentioned earlier, this will usually be outputs in the form of screen and print layouts extracted from the Function Catalogue. We

Pay No	Name	Branch	Div
2234	Smith	D4	HQ
1241	Jones	L2	PUR
1417	Peters	L4	SAL
8063	Brown	S5	MAR
1412	Rogers	D1	HQ

Div	Name	Staff
HQ	Headquarters	14
MAR	Marketing	17
PUR	Purchasing	11
SAL	Salaries	9

Fig. 11.5   Foreign keys

would not normally perform Relational Data Analysis on each and every output as this would take far too long. Usually we select those outputs that are considered to be of some importance.

2. *Produce dependency diagrams.* We will produce one such diagram for each document we have collected. The technique will be described in detail later.

3. *Write relations in third normal form.* These are taken directly from the dependency diagrams, each diagram generating a number of relations.

4. *Rationalize the relations.* Many of the relations coming from different dependency diagrams will 'overlap'. This task is concerned with amalgamating all the relations.

5. *Produce a structure model.* Applying fairly mechanical rules we can produce a Logical Data Model type of structure from the rationalized relations.

6. *Produce an enhanced Logical Data Model.* The structure produced from activity 5 is compared with the Required Logical Data Model as produced in step 320. Any information found missing as a result of this check is incorporated into the Logical Data Model.

Note that as we are not considering *all* inputs and outputs in activity 1, the model we produce in activity 5 is likely to be a partial model, and hence the checking in activity 6 is not complete. For this reason, it might be convenient to perform the activities a number of times, using a different set of input and output documents on each pass in order to examine specific portions of the Logical Data Model. Before applying this technique to any data items we first need to describe dependency diagrams.

11.6 DEPENDENCY DIAGRAMS

The basic notation used in dependency diagrams is as shown in Fig. 11.6. Here A and B stand for data items within a relation. The notation states that A determines B, or that B is functionally dependent on A, i.e. given a value for A, there is a unique value for B. An example of such a dependency is shown in Fig. 11.7. Here Employee Number uniquely determines an Employee Name. Obviously the arrow cannot travel in the opposite direction, since an Employee Name does not determine an Employee Number. (There may be several Smiths, for example.) Note also that arrows normally emanate from keys.

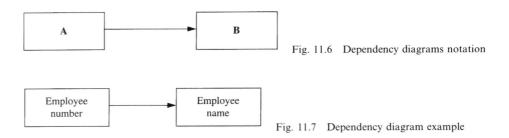

Fig. 11.6   Dependency diagrams notation

Fig. 11.7   Dependency diagram example

On the other hand, the situation in Fig. 11.8 is not valid. This is because an invoice might be for many products, and therefore Invoice Number does not determine a unique Product Number.

We will normally produce a dependency diagram for each form, screen or print layout. In doing this there are a number of guidelines we can follow:

1. Write down all the data items in boxes.
2. Identify primary keys.
3. Add dependency arrows.
   i. Ensure that all non-key items are connected to a primary key.
   ii. Explore the relationship between the keys.
4. Add 'extra' primary keys.
5. Remove indirect dependencies.
6. Identify link boxes.

This is not really a step-by-step guide, more a set of principles that need to be applied. We will see how it works in the three examples that follow.

One point to get clear right from the start is that in our approach to dependency diagrams arrows will *only* emerge from primary keys—that is, those data items that have already been chosen to be keys in the system. Other authors allow dependency arrows to emerge from any candidate key.* Thus in Fig. 11.7, if Employee Name were also to be a candidate key, there would also be an arrow from this box to Employee Number. In effect a two-way arrow would exist. This is not the end of the matter, though, for not only would every other dependent data item be connected to Employee Number, it would also be connected to Employee Name. The diagrams would then become busy and confusing. For this reason in Rapid SSADM arrows can only emerge from primary keys.

11.7 DEPENDENCY DIAGRAMS—EXAMPLE 1

As an example of how to produce a dependency diagram, consider the form in Fig. 11.9. The first thing we need to do is to place all data items in boxes. All primary keys are specially identified on the diagram and then the dependency arrows are introduced. We do this by visiting each non-key item in turn and determining which key item it is

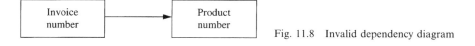

Fig. 11.8 Invalid dependency diagram

---

*See, for example, Date (1990). Date uses dependency diagrams to illustrate the various concepts underlying normalization. If we wish to use the diagrams to *achieve* normalization, we have to be far more restrictive about their use. In most books on SSADM dependency diagrams are not stressed. One exception to this is Skidmore *et al.* (1992). However, again Skidmore uses the diagrams for understanding the data, rather than generating relations.

Happy camping training list

Course No   CB/78/977

Course Title   Tent management for beginners

Start date   4/4/91

End date   5/4/91

Rep No	Rep name	Course grade	Office No	Tel No
47	T. MacDermott	A	10	0494 455667
66	A. Chung	B	13	081 566 7888
67	B. Strutt	F	10	0494 455667
91	A. Stein	C	11	021 447 8899
22	M. Patel	B	11	021 447 8899

Fig. 11.9   Happy Camping Training List example

dependent on. Finally, we explore any possible dependencies between the key items. The resultant diagram will look like that in Fig. 11.10.

Note that the symbol † is used to denote a primary key. All dependency arrows must emerge from a box containing such a key or keys. Note also the use of the large enclosing box to denote a compound key. Course Grade is dependent upon this compound key.

Having produced the diagram we write the relations directly into third normal form. The relations consist of the key items and their dependent data items. Thus the relations in third normal form are

Course Number
Course Title
Start Date
End Date

Office Number
Tel Number

Rep Number
Rep Name
*Office Number

Course Number
Rep Number
Course Grade

Conventionally, asterisks are used to denote foreign keys.

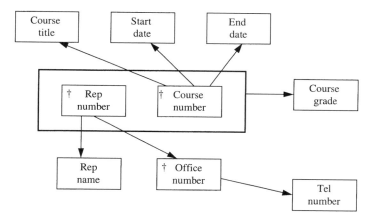

Fig. 11.10 Happy Camping Training List dependency diagram

11.8 INDIRECT DEPENDENCIES

The dependency arrows are meant to show direct dependencies. In our example, suppose we decide that the Telephone Number depends on the Representative Number and also on the Office Number. This situation is depicted on the left-hand side of Fig. 11.11.

This is incorrect since it contains an indirect dependency. A representative only has a given telephone number because he or she happens to work in an office with that telephone number. In other words, the telephone number is more correctly filed under office, rather than representative. This is the situation on the right-hand side of Fig. 11.11.

In general, a triangle (or any other polygon) on a dependency diagram betrays the presence of an indirect dependency.

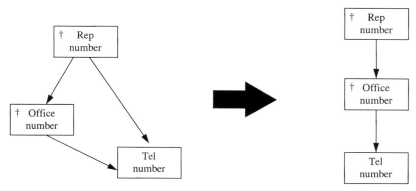

Fig. 11.11 Indirect dependency

11.9 DEPENDENCY DIAGRAMS—EXAMPLE 2

As a second example consider the screen used for Customer Bookings. This is shown in Fig. 11.12. (On the screen PC stands for Promotion Code. This refers to a Special Promotion in which all bookings made under the terms and conditions of the promotion would attract a discount.) The screen generates the dependency diagram of Fig. 11.13.

Obviously there are some problems with this dependency diagram:

1. The screen is all about customer bookings. This is what links a Site, say, with a Customer. However, when drawing the dependency diagram there appears to be no obvious way of making this link. This is because the linking data item—Booking number—is absent from the screen. (This might be because the booking number is automatically generated and appears elsewhere, perhaps on a second screen.) Nevertheless, to complete our Relational Data Analysis, we need to include it on the dependency diagram.

2. A similar problem occurs in connection with the data items that refer to the various individuals who make up the party. To identify each person uniquely, we have to generate another data item—person number. This will take the values 1, 2, 3, . . . ,

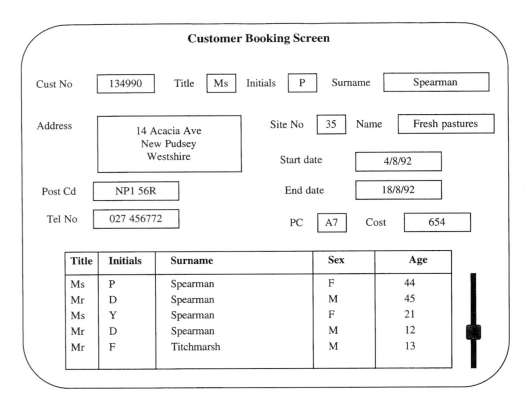

Fig. 11.12   Customer Booking Screen

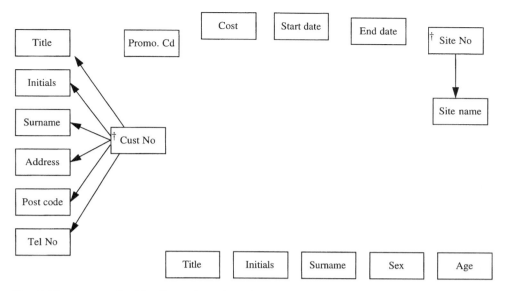

Fig. 11.13 Customer Booking Screen dependency diagram 1

etc. on each booking, and so lead to a composite key consisting of booking number and person number.

Adopting these two further data items we can generate a further dependency diagram which is shown in Fig. 11.14. Note that a composite key is shown by a large box enclosing two other boxes, only one of which is a key.

The relations in third normal form are therefore:

Customer No	Booking No	(Booking No)
Title	*Customer No	(Person No)
Initials	*Site No	Title
Surname	Start date	Initials
Address	End date	Surname
Post code	Promotion Code	Sex
Tel No	Cost	Age

Site No
Site Name

11.10 DEPENDENCY DIAGRAMS—EXAMPLE 3

As a final example let us consider the report of Fig. 11.15. The dependency diagram for this is in Fig. 11.16. Unfortunately we appear to have lost any connection between a mailshot and the customers. This is because Mailshot Number and Customer Number are independent keys. What is needed is something akin to a link box.

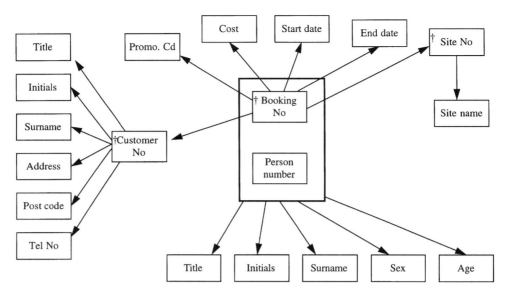

Fig. 11.14   Customer Booking Screen dependency diagram 2

Happy Camping Mailshot

Mailshot No	2344
Mailshot Title	1993 Yorkshire trawl
Mailshot date	7/5/93

Customer No	*Customer Name*	*Customer Address*
126554	Ms A Higgins	123 Oakfield Cres, Scarborough
128775	Mr P L Wade	23 Land of Green Ginger, Hull
134008	Mr T P Shah	12 Whip-ma-whop-ma-gate, York
134009	Mr A Bleasley	23 Briggate, Leeds
156442	Mrs Q Z Armley	12 Attercliffe Road, Sheffield

Fig. 11.15   Happy Camping Mailshot

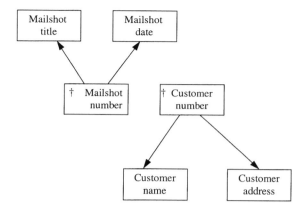

Fig. 11.16 Happy Camping Mailshot dependency diagram 1

Whenever we produce a dependency diagram with two apparently unrelated structures, we need to go back to the original form or screen, and ask if there is a relationship between the two keys. In other words, would a 'key only' relation consisting of Customer Number and Mailshot Number make any sense? Obviously, in this case it would. It is the only way of recording which customers have been included on a particular mailshot. Another way of looking at this is to notice that on the original form Customer information repeats within each mailshot. Whenever this occurs we should consider establishing a compound key, in this case that of Customer Number within Mailshot Number (Fig. 11.17).

Note, however, if we did have two unrelated chunks of information—perhaps obtained by a random pasting together of two unrelated forms—the dependency structures would still be separate.

11.11 OTHER POINTS ARISING FROM DEPENDENCY DIAGRAMS

On a dependency diagram all dependency arrows must emerge from key data items. Thus the only sources of arrows are as shown in Fig. 11.18. (Obviously, each of these

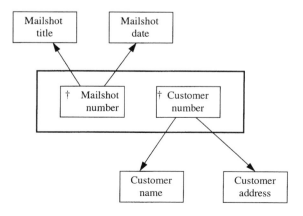

Fig. 11.17 Happy Camping Mailshot dependency diagram 2

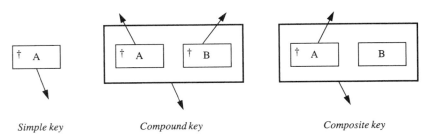

Simple key   *Compound key*   *Composite key*

Fig. 11.18   Possible dependency arrows

keys can also be the destination point of arrows by being dependent on other keys, something we have seen in our examples.) Note in particular that for the composite key, an arrow can emerge from the higher part of the key, but not from the lower. Also it should be noted that Compound and Composite keys are not limited to two data items. A compound key of three or more elements is perfectly possible. The main point to note, however, is that no arrow can emerge from a non-key box.

Another situation that is not allowed is shown in Fig. 11.19. Here A and B appear to form a compound key which determines data item C. However, data item B is dependent upon data item A. Thus, the diagram is saying, on the one hand, that both A and B are required to determine B, but, on the other, that A by itself determines B and therefore C as well. Obviously this is inconsistent. Either A determines B in which case A determines C (either directly from A itself or indirectly via B), or A and B are independent, in which case the compound key will remain but the arrow between A and B will disappear. The three possible alternatives are shown in Fig. 11.20.

Derived information, such as totals and averages, sometimes presents difficulties. The first question to ask is whether this information is required at all. Unfortunately, there is no standard answer to this question. Leaving such data in the model will lead to

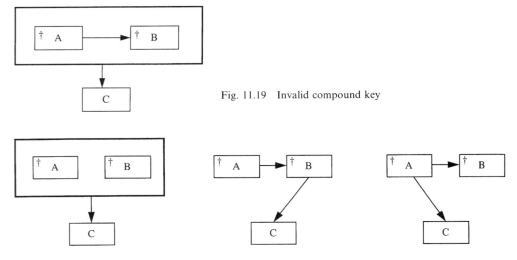

Fig. 11.19   Invalid compound key

Fig. 11.20   Alternatives to Fig. 11.19

update problems. If, for example, Customers were classified by region and if the Region entity contained an attribute Total Value of Orders, then the receipt of each and every order from a customer in the region would lead to the updating of this total. On the other hand, omitting such items could lead to access problems. To go back to our previous example, if we had to calculate the total value of orders in a region every time region data was displayed, the response time could well be unacceptable. It might be argued that this issue is really only one of physical design, but leaving decisions until then might involve a considerable amount of reworking.

Suppose we do include derived information. Then these items are no different from other items when dependency arrows are inserted. If they depend upon anything, they can only depend upon keys. A common mistake is shown in Fig. 11.21. These three items are taken from an invoice line. Obviously, the amount charged for a particular product equals the quantity ordered multiplied by the unit price. Thus the temptation is to produce something like Fig. 11.21. This is wrong! First, dependency arrows can only emerge from keys. There is no way in which Quantity ordered, or for that matter Unit price, could ever serve as the key of a relation. Second, even if these items could be made into keys, the dependency arrows would state that given Quantity Ordered there is one and only one Amount Charged, and also given Unit Price there is one and only one Amount Charged. Dependency arrows do not imply multiplication (or addition, subtraction or division for that matter)!

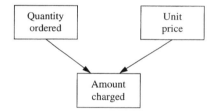

Fig. 11.21   Invalid derived data example

11.12 RATIONALIZATION

Once we have finished with each of the individual forms, screens and print layouts we will use the relations which are in third normal form to build a structure which we can compare directly with the Logical Data Structure. Obviously, before doing this we need to remove any duplication from the relations that we have discovered. This process is known as rationalization. In it we amalgamate all relations with a common key into a single relation. So, for example, if we obtain the following relations

<u>Customer No</u>	<u>Customer No</u>
Title	Mailing Indicator
Initials	Name
Surname	Address
Address	
Post code	
Tel No	

We would merge the two relations into a single relation

> Customer No
> Title
> Initials
> Surname
> Address
> Post code
> Tel No
> Mailing Indicator

Note that in the above we are assuming that Name in the second relation would be covered by the data items Title, Initials and Surname in the first. Obviously, this would have to be cleared with the user. Another thing to be aware of is the presence of synonyms. These are different names used for the same data item. As an example it could well be that what the Sales Office of a company refer to as 'Customers' might be known as 'Accounts' to the Accounts Department. In this case it is more than likely that the keys Customer Number and Account Number refer to the same thing. When this happens the analyst has to choose which of the potential keys is to serve as the primary key of the relation.

Sometimes we might not wish to combine relations even where they have common keys. For example, suppose a company keeps the following data about Customers who are late in paying:

> Customer No
> Name
> Amount owed
> No of reminders sent
> Date referred to solicitors
> Start date of court case

Clearly we would not wish to record this information for every Customer. It is probably better to have a separate relation, Delinquent Customer say, with the same key.

11.13 BUILDING A STRUCTURE

Having drawn together all the data and produced a group of rationalized relations our next task is to build the data structure that we will use to compare with the Logical Data Structure. Fortunately, there is a mechanical approach to this. In it we

1. Identify all foreign keys on the rationalized relations
2. Make each rationalized relation into an entity
3. Identify relations by making details out of entities with
   - *Compound keys*. All entities with compound keys become details of entities having constituent parts of the compound key as their primary key.

- *Foreign keys.* All entities with foreign keys become details of entities having the foreign key as their primary key.
- *Composite keys.* All entities with composite or hierarchical keys become details of entities having as primary key the major part of the composite key.

As an example of this approach let us consider the rationalized relations based upon our last two Happy Camping examples. These relations are

Customer No	Mailshot No	Booking No
Title	Date	*Customer No
Initials	Mailshot Title	*Site number
Surname		Start date
Address		End date
Post Code	Mailshot No	
Tel No	Customer No	(Booking No)
Mailing indicator		(Person No)
Credit rating		Title
	Site No	Initials
	Site name	Surname
		Sex
		Age

Making each relation into an entity and showing primary and foreign keys we arrive at the situation in Fig. 11.22.

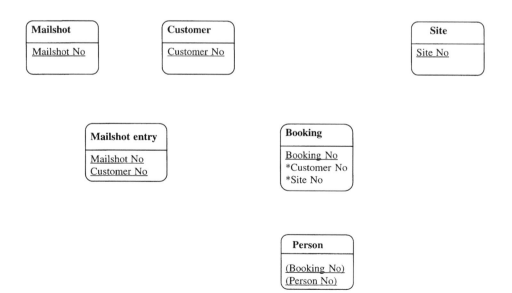

Fig. 11.22   Rationalized relations as entities

Here the entity Mailshot Entry has a compound key of Customer Number and Mailshot Number and so must be a detail of both Customer and Mailshot. The entity Booking has Customer Number and Site Number as foreign keys and so must be a detail of Customer and Site. Finally, the entity Person has a Composite key consisting of Booking Number and Person Number. The major part of this key is Booking Number. Indeed, a Person number only makes sense once a Booking is known. So in this case it becomes a detail of Booking and of Booking only. The structure we produce from this is shown in Fig. 11.23.

As we stated, relations or entities having compound keys must be linked to the entities having as primary keys the constituent parts of the compound key. What happens if such an entity does not exist? This might occur if we had done RDA on a single form where each item depends upon a compound key. In such a case we 'invent' an entity with the appropriate simple key. Thus if in Fig. 11.22 the entity Mailshot did not exist, we would still arrive at Fig. 11.23 as our final model. Similar arguments apply to composite keys.

There is an alternative approach that can be applied in the case of compound keys consisting of three or more parts. Such a situation is depicted in Fig. 11.24. If we had applied our rules in a dogmatic way, the entity with the triple key should have been linked to the three entities with the simple keys. However, the entity with the double compound key consisting of A and B also exists, and so it is possible to link the triple-keyed entity to this. Note that this is only possible if every occurrence of the triple key can be linked to a possible occurrence of the double key. In other words, if there is an occurrence of an entity with the key $A_1B_2C_3$ there must be an occurrence of the double entity with keys A_1B_2. Otherwise we would have orphans. In other words, occurrences of an entity with a key $A_1B_2C_3$ which cannot be tied into masters with the appropriate keys.

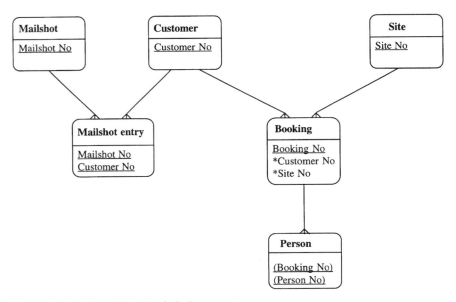

Fig. 11.23   Relational Data Analysis data structure

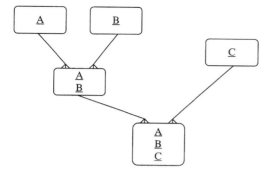

Fig. 11.24   Choice of links for compound keys

11.14 COMPARE THE TWO STRUCTURES

Our final task is to compare the structure that we have obtained with our Logical Data Model (Fig. 11.25). The purpose of doing this is to correct the Logical Data Model and so produce what is called the enhanced Logical Data Model. Before plunging into this and wielding the axe, pruning long-loved entities, it is as well to recognize several facts:

1. Mistakes may have been made in the Relational Data Analysis. This is probably the major cause of differences between the two models. Obviously in this case we would need to rework the Relational Data Analysis model.

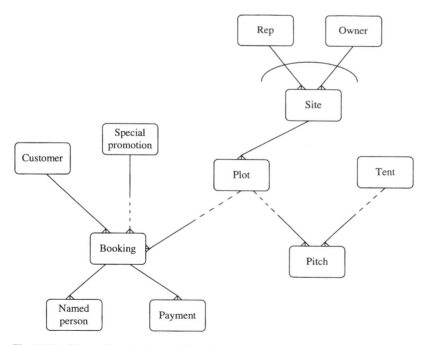

Fig. 11.25   Happy Camping Logical Data Structure

2. The Relational Data Analysis model may not be complete. This is because we normally work only with a selection of forms, and so obtain only a partial view of the system.
3. The Relational Data Analysis model does not contain such extra information as optional and mandatory relationships, link phrases, exclusive arcs, sub-types, etc.
4. One needs to question whether some of the Relational Data Analysis relations need be actually stored on the system. This is especially true if Relational Data Analysis is performed on statistical reports. The result of doing this is to arrive at relations with compound keys of staggering complexity. An example of this might be a relation

> <u>Salesperson number</u>
> <u>Area No</u>
> <u>Month</u>
> <u>Product</u>
> <u>Depot No</u>
> Amount

which shows the amount of a particular product as supplied by a particular depot sold by a particular salesperson in a particular area in a given month (phew!). One really needs to question whether such information has to be *stored* on the system, or whether there are alternative ways of extracting the information.

It has to be said that given the above, the Relational Data Analysis model does tend to be more flexible and produce more comprehensive data models. In our Happy Camping solution there are two points at issue when we compare the models:

1. The Booking appears as a detail of the site. On the Logical Data Model the booking is a detail of the plot which is itself a detail of site. How has this happened? The answer is that, initially, only the site number is entered. The plot would be allocated later. As a result, the Customer Booking Screen contains only site details, and working from the forms and screens in *isolation* there is no reason to connect a booking with a plot. (Perhaps the plot information is displayed on a later screen.) So what do we do about it? There are two possibilities:
   (a) The plot is allocated as part of the booking function. In this case I would ignore the Relational Data Analysis result and go with the Logical Data Model structure.
   (b) The plot is allocated at a later date. In this case both the Relational Data Analysis and the Logical Data Model results would have to be included. This does give rise to an 'indirect relationship triangle', but this is a necessary evil as the sides of the triangle are established at different times.
2. The mailshot and associated link entity. This is totally absent from the Logical Data Model. Before including it on the Logical Data Model, we need to ask ourselves whether we really need it. If we wish to keep a mailing history, the answer is yes, and so it goes on the Logical Data Model. If, however, we are not interested in retaining information about past mailshots, these being things that are merely generated from time to time, we would ignore the Relational Data Analysis model.

11.15 WORDS OF WARNING

Earlier Versions of SSADM tended to place far too much faith in the workings of Relational Data Analysis. In Version 3, for example, the analyst was supposed to collect together each and every form and screen or print layout in the system, perform Relational Data Analysis upon each and somehow combine the lot into a single all-encompassing Relational Data Analysis structure. This would then be *combined* with the Logical Data Model to produce a single data model, called the Composite Logical Data Diagram (CLDD), which was supposed to embody the advantages both of the top-down and of the bottom-up approach.

Needless to say, hardly anyone ever used this approach. It was fine on the usual trivial classroom examples, but when applied to a real-world system with possibly thousands of forms and layouts such an approach presented obvious difficulties. Performing the initial Relational Data Analysis was bad enough, but what followed was worse. Having waded through a morass of forms, the analyst was confronted with the task of constructing a structure of mind-bending complexity. Very few survived such an ordeal.

The Version 4.2 approach is far more pragmatic. In essence, the analyst makes a selection of forms and layouts, constructs a partial model, and performs piecemeal cross-checking. The choice of forms is obviously vital. Clearly, statistical reports showing historical data should not be included. For these, all we need to do is to convince ourselves that the system contains sufficient data to generate the output. This is detailed more formally when we come to Access Path Analysis.

TWELVE

PROTOTYPING

12.1 TYPES OF PROTOTYPING

As far as SSADM is concerned, prototyping was first introduced in Version 4. Prototyping has a much longer history than this, covers a huge range of activities and often means different things to different people. In essence, a prototype is a scaled-down model which can demonstrate certain facets of a system. Prototypes have been used in many different ways. To facilitate the ensuing discussion we need to categorize prototyping activities. For our purposes, we will adopt the following definitions:

Experimental prototyping. This is where a model is developed to see if something actually works. It is usually done when technical difficulties are foreseen. Two examples of this are where a small test is made to see if two machines can communicate and where large volumes of dummy data are stuffed into a database product in order to evaluate response rates.

- *Specification prototyping*. The purpose here is to test whether the requirements have been understood by the analysts and specified correctly. Often it is used to establish further presentational requirements for the user interface. Something similar can also be used in the early stages of analysis if difficulties are encountered in eliciting requirements.
- *Incremental prototyping*. Here the analysis and design is done normally, but the system is built incrementally. The final product is released in stages, each release being a prototype for the whole system. Obviously, small modifications to the requirements can take place during the building of the system, but major changes are impossible after the initial analysis and design.

- *Evolutionary prototyping*. This is different from the incremental method in that analysis and design is not done all at once but proceeds hand in hand with the building of the system. In essence, the approach consists of the unending sequence 'analyse a little, design a little, build a little, test a little, analyse a little . . .'. (This description was applied to Object Orientated methods by Berard, 1990 and repeated in Henderson-Sellers, 1992.) The system evolves out of this, and the final product might look substantially different from the first release.

There is one major difference which further divides these four approaches. In the first two the prototype is developed solely for demonstration purposes, to be thrown away after it has achieved its aims, while in the final two the initial prototype somehow 'grows' into the final system. Although specification prototypes are meant to be disposable items, many analysts find their retention far too tempting and use the prototype as a basis for the system build. This is quite sensible provided neither the aims of the prototype nor the efficiency of the final design are compromised by this decision.

It is worth noting that the changes wrought by each of the prototyping approaches on standard SSADM, or indeed any structured methodology, increases as one moves down the list. Experimental prototyping has tacitly always been part of the SSADM toolkit. It is concerned with a technical evaluation of products and techniques and so is easily incorporated into Technical Options or within the option part of the Feasibility Study. Specification prototyping was first incorporated within Version 4 of SSADM and the rest of this chapter is devoted to a consideration of this topic. The other two approaches are not addressed by standard SSADM but have been incorporated into Rapid SSADM. Incremental prototyping is addressed by 'Rapid Rapid SSADM', a customization of the base method discussed in Chapter 19 while evolutionary prototyping will be described in Chapter 21.

12.2 PROTOTYPING IN STANDARD SSADM

Specification prototyping can be used almost anywhere in SSADM. (For a full description of how specification prototyping can be used in SSADM, see CCTA, 1993.) However, the most usual points are steps 120 and 160 to help establish requirements, and step 350 to confirm the requirements. Step 350 is the place where it is formally placed in Version 4.2 (Fig. 12.1). Basically it consists of demonstrating functions to users, and so the two major inputs to the step are the Function Catalogue and the User Roles. The Logical Data Model is often needed to build the database underlying the model. Outputs from this stage will only really occur if errors or misunderstandings are uncovered. Should this eventuality arise the Function Catalogue or even the Requirements Catalogue would need updating. In the very worst of cases, the analysts might discover that they had been moving in completely the wrong direction, and if this happens, much of the preceding analysis would need reworking. Finally, it should be noted that prototyping is a voluntary activity. Whether or not it is done depends to a large extent upon the tools available. Previously this might have been a major problem, but is less so nowadays with the advent of good 4GLs equipped with screen painters and report generators.

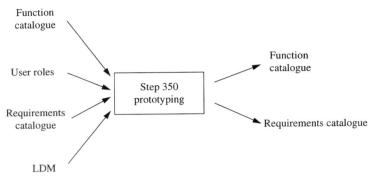

Fig. 12.1 Inputs and products

Having taken one small step towards flexibility by including prototyping, SSADM then shackles the technique with formal management structures and reams of documentation. The recommended management approach is shown in Fig. 12.2. The key issue revolves around the number of times a particular prototype is demonstrated. Most people feel that three times should be sufficient. In the SSADM manual, five different paper products are mentioned in connection with prototyping. This level of bureaucracy seems at odds with the free-wheeling nature of the technique. Obviously, the amount of documentation must be governed by the size of the system and the spread of the user community. For single-user systems implemented on a PC, an interactive session where changes can be made on the spot is probably most useful. For larger user communities this degree of informality is probably not advisable. Even so, there is

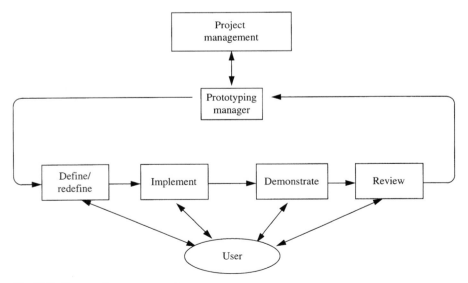

Fig. 12.2 Prototyping management

probably no need for anything more than the document in Fig. 12.3. This does, after all, allow the team to record formally the results of the prototyping session.

Prototyping does, of course, come with advantages and disadvantages. On the positive side there is the increased probability of designing the right system, by trapping of errors and avoiding misunderstandings at an early stage. Ultimately there should be less chance of a damaging system rewrite. Even so, the main benefit of prototyping is the repeatedly observed increase in user commitment to the system. There is, however, a negative side to all this. Prototyping does cost money and can extend system delivery times. More worrying, though, is the rise in user expectations. A prototype is delivered quickly, sometimes has features not available on the target machine and seems extremely efficient on the limited amount of data fed into it. Not surprisingly, users are often frustrated by a long wait for the delivery of the real system. All these difficulties can, however, be overcome by good communications. As a final word, the importance of quick results and the rise in importance of the Graphical User Interface has made prototypes not so much desirable as essential.

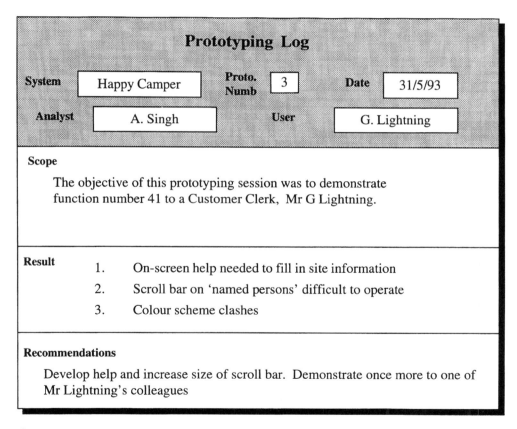

Fig. 12.3 Prototyping log

THIRTEEN

ENTITY LIFE HISTORIES

13.1 PURPOSE

The major purpose of Entity Life Histories is to validate the Function Catalogue. This it does by identifying missed functions. In practice most analysts find that they have only uncovered about 80 per cent of the processing on their first attempt at function identification. For example, quite often deletions are absent from the Function Catalogue, as typically analysts do not worry at first about getting rid of entities. They are usually much more interested in defining the normal day-to-day processing. When constructing Entity Life Histories, however, they are then asked formally what can kill off each entity, and so have to fully define all deletions.

It is often said that Entity Life Histories provide a third view of the system, one that contrasts with the other two views, the Data Flow Model and the Logical Data Model. It is the only view that really involves time. An Entity Life History is really no more than what it says—a pictorial description of the life of occurrences of an entity from birth to death. By providing this third time-driven view, in effect we are cross-checking the Data Flow Model against the Logical Data Model.

Entity Life Histories are constructed in step 360 of SSADM. The major inputs and outputs to this step are shown in Fig. 13.1. Obviously, the Logical Data Model provides the entities whose lives are the subject of this technique. We will compare the processing that this elicits against that already documented in the Function Catalogue. Sometimes it is useful to go back and refer to the Requirements Catalogue and the Data Flow Model in order to clarify the events that lead up to processing. The major output of this step is an updated Function Catalogue. Obviously, any changes to this must also be cross-referenced in the User Roles. If we wished we could also add the newly discovered processing to the Data Flow Model. There is little point in doing this, other than to have consistent diagrams, because the Function Catalogue is now the main repository

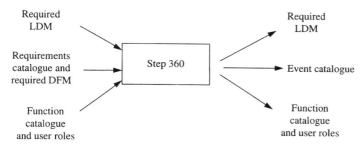

Fig. 13.1   Inputs and products

of the system processing. We will also create an Event Catalogue and may modify the Logical Data Model.

Entity Life Histories are one of the most powerful techniques in SSADM. The use of this technique can reveal hidden aspects of the system processing. For this reason it is essential that it is done in all but the simplest of systems. But before embracing Entity Life Histories with undiluted enthusiasm a note of caution needs to be sounded. Many advocates of Entity Life Histories seem to regard the technique as an all-embracing panacea. They argue that, used properly, the technique will all but solve every single processing problem. Certainly this was the vision held by the designers of SSADM Version 4. They expanded the role of Entity Life Histories from what it was in previous versions of the methodology. The technique itself has grown more complex and, as a result, Entity Life Histories are far bigger and thus more difficult to draw. Many practitioners, on encountering this degree of complexity, rebel and refuse to have any-thing to do with the technique. But this is just a case of the means getting in the way of the ends. So much is missed by a refusal to look at life histories. In this chapter I propose giving a simplified view of Entity Life Histories. I believe that this approach does achieve the majority of the Entity Life History objectives. Anyone, not just the experts, should be able to use our more simplified approach. Although the full treat-ment of SSADM Version 4.2 may reveal yet further processing details, I do not feel that the investment is really worth while. Better to achieve 80 per cent of the objectives than to fail in attempting 95 per cent.

13.2 THE GENERAL APPROACH

Entity Life Histories are defined as follows:

> For each entity, an entity life history shows the events that can create, amend and delete an occurrence of the entity and the order in which these events can take place.

So, in somewhat more physical terms, we are looking for things that can update records. Having decided what can create, amend or delete a record we can place these on some form of time-sequencing diagram. These time-sequencing diagrams are what are usually referred to as Entity Life Histories. The production of the diagrams is really optional. They are meant to aid understanding, and for many entities, especially those with simple life histories, might not be required.

As usual in SSADM, we take a step-by-step approach to Entity Life Histories:

1. Identify events.
2. Complete Entity/Access Matrix.
3. Draw Entity Life Histories.
4. Check derived data.
5. Deal with death events.
6. Allocate events to functions and update the Function Catalogue accordingly.
7. Complete Event Catalogue.

Obviously before going much further we need to decide what is meant by an event.

13.3 EVENTS

An event is something in the outside world that triggers the system to update an occurrence of an entity.* Figure 13.2 illustrates what usually happens in Data Flow Diagram terms. An external entity does something to which the system must respond. It is as well to emphasize the distinction between events and processes. Events are the triggers for the processing. For this reason the more pedantic insist that an event is described by a noun, in contrast to a process, which is described by a verb.

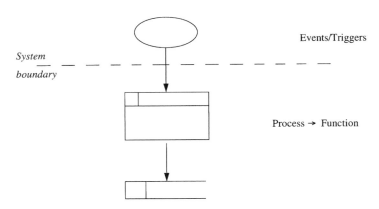

Fig. 13.2 Events

---

*In the Version 4.2 manual an event is defined as 'something that triggers a conceptual model process data to update the system data', (CCTA (1995) p. 6-13). Version 4 stated on RS-EEM-17 (CCTA (1990a)) that: 'Operations within the entity life history represent the discrete components of processing which when combined, constitute events'. The first view will be followed in this book. Robinson and Berrisford (1994) debate this topic at length, concluding that an event is a commit unit. Provided this is a logical rather than a physical commit unit, it does not conflict unduly with our definition.

One thing to be very clear about is that in Rapid SSADM terms, an event is a business trigger that leads to an update. If nothing is updated then there is no event. In other fields of computing the word 'event' might often mean something different, and one often talks about such things as 'mouse-generated events'. Again, it is worth repeating that in SSADM events have a restricted meaning. They are triggers for updates and updates only. To repeat myself *'No update—no event'*.

There are three different types of event

1. Events that come from an external source, that trigger off a process, which in turn updates a datastore. This is the usual way in which an event happens and is as illustrated in Fig. 13.2. A commonly quoted example is to do with customers sending in orders. A customer sends in an order, and so triggers the 'Record order' process, which itself enters details on the order datastore. The event that triggers this processing would be called *Receipt of Customer Order* or something similar (we will use italics to denote events).

2. Events generated by the passage of time. These cause time-triggered updates. As an example, suppose that in a stock control system, at the end of every day, the system searches through all items, reordering those where the current stock level has fallen below a certain level. The event that leads to this updating would be called *End of Day*. It is obviously a time-generated event. A similar time-generated event which appears in many systems is *End of Financial Year*.

3. Internally generated events. These are the least common and occur when the system itself recognizes a certain condition. As an example, let us return to the stock control system. Suppose that the system is searching for products to reorder, and that after every fifty orders the system writes an order summary record to the appropriate datastore. Then the *Sending of Fiftieth Order* would be an internally generated event.

Events are not developed in isolation. Each event will be cross-referenced against the entities that it can change. In fact, we will usually approach events via the entities, by asking for each entity what events affect it, in what sequence these events occur and what processing should the system do for each event. When we say an event affects an entity, what we really mean is that an event can create, amend or delete an occurrence of the entity. In the SSADM literature one often finds this called the *effect* of an event upon an entity.

13.4 THE SEARCH FOR EVENTS

Having now decided what an event is, we need to understand how they are found. From Fig. 13.2 it might appear that the Dataflow Diagrams are the natural place to start the search. All we have to do is to find datastores that have been updated. These are easily recognized as being on the receiving end of arrows. Following the arrows backwards we arrive at the updating process, which is either time triggered or triggered by an external entity. Thus we arrive at the event. Of course, all this must take place on the lowest level of Dataflow Diagram.

In practice, we tend not work from the Dataflow Diagrams. There are three reasons for this. First, the whole point of Entity Life Histories is to elicit extra processing, that processing which is often absent from the Dataflow Diagram. So it would seem sensible to choose a different starting point. Second, the Dataflow Diagrams are somewhat vague documents with processing often covered at an 'overview level'. Entity Life Histories aim to be much more precise. Third, a different approach forces us to ask types of question about the processing other than those that naturally spring to mind when constructing a Dataflow Diagram. This doesn't mean that Dataflow Diagrams are useless as far as events are concerned. Often when there is debate as to whether something actually is an event, a check against the Dataflow Model will resolve any problems.

Our starting point will be the Logical Data Model. For each entity on the Logical Data Model we will ask three simple questions:

What creates the entity?
What deletes the entity?
What amends the entity?

The answers to these questions will be our events. Sometimes we can find them by reference to the Dataflow Model. Sometimes we need only apply our existing knowledge of the business to provide answers. On other occasions, though, we have to go back to the user.

Let us consider how this technique can be applied to our Happy Camping scenario, whose Logical Data Structure is given in Fig. 13.3. We will take as our sample entity Booking.

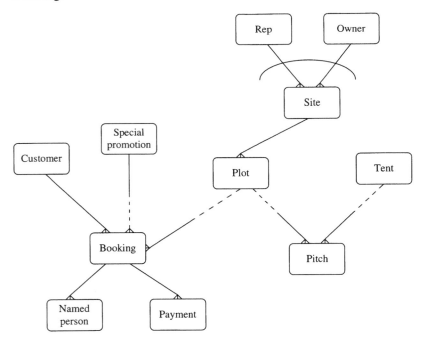

Fig. 13.3   Happy Camping required Logical Data Structure

1. *What creates the entity?* From our knowledge of the system, there appears to be only the one event that does this—*Receipt of Booking*.
2. *What deletes the entity?* The answer to this question is not readily apparent. We will assume, however, that from discussions with the user we have learnt that all bookings must remain on the system for at least three years. The deletion event then becomes *3 years after booking*. (Note that we cannot as yet deal with this event, for we need to add an attribute—Date of Booking—to the entity description, in order to identify when it occurs.)
3. *What modifies the entity?* Here we need to go through the attributes one by one and decide what could change them. Figure 13.4 shows the relevant entity description. Looking at the attributes, the first three do not change once created. As far as the time and place of the holiday are concerned, I will assume, for the sake of simplicity, that once booked it is impossible to change site, plot or dates. With this in mind, site number, plot number and dates do not change after the creation event. A similar statement can be made for the cost. All this is fairly straightforward. The major problem is status. This indicates the state of the booking and can take the values

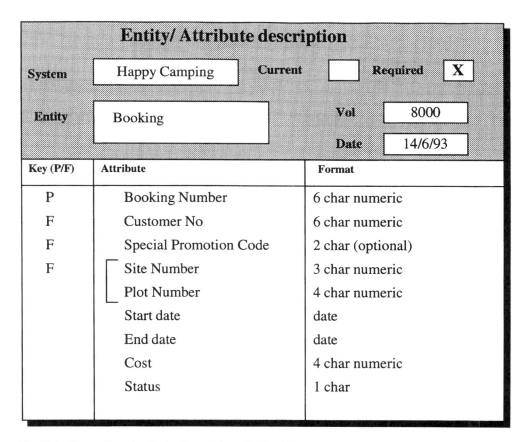

Fig. 13.4 Happy Camping Entity Description—for Booking

P	Provisional Booking	R	Rejection
D	Deposit received	F	Fully paid
N	Non-payment	C	Cancelled
S	Site report received		

Obviously this generates a wealth of events, such as *Receipt of Payment, Receipt of Site Report, Cancellation of Booking, Non-payment of Deposit* and *Non-final Payment*. The last two events are time triggered, and indicate that the dates for deposit or final payment have passed. In the light of this perhaps a better name for these might be *Deposit Due Date + 7 days* and *Final Due Date + 7 days*. Obviously, the processing that would deal with these events would be a batch function run perhaps once a week. Finally, note that the status will take one of the values R or P immediately upon creation.

We do a similar analysis for each entity. The results are then placed on a grid called the Entity Access Matrix. A partial matrix for the Happy Camping system is shown in Fig. 13.5. All the events that have been identified are placed in the first column and all the entities in the system are arranged along the top. If a particular event affects an entity an entry is made in the appropriate square of the matrix. If an entity is being created (inserted) by the event an I is entered, if deleted a D is entered, and if modified, an M. (Full SSADM Version 4.2 uses additional codes to denote other types of access, but we will not use them.)

As we have stated, Fig. 13.5 is a partial Entity Access matrix for the Happy Camping system. On the matrix there are certain entries with both an I and an M, something that might require a few words of explanation.

Events \ Entities	Customer	Booking	Named person	Payment
Receipt of Booking	I/M	I	I	I
Change of customer details	M			
4 years after last booking	D			
Receipt of payment		M		M
Non-payment of deposit		M		
Non-final payment		M		
Ad hoc payment		M		M/I
Receipt of site report		M		
3 years after booking		D	D	D
Addition of person to party			I	
Deletion of person from party			D	
Change of person details			M	
Cancellation of booking		M		

Fig. 13.5   Happy Camping Entity Access Matrix (part)

The first of these dual entries is for a customer. When a booking is received, it is either the first for a customer, when a customer record is created, or is not, in which case the record is modified. (In order to facilitate this, the booking form sent to customers will ask them if they have had previous holidays with Happy Camping.) Thus the event *Receipt of Booking* either creates or possibly modifies an occurrence of the entity Customer.

The other dual entry is to do with *ad hoc* payments. When a Booking occurrence is created, two Payment occurrences, one for a deposit and one for a final payment, are also created. At this stage, these payments really represent payments that are due, rather than payments that have been made. For this reason, the attributes *Payment due date* and *Amount due* are completed, while *Amount paid* and *Date paid* are left null. In the normal course of events, these payments are made in full by the customer some time before the due date. This is catered for by the event *Receipt of Payment*.

What happens, however, if a Customer does not tender sufficient to cover the bill? The processing triggered by the event *Receipt of Payment* would reject the amount proffered as being insufficient. In business terms, leaving the matter like this is not satisfactory from Happy Camping's point of view. The company would like the clerk responsible for entering payments to contact the Customer and ask if the cheque was to be returned or treated as a partial payment. If it were to be returned, the processing triggered by the event would have failed. If the cheque were to be banked, the processing triggered by this new event, which we will call *Ad hoc payment*, would then recognize the amount as an underpayment. It deals with this by changing the Payment occurrence that is due into an interim payment with the amount and amount paid equal to the partial payment, and creating a new Payment occurrence for the remaining balance. Thus a partial payment of a deposit would modify the old deposit record, making it an interim payment, and create a new deposit record for the amount still outstanding. This explains the C and M on the matrix.

Although both these cases appear similar, as they involve an event doing different things to an entity depending upon the situation, they are in fact different. The first, that concerning a Customer, is an example of an event having different effects upon an entity. The second which concerns a Payment, is an example of an entity playing different roles with regard to an event. We will cover this in more detail later when we come to discuss the entity life history technique.

As a final point, note that often we need to modify the Logical Data Model in the light of our analysis. For example, a Customer record is only deleted 4 years after the last booking. Obviously we cannot do this unless the Customer entity has an attribute *Date of last Booking*.

13.5 ENTITY LIFE HISTORY TECHNIQUE

The purpose of the Entity Life History technique is to form a pictorial representation of the life of an entity. This should show all the events would could affect any occurrence of an entity from its birth to its death. Note that not all occurrences of an entity experience the same events. While all occurrences of an *Invoice* entity might be created by a *Billing* event and be deleted by event caused by the passage of several years after the billing date, only a small delinquent minority would be subjected to the full rigours of events such as *Sending of Final Reminder*, *Referral to Solicitors* and *Result of Trial*. The pictures of the lives of entities must of necessity reflect this richness, allowing for abnormal behaviour as well as the normal case.

There are numerous ways in which Entity Life Histories can be represented. The chief among these are:

- Jackson diagrams
- Regular expressions
- State transition diagrams
- Finite state automata
- Event flow diagrams (or syntax diagrams)

Each of these notations has its adherents and its detractors. Each has advantages and disadvantages, and different entity life histories might best be analysed using different techniques. One can prove mathematically that the techniques are formally equivalent (see, for example, Hopcroft and Ullman, 1979). In Appendix 2 an example is illustrated using each of the notations to give a flavour of each approach. Standard SSADM uses Jackson notation and a more detailed description of this is given in the standard SSADM texts. It has to be said that many analysts find Jackson diagrams extremely difficult to use, so much so that the technique is often omitted on many projects. This is rather like throwing out the baby with the bathwater. By not doing Entity Life Histories, an analyst would be failing to get that third view of the system. Many vital questions about the system would remain unasked, let alone answered. It is important that we do not let the notation hinder us from asking these questions even on the smallest systems. For this reason we propose the use of a simpler, more user-orientated approach, that of Event Flow Diagrams. It should be stated that this is merely an alternative approach. If you have been brought up in a structured programming environment, and are happy with Jackson diagrams, by all means use them. The important thing is to do something!

Event Flow Diagrams are not new. They have been used extensively in computer science to illustrate regular grammars for programming languages such as Pascal. When used in this way they are called syntax diagrams. They have also been used for event analysis in other methodologies. In this notation for Entity Life Histories, events are represented by nodes on a diagram, each node being represented by a round-edged box. Figure 13. 6 shows all the possible constructs. The first is that of a *sequence*. This says that event A is followed by event B which is in turn followed by event C. Choice is implemented by the use of the *selection* construct. In our example, either A happens or B happens or C happens. Finally repetition is achieved by use of the *iteration* construct. This comes in two variants. In both of these in Fig. 13.6, event A can happen any number of times. The difference is that in the first A need not happen, while in the second A must occur at least once.

An example of an Entity Life History in practice is shown in Fig. 13.7. The example is taken from the Happy Camping system and represents the life history of the *Named Person* entity. (Recall that this refers to the individuals named on a booking form.) The events that affect the entity are shown in Fig. 13.5, the Happy Camping Entity Access Matrix. Usually, occurrences of the Named Person entity are created when a booking form is received. Sometimes a person is added to the party later which would cause an

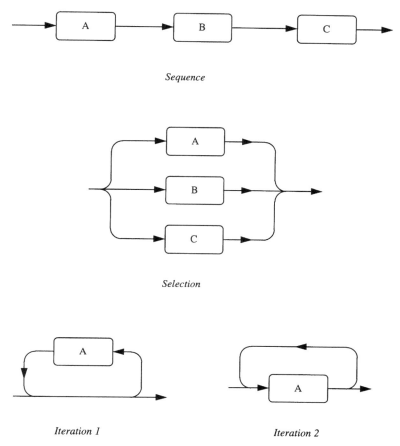

Sequence

Selection

Iteration 1   *Iteration 2*

Fig. 13.6   Event flow constructs

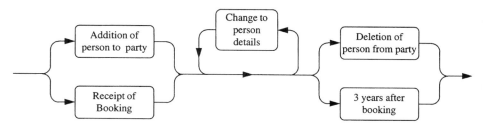

Fig. 13.7   Named Person Entity Life History

extra occurrence of the entity to be created. Thus either of the events *Addition of Person to Party* or *Receipt of Booking* creates an occurrence of the entity. A similar argument applies to the deletion of the entity. Normally, a Named Person occurrence would be deleted with the booking at a date some three years after a booking had been made. Again there is the possibility of an early removal from the booking. Between creation and deletion a person's details might also change, in fact might change several times.

We often speak of creation events and of deletion events. In this case the creation event would be a selection choosing between *Addition of Person to Party* and *Receipt of Booking*. Similar things could be said of the deletion events. This is quite a useful approach to the drawing of Entity Life Histories. First, one identifies the creation event(s), places them on the diagram, does the same for the deletion events and then attempt to sort out the mid-life. For a complicated life history, the mid-life is often the most difficult part to draw and so it is as well to deal with the birth and death events first.

Note that events *must* lead to an updating of the entity. It is quite tempting when looking at life histories to insert extra 'events' because they seem to make sense or be necessary in terms of the life of the entity in question. For example, for the Named Person Entity Life History it is quite tempting to ask if the *Change to Person details* event can ever take place after the party has visited the campsite. Presumably we would not be interested in recording any change to the details of people after the holiday has taken place. Having asked this question, the next step would seem to be the inclusion of the event *End of Holiday* or something similar onto the life history. But before succumbing one must ask whether this is indeed an event which affects this entity. Recall that an event affects an entity, if and only if it updates the entity. At present there is no attribute on Named Person that is updated by this event. One could invent such an attribute, but this seems to be using a rather large sledgehammer to crack a very small nut. If we try to analyse our reasons for including this event, it is really as an error-trapping mechanism for the processing attached to the previous event *Change to Person details*. Rather than overcomplicating the logic of the life history, it is far better to use the Entity Life History to uncover these possible errors, place them on the event catalogue (see later) and via this onto the function catalogue.*

Entity Life Histories provide a wonderful vehicle for asking this type of question. This is the secret of their power. They enable the analyst to uncover aspects of the system that remain hidden with other techniques. Quite often the attempt to draw an Entity Life History will uncover fresh events. These must then be added to the Entity Access Matrix, as it is quite possible that the event could also affect other entities. Indeed, when adding a freshly discovered event to the matrix, it is necessary to examine each entity in turn to ask whether the event could affect it. Obviously, we may then have to modify a freshly drawn Entity Life History for some other entity. However, in spite of the beguiling nature of this power invested in Entity Life Histories, the technique must not become an end in itself. Its major aim is to clarify the processing, not to supplant the processing. The guiding principle must be to keep Entity Life Histories simple. As we have seen, too deep an immersion in the technique could lead to the piling up of more and more attributes for each entity. By all means, errors revealed in the Logical Data Model should be corrected, but the model should not be changed unnecessarily.

---

*SSADM Version 4.2 attempts to use the Entity Life Histories for this error-checking purpose. This it does primarily by the use of state indicators. Questions of referential integrity are further trapped by the use of 'Gain' and 'Loss' operations and the importation of extra death events. Not only does this lead to Entity Life Histories of a baroque-like difficulty, but it can also be proved that full error checking is unattainable. (See Hargrave (1995).)

13.6 EFFECTS OF AN EVENT

Figure 13.8 shows the Customer Entity Life History from the Happy Camping system. One interesting thing about this Entity Life History is the repetition of the event *Receipt of Booking*. The reason for this is fairly obvious. When a booking is first received, the customer will not have been previously recorded on the system, and so an occurrence of the *Customer* entity will have to be created. Subsequent bookings by the same customer may lead to a change to this occurrence of the *Customer*, perhaps because they have changed their address. In this case we say that an event has different effects on an entity depending on where the entity is in its life. When this happens, an event must occupy two different positions on the entity's life history, and each repetition must be qualified. Following each node containing the event must be a word or words in brackets which serves to differentiate the different effects of the event. For the Customer Entity Life History the event is qualified by the use of the words 'first' and 'other'.

It might be argued that this particular scenario is a little unrealistic, since it is only for the regular customers that one would wish to record detail changes from the booking form. Indeed, in the vast majority of cases there is a real practical difficulty in associating a new booking with a previous customer, it is far easier just to create a new Customer occurrence for every new booking. If this were indeed the case then the Entity Life History would be altered and *Receipt of Booking* would be the creation event and the only creation event. However, if there is the slightest possibility of customers having more than one booking then the Entity Life History of Fig. 13.8 must stand. (In fact the practical difficulties of identifying previous customers are eased somewhat by asking on the booking form if they had booked previously.)

Large Entity Life Histories can become a little messy, often with lines crossing and tangling. Sometimes the diagram can be made a little clearer by repeating events on the diagram. In this case, taking our cue from the Dataflow Diagram conventions, we place a small bar across the repeated nodes, as in Fig. 13.9. Obviously this is rather a simple case, and the diagram could be redrawn without repetition. Real-life cases are a little more complicated. Remember that this is purely a drawing convention and it should not be confused with an event having different effects upon an entity.

Talking about alternative ways of drawing a life history, Fig. 13.10 represents two further ways of drawing the Customer Entity Life History. In our original representation, we stuck rather rigidly to the constructs of sequence, selection and iteration,

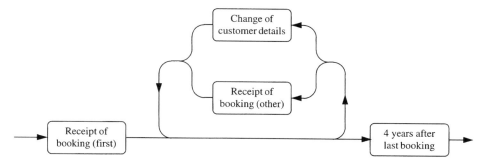

Fig. 13.8   Customer Entity Life History

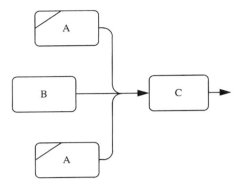

Fig. 13.9   Duplicate symbols

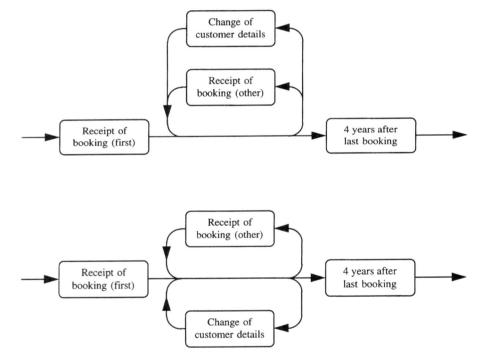

Fig. 13.10   Alternative Customer Entity Life History

primarily because this is the way that standard SSADM would present the life history using Jackson diagrams. As can be seen from Fig. 13.10, alternatives do exist. This is one of the great virtues of this approach. If we want one event to follow another we just connect them by an arrow. The resultant diagrams are user friendly and can be presented in a way most acceptable to users. The drawback is the lack of uniformity in the solutions, with different analysts presenting different pictures.

13.7 QUITS

Returning to the Happy Camping system, let us attempt to draw an Entity Life History for the Booking entity. If we ignore the *Cancellation* event we end with a diagram something like that in Fig. 13.11. Note that we have annotated the diagram to show that if the booking is initially rejected, perhaps because the campsite is full, the top path is taken. (We would still maintain such bookings on the system in order to be able to monitor the demand for certain sites.) We can use such annotation where we need to clarify the diagram. In Fig. 13.11 we also use it when dealing with an *ad hoc* payment which is greater than that asked for. Happy Camping cannot really accept an over-payment as a final payment, and so the event only affects the deposit. The payment can either cover both deposit and final payment or can cover the deposit and only contribute partially towards the final payment. Note that an underpayment does not affect the Status of a Booking. (Why?)

Now let us try to add the *Cancellation* event to the structure. The main problem with this is that it is possible to cancel the booking at any point between the receipt of the booking and the receipt of the site report. Clearly it is possible to rearrange the diagram so that there are possible paths from the event *Receipt of Booking* and the two *Payment* events. However, the diagram could become a little messy, and so an alternative approach is shown in Fig. 13.12.

This 'Quit from anywhere' device is quite useful in the event of abnormal deaths. Its use serves to highlight the different exit routes from the life. As we mentioned previously it is always possible to replace this device with a number of lines and arrows, but the resultant diagram might look messy. Note that the 'Quit and Resume' technique as used in Jackson diagrams in standard SSADM is not required in our approach. If we wish one event to follow another we merely draw an arrow from one to the other. However, if the diagram does become messy, then it is possible to extend the notation by introducing some form of quit.

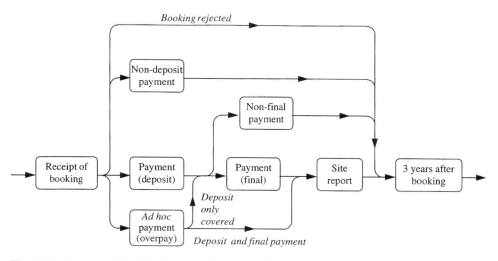

Fig. 13.11 Booking Entity Life History without cancellation

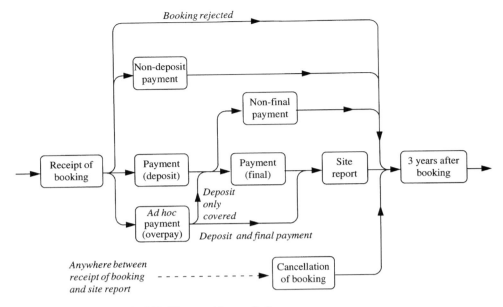

Fig. 13.12   Booking Entity Life History with cancellation

13.8 ENTITY ROLES

We next need to consider the situation when an entity plays different roles with respect to an event. To do this, we will revert to our Happy Camping system and take as an example the life history of a Pitch. Recall that a Pitch entity is the link box replacing the many-to-many relation between a tent and a plot. In some sense it is the record of the stay of a tent in a particular location in a campsite. Also recall that its attributes are

> Tent number
> (Site Number)
> (Plot Number)
> Date erected
> Date taken down
> End of season Code

Tents are normally erected at the start of the season, and taken down at the end. Note that *Date erected* has to be part of the key since it is possible for a tent to occupy the same plot on subsequent years. The End of Season Code is used to record the condition of the tent. So in the normal course of things the Pitch entity is affected by three events—the creation event *Pre-season Allocation*, the modification event *End of Season* and the deletion event *2 years after the end of season*. This seems fairly straight-forward, but what happens if there is a sudden overbooking at one campsite, while there is a dearth of customers at another? In purely business terms, Happy Camping would like to move tents from the under-subscribed site to the over-subscribed one. Obviously the system should be able to cope with this. One way of doing this is to 'archive' the old pitch record and to create a new one for the same site. 'Archiving' is achieved by modifying the occurrence by entering the *Date taken down* and the *End of Season Code*. This explains the situation of Fig. 13.13. The first occurrence of the Pitch entity is created before the start of the season on 1 April 1993. This is for tent number 2133 on plot number 102, site number 45. On 10 July 1993, the tent is taken down and re-erected on site number 49, plot number 23. Thus the event *Transfer of Tent* leads to the creation of a second Pitch occurrence and a modification of the first. Finally, the second occurrence is modified by the *End of Season* event, and both are deleted by the event *2 years after the end of season*.

The Entity Life History for the Pitch entity appears in Fig. 13.14. Note that the event *Transfer of Tent* appears twice on the life history, once as a modification event, once as a creation event. In this case we say that the entity plays different roles with respect to the event, and the two occurrences of the event on the life history are also differentiated by the use of qualifiers.

There is often some confusion between an event affecting an entity in different ways and an entity playing different roles with respect to an entity. When an event has different effects on an entity we are saying that an event either does one thing to an occurrence of the entity or does something else. An example of this is the Customer Entity Life History in Fig. 13.8. Here the event *Receipt of Booking* can affect the Customer entity in one of two ways. It either creates an occurrence of the Customer entity *or* it amends an existing occurrence. Contrast this with the case of an entity playing different roles with respect to an event. Here there are normally two occurrences of an entity involved. One occurrence is affected in one way and the other occurrence in another way. Thus the *Transfer of Tent* event modifies one occurrence of an entity *and* creates another. At a very superficial level this is one way of being able to distinguish between effects and roles. The effects involve one occurrence of an entity with *or*s while the roles involve two occurrences of an entity with *and*s.

As far as the notation is concerned, the qualifiers for the different effects of events use round brackets, while the qualifiers used for the differing roles played by an entity use square brackets. Although this might appear to be a somewhat trivial matter, unless this convention is adhered to the diagrams can become very confusing when effects and roles are intertwined. Figure 13.15 is a case in point. It shows the life history of the Payment entity. Recall that two payment records, one for the deposit and one for the final payment, are set up when the booking is made. Thus in the vast majority of cases, the life is fairly straightforward, consisting of the three events, *Receipt of Booking*, possible *Receipt of Payment* and *3 years after booking*. (In the case of a non-payment, the booking entity is changed, but the payment is left alone.) The only difficulties arise when a Customer wishes to pay more or less than that which is due. This is dealt with by the event *Ad hoc payment*. The effect of this event upon the Payment entity is a little complicated as effects and roles are intertwined.

We have already mentioned what happens if an underpayment is made. The old Payment occurrence, the one that is expecting a payment, is changed into an interim payment, with the attributes *Amount due* and *Amount paid* altered to equal the amount of the underpayment. Nothing further happens to this occurrence until the deletion event. A new Payment occurrence is created with Amount due equal to the balance outstanding. This 'replaces' the old Payment and so is for either a deposit or a final

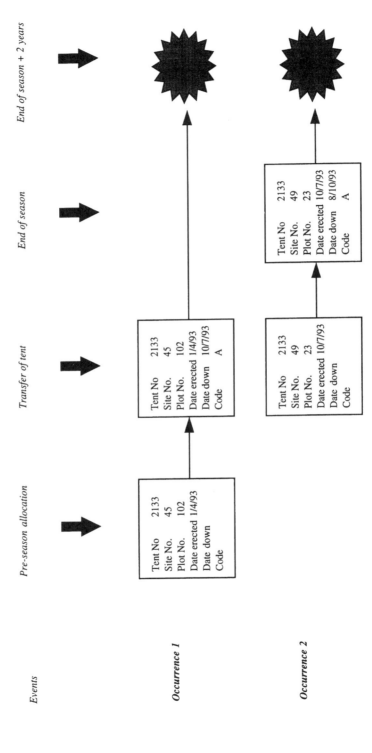

Fig. 13.13   The effect of the 'Transfer of Tent' event on the Pitch entity

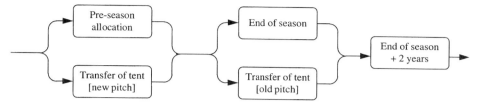

Fig. 13.14   Pitch Entity Life History

payment, whichever is the most appropriate. Note that this way of dealing with under-payments copes with the situation where a number of partial payments are made.

An overpayment can only be made when a deposit is due. In this case the attributes *Amount paid* and *Amount due* on the Payment occurrence corresponding to a deposit are altered to equal the amount tendered. The next event that affects this entity is the deletion event. The *Amount due* on the Final Payment occurrence is reduced to the balance still owing. Obviously, this event can affect the Final Payment only once.

It might be thought that the differences between effects and roles are purely cosmetic, in that if the analyst really knows what he or she is doing, whether it is an effect or a role and what is the shape of the brackets don't really matter. This is correct as far as Entity Life History analysis is concerned, but it will make a difference later when we come to Access Paths.

13.9 SUB-LIVES AND PARALLEL LIVES

Entity Life Histories can become quite complicated even when we use our more simplified approach. In order to reduce the size of the diagrams and to make things more intelligible one can use the concept of *sub-lives*. A sub-life is merely what it says, a portion of the life of an entity. Figure 13.16 shows the concept applied to the life of the Tent Entity from the Happy Camping system.

In order to interpret this diagram recall that the attributes of tent are

> Tent Number
> Model manufacturer
> Cost
> Capacity
> Date of purchase
> Date of sale/destruction
> Date of last pitch
> Date of last inspection
> Condition Code
> Status Code
> (S = in store I = being inspected P = on active pitch)

Note that on the life, events are represented by the use of soft-edged boxes, while sub-lives are represented by hard-edged boxes. In the life of the entity Tent, when we meet

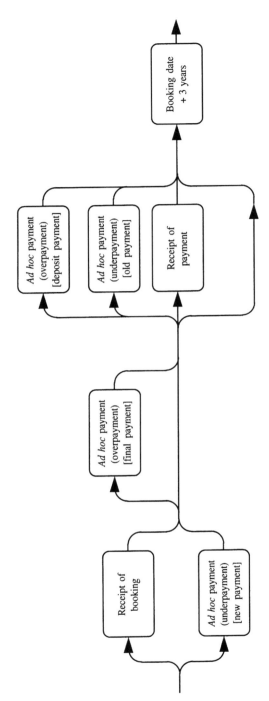

Fig. 13.15 Payment Entity Life History

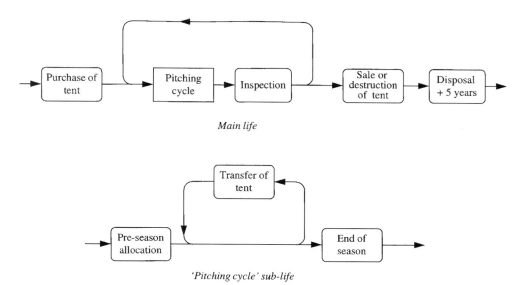

Main life

'Pitching cycle' sub-life

Fig. 13.16   Tent Entity Life History

the box *Pitching Cycle* we jump out of the main life and start on the sub-life. When we come to the end of the sub-life we re-enter the main life and then start on the *Inspection*.

Note that entry and exit from a sub-life are very well defined. An entity can only enter at the start of a sub-life and leave at the end of a sub-life. In this sense a sub-life is rather like a subroutine or procedure in programming. Obviously we could easily draw the life history of a Tent without sub-lives. We merely chose this example for ease of illustration.

Closely allied to sub-lives is the concept of parallel sub-lives. Here two separate sets of events overlap. The notation we use is shown in Fig. 13.17. Here the events that go to make up the sub-lives of A and B cannot be placed in any order—in some sense the two sub-lives take place in parallel. In Fig. 13.18 we illustrate the concept in action by describing the life history of the Rep entity from the Happy Camping system. Here we assume that a Rep must pass a two-stage exam at the start of her or his career. The second stage takes place some months after the first. Thus we have the two events *Stage 1 exam* and *Stage 2 exam*. The personal details of the Rep can change at any time during this process. They can change before the first exam, before the second exam or after the second exam. So the two sub-lives *Exam Life* and *Personal details changes* happen in parallel.

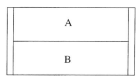

Fig. 13.17   Parallel construct

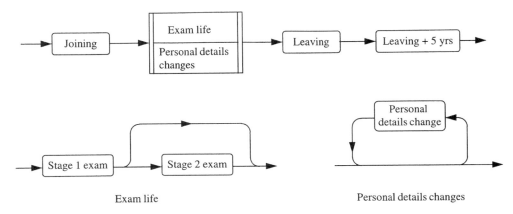

Fig. 13.18   Rep Entity Life History

One common mistake made in connection with parallel lives is to assume that events in the lives can occur simultaneously. Although theoretically possible, in practice this never happens. So to say that two sub-lives happen in parallel is really a misleading use of words which can lead to mistakes. What we should say is that the lives overlap. One common situation in which the construct is used mistakenly is when both sub-lives are just iterations of single events. The two events cannot happen 'at the same time', and so the parallel notation is not necessary. What is needed is a selection within an iteration, in other words, the two events occurring a number of times in a random order. Parallel constructs should not be used too liberally. They are really only necessary if there is some form of sequence in one of the sub-lives. If you can avoid using this construct, by all means do so.

13.10 DERIVED DATA, DEATH EVENTS AND SUB-TYPES

After completing the individual Entity Life Histories for each entity, we need next to consider the effects of events upon groups of entities. In the best of all possible worlds this should not really be necessary, as we should have sufficient insight into the life of each individual entity to be able to foresee all the events that could possibly affect it.

However, being mortal, it is likely that we have missed some events. In particular, we could well have ignored the relationship of one entity to another when the effect of an event upon one entity has a knock-on effect on the other. For this reason we will look at derived information, death events and sub-types in a fairly formalized way.

Consider the entities in Fig. 13.19. Suppose an attribute of Sales Rep is *Total sales this year*, and that the Area entity also has an attribute *Total sales this year*. Then obviously the attribute in Area is the sum of the corresponding attributes in Sales Rep. Thus anything that affects the *Total sales this year* attribute of Sales Rep must also affect the corresponding attribute of Area and so appear on the Area Entity Life History.

So to make sure we do not miss any of these events we need to do the following:

1. List all derived attributes in the system.
2. Identify all the events that affect attributes that determine the derived items.

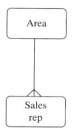

Fig. 13.19 Sales Rep/Area

3. Ensure that these events are on the Entity Life History of the entity having the derived attribute.

After having considered the problems posed by derived data, we next need to consider the ripples emanating from death or deletion events. What we need to do is to look at each relationship and ask two questions:

Does the death of a detail affect the master?
Does the death of a master affect the detail?

Considering the first of these questions, in general the death of a detail has no effect on its master. There are only two cases where we need to be careful. The first is if there are integrity problems. For example, in Fig. 13.20 suppose entity A stands for a 'Bill' and B stands for 'Item on a Bill'. Then any attempt to delete a B without deleting the corresponding A will mean removing an item from the bill without deleting the bill itself, thus corrupting the data. Obviously, we need to remove a bill and all its detail items in one fell swoop. In other words, the death events on the Entity Life Histories for A and B must be the same.

Similar problems arise where entity A contains information derived from its set of Bs, such as total number of Bs, or average value of an attribute of B. In this case a death event for B must appear on A's Entity Life History, but does not necessarily lead to the death of A. It might just mean modifying the derived information in A.

The second case is where death floats upwards. Here the death of the last detail will cause the death of the master. As an example of this suppose we delete customer records when the last order that customer has made is deleted. If the orders are deleted 5 years after the order date, then the event *Order date + 5 years* would have to appear as a deletion event on the master's Entity Life History.

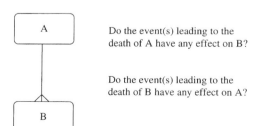

Fig. 13.20 Death events

The second question posed was does the death of a master affect its details? Here we have to be more careful. There are essentially three cases:

1. The death of A removes all existing Bs. Here the event leading to the death of A must appear as a death event on B. (Note that it might not be the only death event on B.)
2. All Bs must have been deleted prior to the death of A. In this case we need to do two things:
   i. If the death events for A and B are time related, the time constraints for B must operate before A. For example, it is obviously wrong to have B being deleted 5 years after the receipt of an order, say, if A is deleted 2 years after the receipt of that order.
   ii. The processing that leads to the death of A must have a check that all the Bs have disappeared. (This might be done automatically by the database in a physical implementation.) In any case, the event catalogue (see later) needs to be annotated with details of this check. Note that we need a way of getting rid of an A if the usual method fails.
3. Any Bs still living survive. Here the foreign key in B needs to be modified to a null value. Thus A's death event must appear as an event on B's Entity Life History.

Again we need to approach death events in a fairly formalized way in order to avoid missing anything. First go through the entities one by one, considering each entity as a detail and asking if its death affects any masters. Next revisit each entity, viewing it now as a master and asking if its death affects any of its details.

Finally there is the question of sub-types. As a sub-type occurrence must always exist in harness with a super-type occurrence, every creation or deletion event appearing on the sub-type Entity Life History must always occur on the super-type Entity Life History. For example, every event that creates an In-Patient occurrence in Fig. 13.21 must also create a Patient occurrence. The converse does not, however, apply. An event which creates a Patient occurrence does not have to appear on *both* sub-type Entity Life Histories. Thus the event 'Heart Attack Notification' is unlikely to create both In-Patient and Out-Patient occurrences. For events other than creations and deletions, there is no *a priori* reason why they should appear on more than one Entity Life History. 'Change of Address', for example, would change the Patient entity, but change neither of the sub-types.

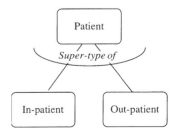

Fig. 13.21   Sub-types

13.11 ALLOCATE EVENTS TO FUNCTIONS AND COMPLETE EVENT CATALOGUE

When all the events have been identified, we need to allocate events to functions and to complete the Event Catalogue.* The Event Catalogue is a somewhat more formal representation of the Event/Entity matrix and is particularly useful when the number of entities is large and, as a result, the matrix becomes cumbersome. It is quite a useful document as being a succinct summary of the basic update operations that are performed within the system. Figure 13.22 shows a portion of the Event catalogue for the Happy Camping system.

To produce the catalogue we first need to allocate events to functions and to update the Function Definition form for updates by listing which events will trigger them. Every event is, by definition, the trigger for update processing within the system, and so must be allocated to an update function. In general, we try to apportion events on the basis that one event to one function. Certainly this should be the case for the vast majority of on-line processing.

	Event Catalogue			
System Happy Camping		**Date** 31/5/93		**Page** 1
Ev. Id	**Event**	**Entities**	**Processing**	**Function**
1	Receipt of Booking	Customer Booking Named Person Payment	I/M I I I	Make provisional booking
2	Change of Customer details	Customer	M	Change of Customer details
3	4 years after last booking	Customer	D	Annual Housekeeping run
4	Receipt of payment	Booking Payment	M–change status M–enter amount (what if not enough?)	Receipt of payment
5	Non-payment of deposit	Booking	M–change status	Weekly payment check
6	Non-final payment	Booking	M–change status	Weekly payment check

Fig. 13.22   Event Catalogue

---

*The Event Catalogue has a somewhat chequered history in SSADM. It was present in Version 3, dropped in Version 4, and reintroduced in Version 4.2, where it is named *The Event and Enquiry Catalogue.* We have not included enquiries since this merely duplicates much in the Function Catalogue.

Sometimes, however, it is the case where more than one event are triggers for the same function. For example, in our Happy Camping system, the two time-triggered events to do with non-payment, that is *Non-payment of deposit* and *Non-final payment*, are catered for by the one function, the weekly payment cheque. This is quite usual with off-line functions, especially housekeeping functions. It can sometimes happen also with on-line functions. In this case it is usually caused by events being 'too small'. To take a trivial example, we might have identified two events *Change to Customer details being notified by phone* and *Change to Customer details being notified by post* which are dealt with by the same function. Such increases in granularity do not really affect the processing and are best avoided as they mess up the Entity Life Histories.

It is sometimes the case that one event triggers several processes. A classic example of this is the event *End of Financial Year*. This can trigger all manner of processing. Although not strictly correct, one might deal with this situation by splitting this event into sub-events, End of Financial Year(Purchasing), End of Financial Year (Accounts), . . . Each of these sub-events could be allocated its own function. In our approach to Entity Event modelling, the precise designation of events does not really matter, as the events are only used to identify the functions, which carry the burden of the processing. In SSADM Version 4.2, matters are not so simple. Here processing is attached to the events and so their precise identification and granularity is important. Attaching processing to events such as *End of Financial Year* is a real problem.

We may end up with some events that are not dealt with by any functions in the Function Catalogue. In this case we will have to generate new functions triggered by these events and complete the appropriate documentation before placing them in the Catalogue. Note that for these new functions we are redoing step 330, so we should in theory also revisit all the intervening steps. It might appear that by doing this we enter some never-ending circular route visiting each of the steps 330, 340, 350 and 360 in turn. In practice, this never occurs.

Our final task is to complete the Event Catalogue. The Event Catalogue is useful, but not strictly essential, as all the information in it is contained on other documents. (It could be replaced by the matrix with a couple of extra columns.) All this information will eventually be transferred in one form or another to the Function Catalogue. If it is proposed to complete an Event Catalogue, this task should not be left until the end of the step, but started as events are identified and Entity Life Histories are drawn. The processing column is not intended to be complete. It is merely an *aide-mémoire*, the repository of random jottings that are to be expanded in later documents.

FOURTEEN

ACCESS PATHS

14.1 PURPOSE

In SSADM the processing, as documented in the Function Catalogue, is really developed in isolation from the data model. Functions were first identified in step 330 as jobs that the user wanted the system to do. When defining a function we were primarily concerned with how it will appear to the user and in broad terms what it will do. The Logical Data Model hardly rates a mention. We first consider the relationship between the Logical Data Model and the functions in step 340 as part of Relational Data Analysis. Here we check that the entities have sufficient attributes to produce the required output, sometimes building a partial model as part of the checking process. This can, however, be a somewhat haphazard process, as we do not analyse every input and output, but pick and choose, doing only those that time will allow. Even if we could go through every single function, we still might miss those data items, such as the 'status' of an entity, required by the processing but which do not appear on any output. We next visit the Logical Data Model when constructing Entity Life Histories in step 360. Here, however, we are really using the Logical Data Model to check the functions, not the functions to check the Logical Data Model. What is needed is some form of guarantee that the functions as we have defined them will really work. In other words, will the Logical Data Model support the processing burden?

Access Paths are a rigorous way of seeing that this is so. More precisely, the purpose of Access Paths is as follows:

1. To describe a possible navigation path around the Logical Data Model for each function. Note that we are only talking about possible navigation routes. We are not deciding how each function will work, merely verifying that it can work. With older technology we might be able to specify the processing and hence the navigation in

precise detail, but with more modern fourth generation facilities the 'system' itself will generally decide how to move around the Logical Data Model, in other words, which entities it will visit and in which order. For such environments, all we can do at this stage is to check that a navigation route is possible but leave its precise determination to the system.

2. To validate the Logical Data Model. This is probably the most important job done by Access Path analysis. We will check that all the entities, relationships and data items needed for processing are in fact present.

3. To define the processing for each function. The access paths will be annotated by the use of Access Path Descriptions which will define the processing to a depth sufficient for most projects that do not wish to be involved with detailed program design.

4. To identify possible performance problems. This is done by attaching volumetrics to the Access Path, calculating how many times each entity is accessed and then forming a rough estimate as to how long each function should take.

Access Paths are defined in step 365.* As can be seen from Fig. 14.1, the major inputs to this step are the Function Catalogue, the Event Catalogue and the Required Logical Data Model. The parts of the Logical Data Model of particular interest to us are the Logical Data Structure, the Entity Descriptions and the Volumetrics. We require two types of volumetric information. The first is about the numbers of occurrences of each entity. The second refers to what are called the dependent volumes. These show how many details are possessed by each master on average. The outputs from step 365 are the Function Catalogue, enhanced by the Access Paths, and a possibly updated Logical Data Model.

14.2 THE TECHNIQUE (ENQUIRIES)

We will consider enquiry and update Access Paths separately. Although the end results look similar, updates are slightly more complicated, and so are best left until later.

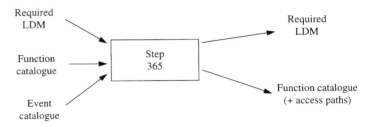

Fig. 14.1 Inputs and products

---

*In standard SSADM Access Paths are produced in step 360. This step also contains the Entity Life Histories. This strikes me as much too much for a single step, and for this reason we have introduced a new step (365) specially for Access Paths.

SSADM Version 4.2 goes a little further than this by having two separate names, Enquiry Access Paths and Effect Correspondence Diagrams, for enquiries and updates, respectively. As is usual in SSADM we have a step-by-step approach to the production of Access Paths. For each enquiry function we will:

1. *Identify the output required.* We need to find out what the function will actually produce. We usually do this by referring to the appropriate screen and print layouts. (We might also use actual physical screens appearing in the guise of agreed prototypes.) Note that we are not so much interested in the appearance or format of the screens and reports, but more in the individual data items that make an appearance on the output. For this reason we ignore such things as system messages, menu choices, error messages and the like. As an alternative interpretation of this viewpoint, consider a function represented as a Dataflow Diagram process. The output that interests us here is the content of dataflows flowing across the system boundary from the process to external entities.

2. *Identify the input.* What item(s) of data are required from the user or initiator of this function? In particular, which items of data are required to trigger the function? For on-line enquiries, these are usually data items input from a user via a keyboard. For off-line functions, the input trigger can be a little more difficult to determine. Often it is something like a date provided by an operator or the operating system. Note that again we are interested in data items obtained from the operator or the system, not in commands or decisions made. Furthermore, it is important to stress that at present we are only concerned with data that emerges from an external source. We are not interested in internally generated data, in particular that obtained from the database. This is the particular concern of tasks 3 and 4.

3. *Work out which entities to access.* We need to identify which entities hold the data that is to appear on the output. We do this by reference to the entity descriptions. Note that some items of data might appear in more than one entity. This is certainly the case with foreign keys. For the present we make no decision as to which of the entities we will use, but merely note their names.

4. *Identify possible navigation paths around the Logical Data Structure.* The input data we have uncovered in task 2 will normally define the function's entry point to the Logical Data Model. This tells us which entity we need to read first. From task 3 we have a list of entities to visit. Using the Logical Data Structure we can define a possible navigation route. Usually there is only one possibility. Sometimes, however, there is a choice, and then we have to decide which of several alternative routes around the Logical Data Model is the best. A decision is usually made on the basis of least accesses. Very occasionally we encounter navigational problems in that some entities appear unreachable by the function. If this should ever happen we have to do one of two things. We must either provide the function with more input, usually the primary keys of the inaccessible entities, or construct extra relationships to enable us to move to other parts of the Logical Data Structure. This latter course of action could have unfortunate consequences, in that adding an additional relationship implies another foreign key in an entity, which could impact on the Entity Life Histories.

5. *Draw the Enquiry Access Path.* For this we use a 'pseudo-Jackson' notation that will be described later. For the present, suffice it to say that this is the point at which we consider any decisions that have to be made in the processing.
6. *Produce Access Path Descriptions.* This is used to document the processing in more detail.
7. *Define volumetrics.* What we attempt to do here is to define the number of entity occurrences read by a function. Doing this will normally give us a feel for the length of time a function takes and should highlight any potential problems.

14.3 ACCESS PATH CONSTRUCTS

An Access Path is a diagram which shows us how a function might navigate the Logical Data Structure. It can be made up from entity nodes, navigation arrows and the Jackson constructs of iteration and selection. One of the simplest Access Paths, that depicting detail to master navigation, is shown in Fig. 14.2. Here we first read an occurrence of entity B, then use the relationship between the two entities to access its master A. The arrow in the access path really means 'read next'. We always assume that it is possible to go directly from a detail to its master, to traverse the relationship in an 'upward' direction. At the moment we are not concerned with how this might be implemented, just that it is possible.

On the other hand, in navigating from a master to a detail, we read a single occurrence of the master, but possibly more than one occurrence of the detail. Figure 14.3 shows us how this is documented on an access path. After reading an

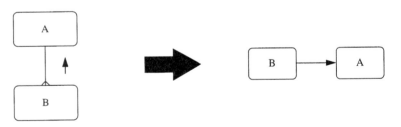

Fig. 14.2   Detail to master navigation

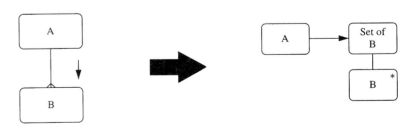

Fig. 14.3   Master to detail navigation

occurrence of entity A, we access a set of occurrences of entity B. This set consists of the details of the original A, and is denoted on the access path by the use of a structure box 'Set of B' connected by a vertical line to an entity box for B. The entity box has an asterisk in the upper right-hand corner to denote that there are zero or more occurrences of B in the set. (Note that the asterisk does denote a possibility of zero occurrences, in other words, an empty set.) Using Jackson terminology, we would say that the upper box, the 'Set of Bs', is an *iteration* of B. Again we always assume that we can traverse a relationship in this way without worrying about how this might be achieved physically.

Our final example of data navigation demonstrates an Access Path using the Jackson *selection* construct. This is used when a choice has to be made. Figure 14.4 shows an example of the construct used in practice. Here we are only interested in reading the Area of a particular Customer if the credit rating is an 'A'. Thus after arriving at the desired Customer occurrence a choice has to be made. This choice is depicted by the use of the Jackson selection, which here consists of the two boxes under the Customer. To show that there is a choice, and that only one of the boxes can be chosen, we place a small 'o' in the top right-hand corner of each. Thus, only in the case of a customer with the correct credit rating do we move on to the Area entity.

An Access Path will consist of all these constructs joined together in an appropriate fashion. We will show how such paths are constructed by means of worked examples. Before doing this, however, we need to revisit some essential documentation.

14.4 THE HAPPY CAMPING LOGICAL DATA MODEL

All our examples are based on the Happy Camping system. To be able to develop Access Paths we need to refer frequently to the Logical Data Model. To aid us in this, we have reprinted the appropriate parts of the Logical Data Model, in particular the Logical Data Structure in Fig. 14.5 and the entity descriptions in Tables 14.1 and 14.2. We have

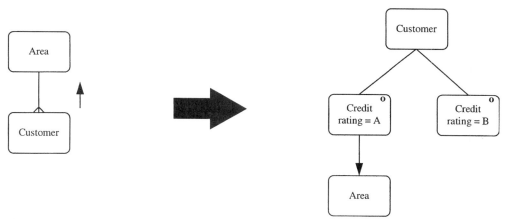

Fig. 14.4   Selection constructs

Table 14.1 Happy Camping entity descriptions

Customer	Special Promotion
Customer No.	Promotion Code
Name	Promotion Description
Address	Percentage Discount
Tel No	Start date
Credit rating	End date
Date of last booking	

Booking

Payment

Booking No
*Customer No
*(Site No)
(Plot No)
*Promotion Code
Booking date
Holiday date (start)
Holiday date (end)
Cost
Status

(Booking Number)
(Payment Number)
Payment due date
Amount due
Amount paid
Date paid
Type of payment

Status Codes

Payment Types

P	*Provisional Booking*	D	*Deposit*
R	*Rejected Booking*	F	*Final payment*
D	*Deposit received*	I	*Interim payment*
F	*Fully paid*		
S	*Site report*	**Site**	
N	*Non payment*		
C	*Cancelled*	Site Number	
		*Owner Number	
Named Individual		*Rep Number	
		Site name	
(Booking Number)		Site address	
(Individual Number)		Tel Number	
Name		Cost per tent per night	
Sex			
Age			

also added the volumetrics in Figs 14.6 and 14.7. Figure 14.8 shows the total number of occurrences of each entity, while Fig. 14.9 shows the average number of details possessed by each master.

14.5 CUSTOMER BOOKING HISTORY EXAMPLE

As mentioned earlier, we will approach Access Paths via worked examples. So consider the enquiry function that delivers details of the bookings made by a particular customer this year. In constructing the Access Path we will follow the step-by-step approach given earlier.

Table 14.2 Happy Camping entity descriptions—part 2

Plot

(Site number)
(Plot number)
Facilities

Tent

Tent Number
Model manufacturer
Cost
Capacity
Date of purchase
Date of sale/destruction
Date of last pitch
Date of last inspection
Condition Code
Status Code

> *(S in store*
> *I being inspected*
> *P on active pitch)*

Pitch

Tent Number
(Site Number)
(Plot Number)
Date erected
Date taken down
End of season Code

Owner

Owner Number
Name
Address
Telephone number
Start of contract date
Contract review result
Last renewal date
Contract termination date

Rep

Rep Number
Name
Address
Tel Number
Result of 1st exam
Result of 2nd exam
Date of joining
Date of leaving

1. *Identify the output.* This is shown in Fig. 14.6. As mentioned earlier, we are not interested in everything on the screen, just the data items.
2. *Identify the data input.* In other words, what data item(s) will the user need to input in order to obtain the screen of Fig. 14.6? Fairly obviously, the whole processing is triggered by the input of a Customer Number. No further data items are required.
3. *Decide which entities to access.* For this we need to identify the locations of the data items of task 1, minus those of task 2. So for our example we have:

Data Item	*Entity*
Customer Name	Customer
Customer Address	Customer
Booking date	Booking
Booking Number	Booking, Payment, Named Individual
Payment dates	Payment
Payment amounts	Payment
Status	Booking

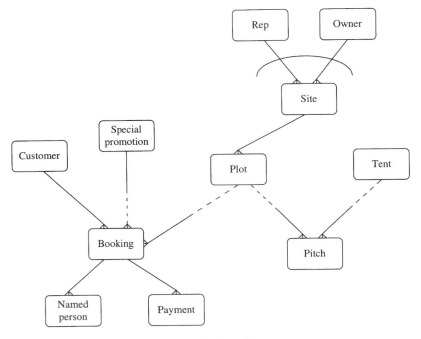

Fig. 14.5   Happy Camping required Logical Data Structure

Customer number	125685
Customer name	Aerobic Retirement Home
Customer address	Wallsend Lane
	Huntington
	York

Booking date	Booking number	Payment dates	Payment amounts	Status
2/3/93	112567	16/3/93	121	Fully paid
		8/7/93	1081	
4/3/93	112577	18/3/93	84	Cancelled
6/4/93	112622	20/4/93	250	Payment due

Fig. 14.6   Customer Booking History example

4. *Decide upon a possible navigation path.* As we have already mentioned, Customer Number is the data input trigger for the function, and so the entry point to the Logical Data Model must be via the Customer entity. Task 4 gives us a list of entities we need to visit. In choosing a navigation path, we might find it helpful to produce a partial view of the Logical Data Structure as in Fig. 14.7. (Note the use of arrows to denote a navigational direction.)

5. *Draw the Access Path.* This is shown in Fig. 14.8. It is really no more than a stylized version of the required view of the Logical Data Model as produced in task 4. Interpreting the diagram, we first start with the Customer Number, which will enable us to read the appropriate Customer occurrence. From this we can go on to read the complete set of Bookings made by the Customer. As mentioned earlier, the asterisk at the top of the Booking box indicates that there are an indeterminate number of Bookings in the set. A booking can be for this year, but could be for other years. Only in the case of this year's bookings do we need to proceed to the payment records. Again, the choice, called a selection, is indicated by the presence of a small 'o' in the top right-hand corner of the box. For each booking made this year, we then go and read the set of payments for the booking. This is shown by another iteration.

14.6 ACCESS PATH DESCRIPTIONS

Our next task is to annotate the Access Path and complete the Access Path Description. To do this we need to go back to the Access Path and differentiate between those nodes on the diagram that refer to actual accesses of the entities and those nodes that are Jackson constructs or merely give navigational advice. Figure 14.9 shows this done for our particular example, with the 'access nodes' highlighted. We have marked each of the access nodes with an access type code. For enquiries this is always an 'R', indicating a read. Thus the first node represents the reading of a customer record, and for each occurrence in the set we read a Booking. In future we will not highlight the access

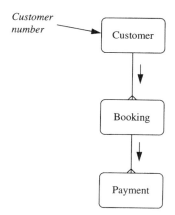

Fig. 14.7   Customer Booking History required Logical Data Structure

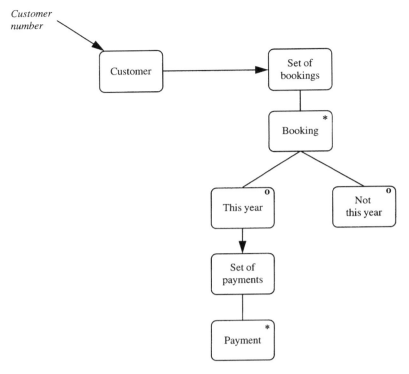

Fig. 14.8   Customer Booking History Access Path

nodes, only use the access type codes. In general, the Jackson boxes containing the words 'Set of . . .' will never be an access node. Other than this one cannot make any general rules, since boxes containing an asterisk, the iteration symbol, and an 'o', the selection symbol, can all serve as access nodes.

After identifying the access nodes we next complete an Access Path Description form, as in Fig. 14.10. On this form we make one entry, numbered sequentially in the first column, for each access node. The second column is used to record the entity accessed, while the third records the access type. For enquiries this will always be an 'R', standing for 'Read'. The final column, entitled 'Operations/Comments', is reserved for statements indicating what will be done with the entity occurrence accessed. For the majority of enquiries, this will merely indicate which data items are retrieved for the output. However, for calculations, for example those of a statistical or actuarial nature, this space could be used to record the formulas used. Alternatively, we could use pseudo-code, decision tables or even flowcharts to describe such tricky operations.

In SSADM Version 4.2, the processing is documented by means of adding operations to the Access Paths (see CCTA (1995)). This achieves exactly the same results as our approach but is really only suitable for those having an appropriate CASE tool.

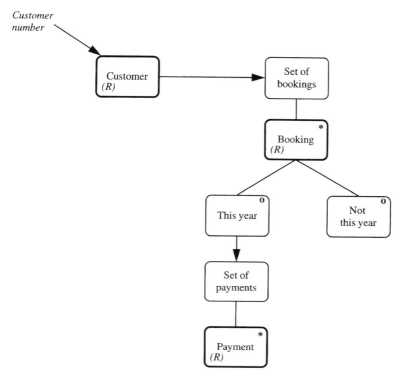

Customer number

Fig. 14.9   Identification of access nodes

14.7 VOLUMETRICS

Our final task is to add volumetric information to the diagram. The purpose of doing this is to highlight any possible problem areas with regard to response times. Adding volumetrics to the access path is done in two stages. First, we add the dependent volumes as in Fig. 14.11. What this says is that to each Customer there corresponds one and only one set of Bookings, and that each of these sets will consist, on average, of four Booking occurrences. Finally, for each Booking encountered there is a 75 per cent chance that it is for the current year. These figures are obtained from Tables 14.3 and 14.4 or from further discussion with the user. When we have added these dependent volumes, the net result will be that all the lines on the access path have a number attached to them. It is worth making the following observations about what these numbers might be:

1. Arrows always show a one-to-one correspondence and therefore attract a dependent volume of 1.
2. Selections always attract fractional values. These fractional values must add up to 1.

Access Path Description					
System	Happy Camping	**Date**	12/6/93	**Page**	1

Func Id	109	**Function**	Customer Booking History		
Seq	**Entity**		**A.T.**	**Operations/Comments**	
1	Customer		R	Retrieve Customer name, Customer address	
2	Booking		R	Retrieve Booking date, Booking number, Status	
3	Payment		R	Retrieve Payment due date, amount paid	

Fig. 14.10 Customer Booking History Access Path Description

3. Iterations usually attract values greater than one. Obviously this is normally because a set will consist of more than one occurrence. Other values are, however, possible. For example, if only one in a hundred masters has any details, but the average number of details in such a set was twenty, then the dependent volume on the iteration would be 0.2.

Table 14.3 Entity volumetrics

Entity	Occurrences
Customer	6 000
Special Promotion	15
Booking	24 000
Named Person	96 000
Payment	48 000
Rep	10
Owner	10
Site	100
Plot	500
Tent	625
Pitch	1 250

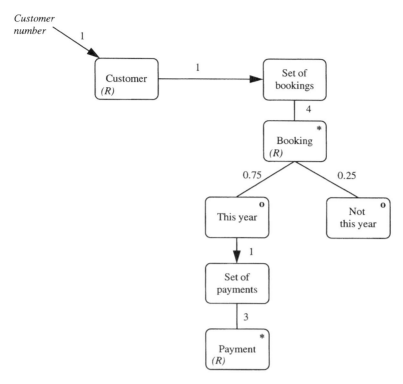

Fig. 14.11   Customer Booking History Dependent Volumes

After adding the dependent volumes, we work out the number of times each node occurs. This is really no more than a simple multiplication exercise. In Fig. 14.12 we have placed our results in the bottom left-hand corner of each node. Thus, for example, Bookings would occur four times, while the selection node entitled 'This year' would occur $4 \times 0.75 = $ three times.

Table 14.4 Dependent volumes

Master	Detail	Occurrences
Customer	Booking	4
Special Promotion	Booking	200
Booking	Named person	4
Booking	Payment	2
Rep	Site	7
Owner	Site	3
Site	Plot	50
Plot	Pitch	2.5
Tent	Pitch	2
Plot	Booking	48

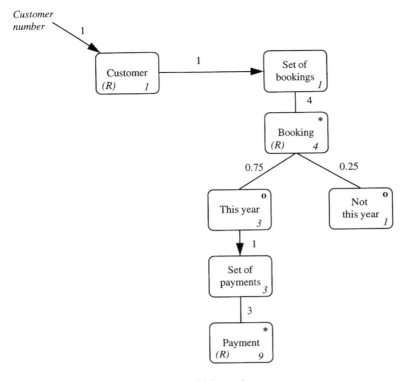

Customer number

Fig. 14.12   Customer Booking History Volumetrics

Finally, we calculate how many occurrences of each entity we need to read. This is done by tying up the access nodes with the numbers contained in the boxes. So from Fig. 14.12 it is evident that one Customer occurrence, four Booking occurrences and nine Payment occurrences are read—in all a total of 14 records. Putting a time to each of these 'logical reads' would give us a rough-and-ready estimate as to how long the function should take to access the data.* For instance, if a 'logical read' took, on

---

*There is some argument as to whether a read of an iteration involves an extra read. Thus in the example above some would argue that reading the set of bookings would take five rather than four reads. This is because one does not know that the end of the set of bookings has been reached until one has attempted to read the fifth booking (to no avail). Using this approach we would add one to each iteration, and so the number of logical reads would be

$$1 + (4+1) + 3 \times (3+1) = 18$$

Whether or not this really makes any difference depends upon the nature of the physical database. In a CODASYL database, for example, you know you have got to the end of the set when the next pointer points back to the master. On a relational database using B-trees to implement a relationship, the keys of the details would be on the lowest level of index which might well be held in memory. Again it is not necessary to physically read any further records to know that you have come to the end of a set. As we are looking only for rough-and-ready estimates, it seems best to keep matters simple and just use the number of records in the set.

average, 50 milliseconds our function should take 0.7 second. As we have stated, these timings are approximate and give us a very rough idea as to how long a function would actually take. Obviously, we are only concentrating on the disk accesses, ignoring such things as screen response and printer timings, and extraneous factors such as the number of users on the system, all of which would add to the function's timing. Nevertheless, our calculations should give us some idea of the minimum time each function might take, and so would serve to highlight any obvious areas of concern.

There are three final points I would like to make about volumetrics. First, Fig. 14.12 does look rather busy. This, however, was done merely for the purpose of illustration. In practice we would probably not annotate every single line and box. As long as we can accurately calculate the number of occurrences to be accessed, we can include or omit the other numbers as we wish. For this, it is usually sufficient to place dependent volumes on the iterations and selections. Moreover, usually it is not necessary to calculate volumetrics for every function, only for those that are liable to cause us concern. These would tend to be those functions which are performed frequently, are time critical or are visible to senior management.

The second point concerns the nature of the volumetric information we have used. So far we have been a little coy about defining exactly what these figures are. Are the dependent volumes the average number of details, or the maximum? Are there seasonal variations? As far as the technique is concerned this does not really matter. If we wish to obtain the average time for a function and also the worst case, we just apply the technique twice with different starting data. Do try to avoid placing both sets of numbers on the same diagram! A judicious use of the photocopier could be the answer here.

Finally, if volumetrics are developed for every function, a picture of the global traffic on the system will soon emerge. The function definition forms contain information about the frequency of a function, that is, how many times it will be executed every day or every hour. Multiplying the logical reads on the Access Path by this figure will provide information on how often the function accesses each entity. Global information is obtained by summing over the whole Function Catalogue. Similar remarks apply to the relationships.

14.8 ENTRY POINTS

As we have seen earlier, entry points can come in a variety of different forms. We can start with a unique occurrence of an entity or with many occurrences. The differences are summarized in Fig. 14.13. The example on the left-hand side shows entry via a primary key. Here we obtain the one and only occurrence of the entity. The middle example shows access by an attribute of Customer other than the primary key. In general, this will not identify a unique customer and so we must employ an iteration. When we come to physical design we will normally implement this entry point by means of a secondary index. The case on the right-hand side illustrates a full serial search. Here every single occurrence of Customer is read. Note the use of the arrow without an attribute to indicate this type of search.

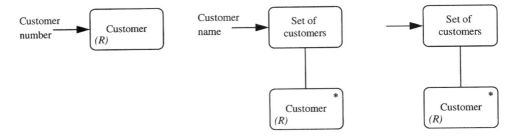

Fig. 14.13   Entry Points

14.9 ACCESS PATHS—POINTS TO NOTE

Before going on there are a few additional points we need to make about Access Paths. The first of these concerns the traversal of exclusive arcs. In going from a detail to a master, this will always involve a selection, as is clear from Fig. 14.14. A second point which often leads to confusion concerns the emergence of multiple routes from a node. Consider the situation depicted in Fig. 14.15, which is taken from the Happy Camping system. Suppose that for a given Booking we wish to retrieve details of the Customer and of the Plot and Site. The required Logical Data Model is given on the left-hand side of the figure, the access path on the right. In the access path, two arrows emerge from the Booking node. This is perfectly acceptable. All it is saying is that after reading the Booking occurrence we go on to the Customer and also to the Plot. The diagram does not state which of these is done first. A third point concerns the treatment of sub-types. This is really no problem, provided it is recognized that sub-types and their associated supertypes are treated as distinct entities. An illustration of the technique is depicted in Fig. 14.16.

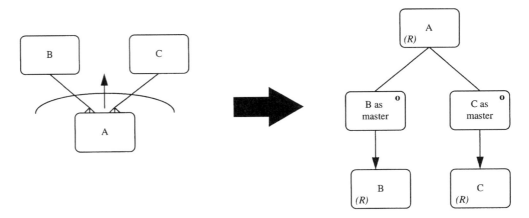

Fig. 14.14   Traversal of exclusive arcs

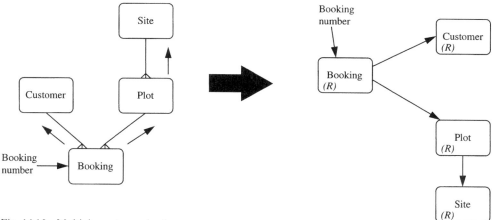

Fig. 14.15   Multiple routes navigation

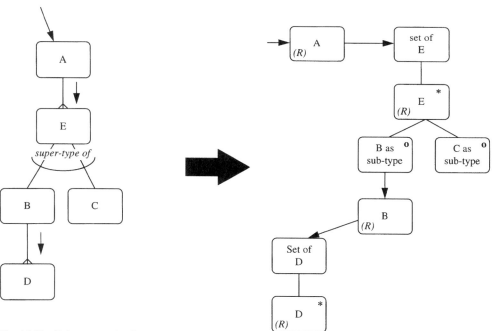

Fig. 14.16   Sub-type navigation

A fourth point concerns partial set searches. The technique as we have seen it so far forces us to read every occurrence in the set when navigating from a master to a detail. Sometimes we only wish to read some items in a set and ignore the others. As an example, suppose we wish to list all customers who placed a booking with Happy Camping in 1990. For any particular customer, once we have found a 1990 Booking, there is no point in reading further Booking occurrences. This is called a partial set search and the way in which it is documented is shown in Fig. 14.17. Note that the iteration is not now an access node. Attaching volumetrics to these partial set searches can be a little tricky. On average, a Customer has four bookings. Let us suppose that, averaged across the whole of the Customers, a 1990 Booking occurs on the second read. Thus, on average, one Booking occurrence in the set is read and discarded, one is found to be 1990, and two are ignored. This should explain the dependent volumes in Fig. 14.17.

A fifth point concerns the situation where a function arrives at an entity by two different routes. There is no obvious example of this on the Happy Camping system as it exists at present, and so we will temporarily extend the scenario by assuming that campsites not only contain plots but also have mobile homes for rent. Thus a booking must be made either for a plot or for a mobile home. The relevant portion of the extended Logical Data Structure is shown in Fig. 14.18. Now let us suppose that for a particular site we wish to list all bookings. At first sight, the access path might be thought to look like Fig. 14.19. However, this is wrong, since this access path implies that to each plot there corresponds a set of bookings, and that the same set corresponds to a mobile home. If we tried to add volumetrics to such a diagram we would soon appreciate why it is wrong. The correct situation is as depicted in Fig. 14.20. Having made this point, we will now remove mobile homes from the Happy Camping scenario.

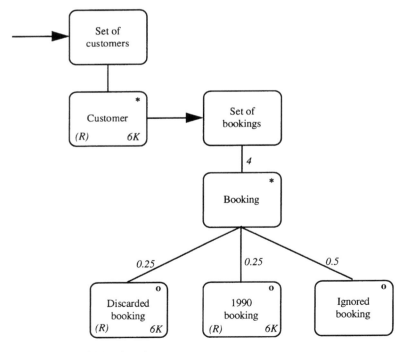

Fig. 14.17 Partial Set Searches

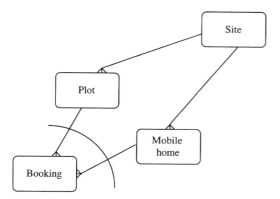

Fig. 14.18   Common Detail Logical Data Structure Extension

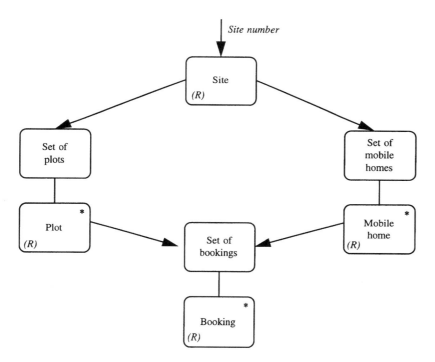

Fig. 14.19   Invalid Common Detail Access Path

Finally, it is worth noting that for all the functions considered so far, one Access Path is sufficient. In those rare cases where a function is split between two or more logical processes, an Access Path should be developed for each process. The only example of this that we have come across was the 'Send Statement' function for a cash machine in Chapter 10. This particular function consisted of an on- and an off-line process. Each should have its own Access Path.

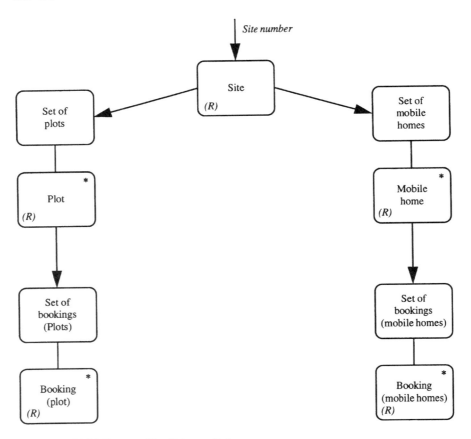

Fig. 14.20   Valid Common Detail Access Path

14.10 VIRTUAL ENTITIES

Returning to our original Happy Camping system, suppose that we wished to produce a report showing for a particular customer, all the bookings placed at Happy Camping owned sites, the name of the Rep responsible for each site and details of payments made. A typical output is shown in Fig. 14.21. Note that we are not interested in the privately owned sites.

At first, the Access Path for this enquiry might be thought to look like Fig. 14.22. There is, however, a serious flaw with the diagram. It seems to imply that we would access a set of Payments for every Booking encountered. This is wrong, as we are only interested in Bookings for the Happy Camping owned sites, in other words, those with a rep. If we added volumetrics to the diagram we would find ourselves reading far more payments than was necessary. The solution to this problem is to use the concept of a virtual entity. This is denoted by the dotted box in Fig. 14.23. A virtual entity is used whenever we wish to revisit an occurrence of an entity. Thus in Fig. 14.23, for each Booking, we visit the Plot, then the Site, and finally the site's Rep or Owner. Only for those sites with a rep do we revisit the Booking and then access the set of Payments.

OWN SITE BOOKINGS

| Customer Number | **327634** |
| Customer Name | **Elviga Systems Ltd** |

Booking	*Site*	*Rep*	*Total Pay*
234961	**Rolling Fields**	**A Patel**	**234.56**
235555	**Roofs 2**	**B Shermann**	**112.33**
236112	**Cow Meadows**	**A Patel**	**455.90**

Fig. 14.21   Own Sites Payment example

Attaching volumetrics to Fig. 14.23 will now produce the correct number of occurrences to be accessed. Note that a virtual entity generates no accesses. The Access Path Description for this enquiry is shown in Fig. 14.24.

Virtual entities can also be used where we wish to report on a group of occurrences of an entity. For example, suppose we wish to calculate the average payment for a booking at each site. Then the Access Path would be as in Fig. 14.25, with the Access Path Description shown in Fig. 14.26. The Site virtual entity is used to revisit each occurrence merely for the purpose of calculating the averages. If we also wish to calculate the average cost per booking over the system as a whole we need a 'Summary' entry in the Access Path Description. This type of entry is also used where we need to sort the entries.

14.11 THE TECHNIQUE (UPDATES)

Access Paths are also used to document update functions. (Version 4.2 of SSADM bases Effect Correspondence Diagrams on events rather than functions. In most cases where there is one event per function this does not matter. In other cases, there is always a problem in combining the two.) The technique for this is similar to that for enquiries. For each update function we need to:

1. *Identify the output required.* As with enquiries, screens and reports are a useful source of information. For updates, however, these are usually fairly trivial, often consisting of no more than a confirmation or failure message. What is impor-

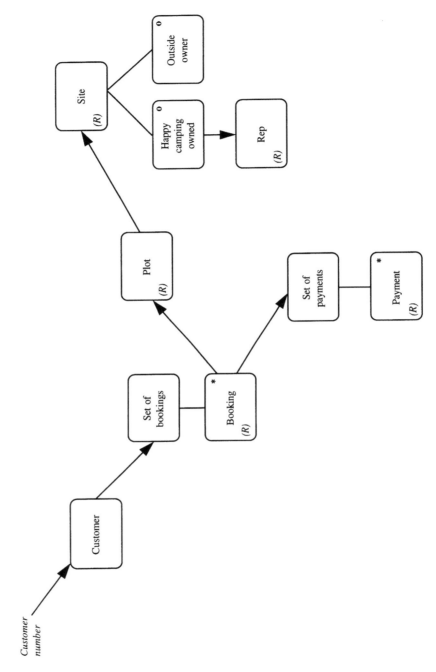

Fig. 14.22   Invalid Own Sites Payment example

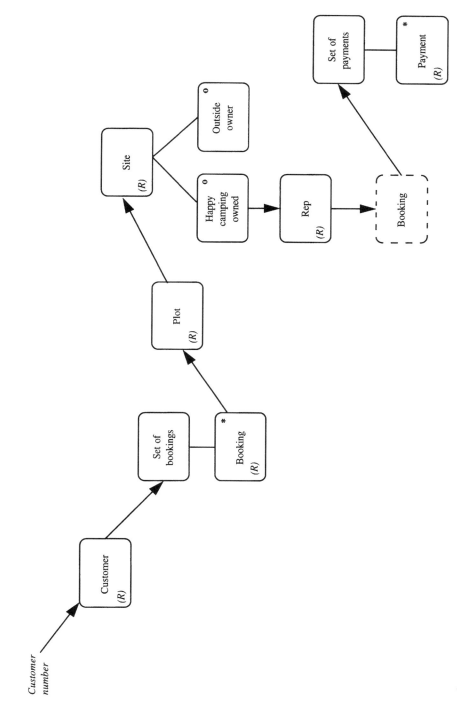

Fig. 14.23   Valid Own Sites Payment example

181

\multicolumn{4}{c}{**Access Path Description**}			

System	Happy Camping	**Date**	12/6/93	**Page**	1

Func Id	156	**Function**	Own Site Payments

Seq	**Entity**	**A.T.**	**Operations/Comments**
1	Customer	R	Retrieve Cust name
2	Booking	R	Retrieve Booking number
3	Plot	R	
4	Site	R	Retrieve Site Name
5	Rep	R	Retrieve Rep Name
6	Booking (re-visit)		
7	Payment	R	Retrieve amount paid, add to total for booking

Fig. 14.24   Own Sites Payment Access Path Description

tant from the point of view of the updates is the Event Catalogue. This shows which entities are changed by the function. The Happy Camping Event Catalogue is shown in Fig. 14.27.

2. *Identify the input.* Which data items are needed by the function? In contrast to enquiries, this could be quite a substantial list. We are, after all, often creating new occurrences of entities.
3. *Work out which entities to access.* This is usually fairly apparent from the Event Catalogue.
4. *Identify possible navigation paths around the Logical Data Structure.*
5. *Draw the update Access Path.*
6. *Complete the Access Path Description.* This is probably more important for updates than enquiries, since often the changes made to an occurrence are not readily apparent.
7. *Define volumetrics for the function.* This is probably less useful for updates than for enquiries, as the link between logical accesses and physical reads becomes a little more tenuous. As an example, suppose we are creating an occurrence of an entity. This involves one 'logical write'. However, when we physically create the corresponding record, we might have to perform many physical writes. This is especially true if a large number of secondary indexes are attached to the record.

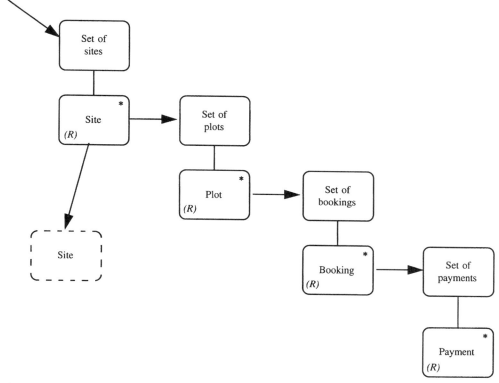

Fig. 14.25   Average Payments Access Path

We will illustrate the technique by means of worked examples. For reasons of conciseness, in all our examples we will ignore any screens or reports. As we mentioned earlier, for updates their content is usually trivial. If, however, they were to be significant, we would obviously need to include them at step 1.

14.12 RECEIPT OF PAYMENT UPDATE

As our first example let us consider the 'Receipt of Payment' function taken from the Happy Camping system. From the Event Catalogue it is clear that both the Payment and the Booking are modified. The Access Path for the update is given in Fig. 14.28 and the Access Path Description in Fig. 14.29. Note that the access type can now take one of four values:

> R   Read
> M   Modify
> I   Insert (Create)
> D   Delete

Access Path Description

System	Happy Camping	Date	12/6/93	Page	1

Func Id	183	**Function**	Site - Average Payment for Booking report

Seq	Entity	A.T.	Operations/Comments
1	Site	R	
2	Plot	R	
3	Booking	R	Add 1 to Bookings/Site
4	Payment	R	Add Payment to Payments/Site
5	Site (re-visit)		Calculate Average Payment per Booking for site (Payment/Site divided by Bookings/site) Add Bookings/Site to Bookings/Total Add Payments/Site to Payments/Total (Payment/Total divided by Bookings/Total)
6	Summary		Calculate Overall average payment per booking Sort site information into site order

Fig. 14.26   Average Payments Access Path Description

Obviously, before we can modify an occurrence we need to read it. Usually we do not wish to separate the two operations, and so we use 'R&M' a fifth access type. Figure 14.28 shows this, and illustrates when to use it. As every single Booking read is modified, we use 'R&M'. Only some of the Payments read are modified, thus we split the 'R' and the 'M'. We have not added volumetrics to this Access Path, since there is unlikely to be a problem with response rates. Finally, note that the possible underpayment error is noted on the Access Path Description. We should also check that this has been added to the error section on the function definition form, as this will be needed for step 380.

Two questions are often raised in connection with this Access Path. The first concerns the input trigger. The function does assume that the user knows the Booking Number of the booking for which payment is to be made. It could be argued that the user might receive a payment without knowing the Booking Number, and so needs some form of facility to enter via Customer Number or even to search through all the customers by name. In order to cope with this problem, there are two possible solutions. The first is to extend the function by putting some form of search on the front of the function. This, of course, would affect the access path, making it substantially bigger. The second solution is to keep the function as it is, but to ensure that we have

Event Catalogue				
System	Happy Camping	**Date**	31/5/93	**Page** 1

Ev. Id	Event	Entities	Processing	Function
1	Receipt of Booking	Customer Booking Named Person Payment	I/M I I I	Make provisional booking
2	Change of Customer details	Customer	M	Change of Customer details
3	4 years after last booking	Customer	D	Annual Housekeeping run
4	Receipt of payment	Booking Payment	M–change status M–enter amount (what if not enough?)	Receipt of payment
5	Non-payment of deposit	Booking	M–change status	Weekly payment check
6	Non-final payment	Booking	M–change status	Weekly payment check

Fig. 14.27   Happy Camping Event Catalogue

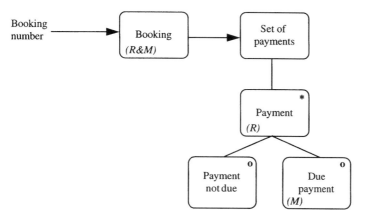

Fig. 14.28   Receipt of Payment Access Path

separate enquiry functions defined to perform the necessary searches. On the function definition form for this function, we would enter the names of these searches in the section allocated to 'Related Functions', thus ensuring that when the user dialogues were designed, this function and all its related searches were bundled together. The first solution is a little old-fashioned, and so of the two I would personally advocate the

Access Path Description

| System | Happy Camping | Date | 12/6/93 | Page | 1 |

| Func Id | 78 | Function | Receipt of payment |

Seq	Entity	A.T.	Operations/Comments
1	Booking	R&M	Retrieve Status Change Status if P to D, if D to F
2	Payment	R	Check amount paid and payment type (if booking status = P we are looking for a deposit payment, otherwise a final payment) If payment not correct, abort
3	Payment (due)	M	Enter Amount paid

Fig. 14.29   Receipt of Payment Access Path Description

second, especially since in more modern systems transferring data from one function to another can usually be done via some form of 'cut and paste' technique. (What we wish to avoid is the situation where the user has to enter the Customer Name to obtain the Customer Number using one function, re-enter this number on a second function to obtain a list of bookings with numbers, and finally re-enter the Booking Number for this function.)

The second problem concerns the 'Read and Modify' operation on Booking. The modify part of the operation changes the status of the Booking occurrence to reflect the fact that a payment has been made. But what happens if there isn't enough money? From the Access Path Description, it would appear that this would abort the function. Surely the modify operation to the Booking should take place after the Payment occurrence has been successfully updated? In practice this does not really matter. We assume that a function operates as a single logical success unit, in other words, it either succeeds or fails as a whole. If the function is aborted, nothing on the database will be changed. Obviously, this could cause problems with 'long' updates, especially those done off-line, but this is a problem that we will resolve at physical design. For the moment we will assume a function either succeeds *in toto* or nothing is changed. Thus whether we modify the Status of a Booking at the start of the function or at the end doesn't really matter.

14.13 WEEKLY PAYMENT CHECK

Let us now turn to the function 'Weekly Payment Check'. As can be seen from the Event Catalogue, this function deals with the events 'Non-payment of deposit' and 'Non-final payment'. In other words, the function is looking for those bookings with a payment due seven days ago, but which have so far received no payment. These bookings will be cancelled by Happy Camping. The Access Path for the function is shown in Fig. 14.30, and its associated description in Fig. 14.31. We have added volumetrics to the Access Path. The function will perform a full serial read of all Payment occurrences, of which there are 48 000. Only 5 per cent of the payments are outstanding. For these we need to visit the corresponding Booking occurrences. We first need to check whether a letter has already been sent for this booking. We do this because outstanding payments for previously cancelled bookings remain on the system for three years. Ninety-eight per cent of outstanding payments fall into this category. Only for the remaining 2 per cent, some forty-eight bookings in all, do we send a cancellation letter.

If we do the necessary arithmetic, it is clear that 50 448 occurrences of the various entities are read on average by this function, while only forty-eight are written to the database. As a very rough-and-ready estimate, if we assume that each logical read takes 50 milliseconds and that each logical write takes 100 milliseconds, then the function will take about 42 minutes. It is left as an exercise for the reader to determine whether there are more efficient navigational routes.

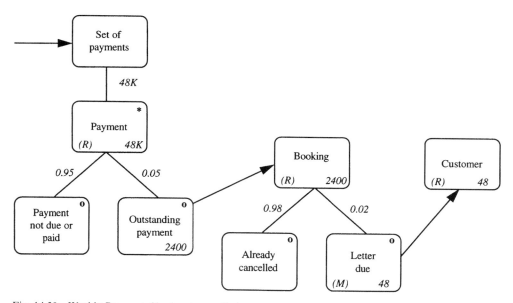

Fig. 14.30 Weekly Payment Check—Access Path

Access Path Description				
System Happy Camping		**Date** 12/6/93		**Page** 1

Func Id 17	**Function**		Weekly payment check	
Seq	**Entity**	**A.T.**	**Operations/Comments**	
1	Payment	R	Check amount paid and due date. (We are looking for records where nothing has been paid and the due date is 7 or more days ago.)	
2	Booking	R	Check status–if already N ignore	
3	Booking	M	Change status to N	
4	Customer	R	Retrieve name and address for snotty letter	

Fig. 14.31   Weekly Payment Check—Access Path Description

14.14 CREATION EVENTS

Consider the function that creates a new Site occurrence together with all its associated Plots. The Access Path for this function is shown in Fig. 14.32. There are a couple of points to make about this. First, one is forced to interpret the arrow in a different way from that done previously. In all the other Access Paths that we have so far constructed, an arrow between an entity and a set meant that we were reading a set of details, using the relationship on the Logical Data Structure to do so. Obviously this cannot be the case here, since before the function takes place no plots exist. So when a creation is

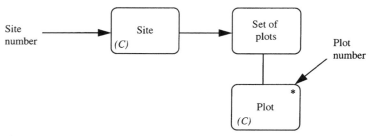

Fig. 14.32   New site—Access Path

taking place the arrow must be interpreted as meaning 'do next'. Thus in Fig. 14.32, after creating the Site occurrence, we next create a set of Plot occurrences. The second point concerns entry points. Here they have been provided for the Site entity, and also for each Plot occurrence. This is because the Site Number and the individual Plot Numbers are provided by the user. If this information was system generated, we would have no arrows on the Access Path.

As a second example of creation events, consider the function 'Make Provisional Booking'. From the Event Catalogue in Fig. 14.27, we see that the Customer entity is either created or modified, while the entities Booking, Named Person and Payment are created. This is slightly vague, since from our knowledge of the system it is clear that when this function is run, one Booking occurrence, one set of Named Person occurrences and two Payment occurrences are created. The two payments correspond to a deposit and a final payment, and when first created, really represent payments that are due. The date of payment and amount paid will be filled in later. This explains the Access Path in Fig. 14.33. The first thing we do is to deal with the Customer. The Customer is either new or existing. In the first case we create a new Customer occurrence. Note that no data item serves as an input to this node, which leaves us to conclude that the key, Customer Number, is system generated. For an existing Customer, however, we display details and give the user an opportunity to update the record. After dealing with this occurrence, we create the other entity occurrences.

There are three points to note about this example. First, for a general creation function such as this, there is often some debate as to the order in which the occurrences are created. Figure 14.33 seems to imply that the Booking is created before the Named Persons, which in turn are created before the Payments. In practice this doesn't really matter too much, since the ordering of the creations could easily be changed without affecting how the function might appear to a user. Indeed, it is quite possible to avoid this issue by having all the other entities on the receiving end of arrows emerging from the top Customer node as in Fig. 14.35. Since the whole function acts as a logical success unit, either all the occurrences are created or none are. The important point to note is that to every Booking created, there is one and only one set of Named Persons, and exactly two Payments.* The other points concern the relationship between the Logical Data System and the Access Path. On the Logical Data System, the Customer entity occurrence owns many Booking occurrences, but on the Access Path the Customer does not correspond to a 'Set of Bookings' but instead to a single Booking. This is because for *this particular function*, we are creating only one Booking occurrence per Customer. Also, rather than having a set of payments corresponding to a Booking we have been more specific in that we create exactly two occurrences.

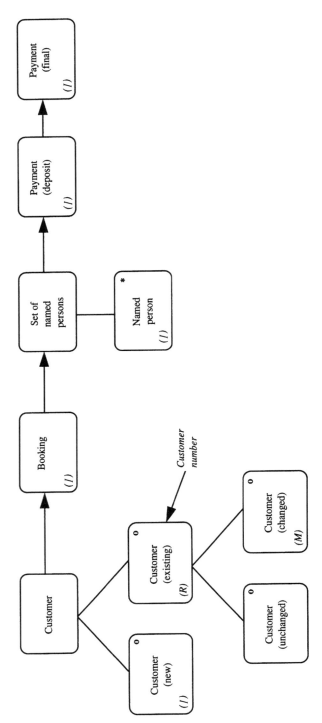

Fig. 14.33 Make Provisional Booking—Access Path

Access Path Description

| System | Happy Camping | Date | 12/6/93 | Page | 1 |

| Func Id | 40 | Function | Make provisional booking |

Seq	Entity	A.T.	Operations/Comments
1	Customer(new)	I	
2	Customer(existing)	R	Check credit rating. Abort if not 'A', otherwise display full details
3	Customer(changed)	M	Change any data items that are required
4	Booking	I	
5	Named Person	I	
6	Payment(deposit)	I	
7	Payment(final)	I	

Fig. 14.34   Make Provisional Booking—Access Path Description

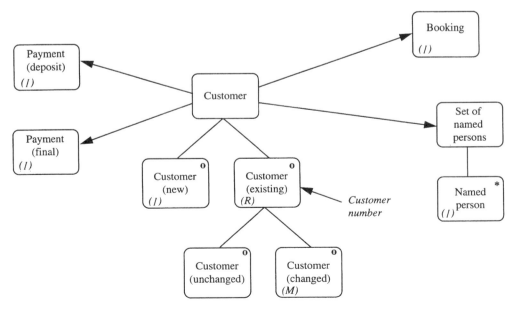

Fig. 14.35   Make Provisional Booking (alternative Access Path)

14.15 EFFECTS AND ROLES

The outputs for each update function are mainly determined from the content of the Event Catalogue. So far we have used it just to identify which entities are affected by the function, and the way in which they are updated. The Event Catalogue does also cross-reference the events against the functions. When in step 360 we looked at the interaction between events and entities, we noted that sometimes an event has different effects upon an entity, and that an entity occasionally plays different roles with respect to an event. The question arises as to whether these two concepts, effects and roles, make any difference to the Access Path for a function.

Turning first to the case where an event has different effects upon an entity, Fig. 14.36 illustrates the Entity Life History for a Customer, where the event 'Receipt of Booking' has two different effects upon the entity. The access path for the corresponding function 'Make Provisional Booking' is shown in Fig. 14.33. Thus the function either creates a Customer occurrence or possibly modifies an existing one. In general, different effects of an event on an entity will lead to a selection on the Access Path.

It is worth noting that when comparing the Access Path in Fig. 14.33 with the Entity Life History in Fig. 14.36, people often try to go back and change the Entity Life History. The argument put forward is that for an existing Customer occurrence, the Access Path appears to show that the function may change the occurrence, while the Entity Life History appears to indicate that if the event does happen it will change the entity. This, however, is to misunderstand the purpose of the two diagrams. The Access Path looks at the world from the point of view of the function (or event). Whenever the event happens, an existing Customer may or may not be updated. On the other hand, the Entity Life History looks at the world from the point of view of the entity. It depicts what could possibly change the entity. From an entity's point of view, after creation it can only be affected by the events 'Change of Customer details' and 'Receipt of Booking' before it is deleted. If an event causes no change to an existing Customer occurrence, it will not register on the Entity Life History at all.

What about the case where an entity plays different roles with respect to an event? Returning to the Happy Camping scenario, consider the event 'Transfer of Tent'. As we discussed in Chapter 13, the entity Pitch plays two roles with respect to this event. The

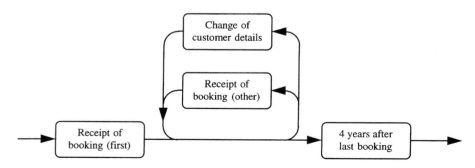

Fig. 14.36   Customer Entity Life History

Entity Life History for Pitch is shown in Fig. 14.37. Recall that when a tent is transferred from one pitch to another, we have to modify the old Pitch occurrence by completing the attribute 'Date taken down', and we have to create a new Pitch occurrence. Looking through the entity descriptions in Tables 14.1 and 14.2 it is clear that the only other entity affected by the event is Tent. We have reproduced the Entity Life History for a Tent, complete with sub-life, in Fig. 14.38. Assuming that there is a single function that deals with this event and this event alone, it is clear that the Access Path for the function is as shown in Fig. 14.39. In general we can make the rule that *if an entity plays different roles with respect to an event then the entity will appear on the Access Path with distinct boxes for each of the different roles.* (Although Access Paths do not really possess any concept of sequence, those familiar with Jackson ideas can easily see how roles could be translated into something not too far away from a sequence. This contrasts with effects being translated into selections.)

14.16 DELETIONS

Deletions often cascade down through the Logical Data Structure, the deletion of one entity triggering off deletions of another. An example is given in Fig. 14.40. This is the Access Path for the 'Annual Housekeeping Deletion Run for Bookings'. The function takes place once a year, when all bookings and associated details that are over three years old are deleted. Thus the event that this function deals with is *Booking Date + 3 years.* (Strictly speaking, this event does not immediately trigger the deletion function, as most bookings are somewhat older than this when removed. The event is more in the nature of a slow-acting fuse than an immediate trigger.)

One question often raised in connection with deletions is whether we need to actually read an occurrence before deleting it. Obviously in some cases it is logically necessary, as for the Booking entity in Fig. 14.40. We need to read an occurrence to find out if it is more than three years old. The other entities, Named Person and Payment, get deleted come what may. It is not logically necessary to read them first. As far as the physical implementation is concerned, some systems need to read a record before deleting it, others merely change a pointer, so there seems little point in worrying about this at this stage.

A second physical issue, that often concerns people when deleting entities, is the order in which they take place. It is often argued that one cannot get rid of the master before getting rid of the various details. Following this reasoning one would have to

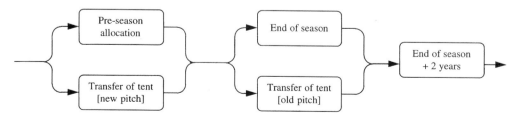

Fig. 14.37   Pitch Entity Life History

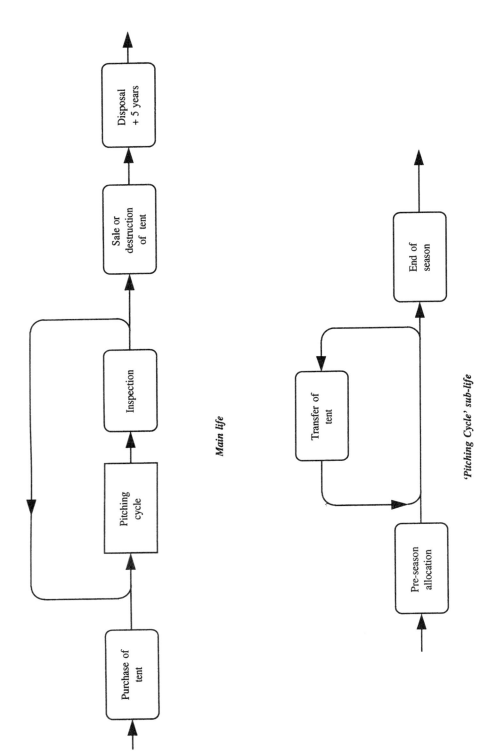

Main life

'Pitching Cycle' sub-life

Fig. 14.38   Tent Entity Life History

194

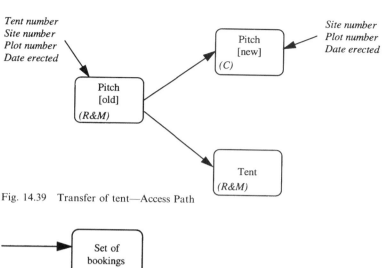

Fig. 14.39   Transfer of tent—Access Path

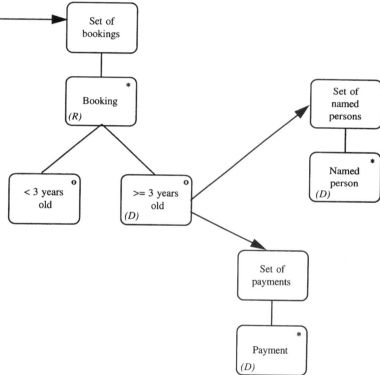

Fig. 14.40   Three years after last booking

navigate down to the lowest detail and then climb back to the master deleting as one went. This, however, is to confuse the logical situation with a particular physical implementation. Again we assume that the function acts as a logical success unit, and that occurrences are merely branded as due for deletion. Their actual removal will take place when the changes are committed to the database.

14.17 UNACCEPTABLE VOLUMETRICS

In all the examples seen so far, the response rates as calculated from the volumetrics are likely to prove to be acceptable. However, this does beg the question as to what could be done if the figures from any possible navigation route prove unacceptable. The simple answer to this is, as little as possible. Changing the overall design to speed up functions is fraught with difficulty. Often speeding up one process will slow down another. If the response rates are marginally unacceptable, perhaps the simplest solution would be to opt for a faster machine or processor when we come to choose technical options.

One thing that can be done without much repercussion is to explore the possibility of secondary entry points. As an example, suppose we wished to obtain a list of Customers in the Happy Camping system with a Credit rating of X. Figure 14.41 shows us two different approaches. The left-hand side of the picture illustrates the Access Path for a full serial scan. This would involve reading 6000 occurrences, obviously far too long if the function were to be on-line. The right-hand side shows the Access Path using the secondary entry point via the Credit Rating. This might involve, say, the reading of only ten occurrences, a far more acceptable figure. (When it comes to physical design, such a secondary entry point would probably be implemented via a secondary index.)

In the above example a convenient attribute, Credit Rating, already existed. Sometimes we might have to introduce extra data items to speed up the search. Again from the Happy Camping system, suppose we wished to calculate the total income earned by a site to date. Given the attributes of Tables 14.1 and 14.2, this would mean summing the Cost attribute for all the bookings for that site to date, some 2400 in total. If the user insisted on having this information placed on-line, our only solution would be to add a further attribute—Total Income to Date—to the Site entity. This, of course, is derived data, and so its introduction could impact on the entity life histories. Thus any event appearing on the Booking Entity Life History which affects the cost of a Booking must also appear on the Site Entity Life History.

Extra relationships can also be added to the Logical Data Model. Figure 14.42 illustrates a case where this might be useful. We have added dependent volumes to the

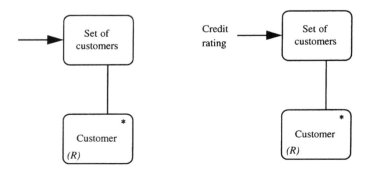

Fig. 14.41 Customer Credit rating search

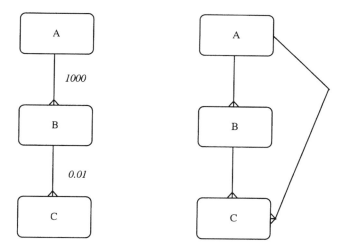

Fig. 14.42   Extra relationships

Logical Data Structure to illustrate the argument. Suppose we wish to access an occurrence of entity A and all the related occurrences of entity C. These are details of details. If we do this via the normal relationships as shown on the left-hand side, we need to read the A occurrence and its 1000 B details. From the Logical Data Structure, on average only one B occurrence in a hundred has any details, and so we will read ten C occurrences. Thus the total number of entity occurrences read would be 1011. However, adding the relationship as on the right-hand side would reduce the number of reads to eleven. A word of warning here. Adding extra relationships would involve the creation of extra foreign keys which could again affect the Entity Life Histories.

Quite often what appears to be a problem at the logical stage may disappear at the physical stage. If the data is sorted, then often several logical reads may be accomplished by a single physical read. As an example consider the situation of Fig. 14.43. The attributes of Order would be things like

> Order Number
> Customer Number
> Date of order......

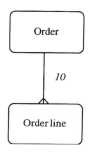

Fig. 14.43   Rolling up details

whilst the attributes of Order Line would be like

(Order Number)
(Line Number)
Product Number
Quantity.......

where the Lines are Numbered 1,2 . . . for any particular order. Assume that, on average, an order has ten items. Then to access an Order and the corresponding Lines we need to perform eleven logical reads. However, if the Order Lines on the physical database are ordered by Line Number within Order Number, one physical read is liable to pick up all the Lines for an Order. Thus one thing we might wish to do at this stage is to consider the keys for each entity. Composite keys often cut down the number of accesses as shown above.

A final thing we could do is to consider rolling up details into masters. Again going back to Fig. 14.43, rather than separating Orders from Order Lines, we could form one gigantic record consisting of an Order and all the associated Lines. This, however, does pose a problem. We must either have the ability to form variable-length records on the target database, something which is not often possible, or we must decide on a maximum number of lines. In either case the attributes of the composite record would be

Order Number
Customer Number
Date of order
Number of lines
$(Product Number)_1$
$(Quantity)_1$
....
$(Product)_n$
$(Quantity)_n$

With a truly variable record, the number of lines will determine the number of repeating data groups. This, of course, destroys the normalized nature of the record. If, however, the records are of fixed length, then there must be a maximum number of lines on the record. This has the virtue that the data remains normalized, but suffers from the fact that on the majority of records many values will be null. (To be more precise that data is still in first normal form. This is only true while the individual data items can be distinguished—in other words, $Quantity_8$ is different from $Quantity_{12}$. For a discussion as to why this should be so, see, for example, Date, 1990, p. 378.) As a general point, rolling up details with masters is best avoided.

If all these strategies fail, the Service level requirement section on the Function definition form must be annotated with details of the problem. This will enable us to do one of two things. In step 390, when we come to confirm System Objectives, we could negotiate with the users to ease the required response time. Failing this, Technical Options provides us with the opportunity of specifying a larger machine.

14.18 DO WE NEED ACCESS PATHS?

Finally we need to answer the question as to whether Access Paths are really needed at all. Furthermore, if Access Paths are worth doing, can the same be said about Access Path Descriptions?

Given that one of the major purposes of this step is to validate the Logical Data Model, the extent to which this does succeed depends to a large extent upon the thoroughness with which the documentation is done. At one level, by checking the relationships of the Logical Data Structure against the function in one's head, one could do a very superficial validation. However, writing things down, using a formal notation, makes it far less likely that errors will be missed. Completing the Access Path Descriptions takes this a stage further and ensures that the validation is a little more complete. Unfortunately, all this does take time. Completing the documentation for each and every function is a large task. Obviously, the extent to which one does this must be governed by the particular circumstances of the project. In particular, we need to consider how much time is available and how critical is it to avoid errors. All in all, it must be something of a balancing act.

A distinction must be made between enquiries and updates. What is produced by an enquiry is usually fairly obvious from the output. For this reason, except for very complicated reports, ones involving complex calculations—for example, the Access Paths and associated Descriptions—are only really useful as validation devices. The same cannot be said for updates. Given that we are omitting stage 5 of SSADM, the point at which we would normally define the processing down to the level of programming detail, we need the Access Path Descriptions to describe what each update is trying to do.

The conclusion must be that Access Paths and associated Descriptions are essential for updates in order to fully document the processing of the system, but that they are optional for enquiries, only being needed for those that are complex or critical. Leaving them out will, of course, add to the risk that things could go wrong.

FIFTEEN

ERROR ANALYSIS

15.1 PURPOSE

In step 367 we turn our attention to the question of errors. There is no equivalent to this step in SSADM Version 4.2, as processing errors are supposed to be identified as a byproduct of other techniques, in particular those concerned with Entity Event Modelling.* The danger with this approach is that purely technical considerations tend to overshadow concerns over error identification. After all, when constructing an Entity Life History, most practitioners are worried about how to draw the diagram, rather than ensuring that all errors have been catalogued in full. By making errors themselves the focal point of a step, there is less danger that any will be overlooked.

In more detail, the purpose of step 367 is as follows (Fig. 15.1):

1. To identify errors that might arise in the system being developed. To be a little more precise, we will look at each function in turn and ask in what ways could the function fail to complete satisfactorily because of errors in the data. Thus we will be concerned primarily with questions of data validation.
2. To standardize and catalogue error messages. If this is not done it is more than likely that separate functions will produce messages and warnings which might look very different, but which have exactly the same meaning. This would be a sure route to confusion, if not chaos!

---

*More particularly, in SSADM Version 4.2 the sequencing errors between events and hence functions are uncovered by the use of state indicators. State indicators are part of the Entity Life History technique and are allocated to the diagrams in step 520. Syntax errors, however, are left until the definition of the Function Component Implementation Map in stage 6.

3. To provide system audit functions. This is the last opportunity before system design to consider the possibility of providing some form of regular system audit. Such an audit could well be implemented as a program or series of programs which periodically trawl the database looking for errors or data inconsistencies.

4. To complete the Function Catalogue. As far as functions are concerned, errors are the final piece of the jigsaw. We started to list error situations for a function when completing the function definition for in step 330, but by now we are likely to have a better understanding of what they might be.

The major input to step 367 is the Function Catalogue. The functions are, after all, the place where errors are trapped and displayed. Another major input could well be any standards for the display of error and warning messages. Most organizations will have some such standards. These are not developed for each project in isolation, but usually apply across broad swathes of projects and systems developed within the organization. The reason for standards is quite clear. In the first place it will avoid unnecessary duplication of effort from project to project. But more important than this, it ensures that projects have a common user interface, something that will speed the acceptance of a project within the user community. In the full SSADM manuals, these standards form part of what is called the *Installation Style Guide*, which is a document produced by an installation to govern every aspect of the human–computer interface. Although such a formal guide may exist in larger organizations, it is quite likely that this will not be the case for the smaller type of team using our approach to SSADM. (If no such standards exist, some thought might be given to creating them.) Our final inputs to step 367 are the Entity Life Histories and the Event Catalogue. These are used to ensure that functions do take place in the correct order. Not all Entity Life Histories need be used, only those for entities having a life in which the events have to take place in a very specific order.

The outputs from this step are the updated Function Catalogue and the Error Catalogue.

15.2 TYPES OF ERROR

Before trying to work out how a particular function might fail to complete successfully, it might be as well to give some thought as to what type of error could cause such a

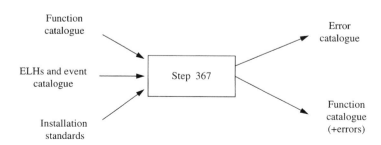

Fig. 15.1   Inputs and products

failure. Broadly speaking, the type of errors we are talking about refer to the data and so should be trapped as part of a data input process. For our purposes, errors can be categorized as follows:

1. Domain errors.* These are errors where a data item is not defined in quite the 'right' way and are usually recognized by looking at a data item in isolation and performing some or all of the following checks:
    i. Presence checks. These ensure that a mandatory data item is not missing. For example, a customer would not be accepted onto a mailing list if their address were absent.
    ii. Size checks. Does a data item contain the correct number of characters?
    iii. Format checks. Does the data item have the correct format or layout? For example, a part number may have to consist of two alphabetic characters followed by four digits.
    iv. Range checks. Does the data item have to fall within a certain range of values? For example, in a some areas of the country, the age of a child in a primary school might have to be in the range of 4 to 7.
    v. Reasonableness checks. Here we are asking if the data is reasonable, in other words, not abnormally high or low. For example, we might question whether we should accept data on an employee if they worked in excess of 60 hours in a given week. Note that such a working week is certainly possible, and so reasonableness checks normally lead to warnings rather than to fatal errors.
    vi. Predetermined value checks. Here a data item can take only one of a limited number of predetermined values. The simplest example of this is sex, which normally takes one of M or F (with possibly some value to indicate 'sex unknown'). Note that if the predetermined values are themselves the keys of another entity, this type of error is more properly called a referential integrity error. Even if the data item in question were not a foreign key, when it comes to physical implementation, we might make it one by placing all the possible values it could take in a separate table or list. We would certainly do this if the list of possible values were large. In this case again we would be performing a referential integrity check.
    vii. Check digits. These are usually applied to attributes which form all or part of a primary key. If a small mistake in the input of a data item were to cause that data item to appear valid but still be wrong, some thought might be given to the use of check digits. For example, suppose we were dealing with bank accounts each of which could be uniquely identified by a number consisting of six digits. Then an account number of 446578 input in error as 445678 might still refer to a valid account. The consequences of such an error slipping through could prove disastrous to both parties concerned! Fortunately, check digits can easily pick up the vast majority of these transposition errors. (For a discussion of check digits and how they can be used, see any introductory computer science or systems analysis text, e.g. Clifton, 1990.)

---

*The SSADM manual calls such errors 'syntax errors'. This can cause confusion to those used to dealing with compilers and the like. The term 'domain errors' is used by Robinson and Berrisford (1994).

2. Integrity errors. These are errors which if admitted would corrupt the database, in the sense that they would destroy the internal consistency of the data in the database. Thus an integrity error arises where one data item disagrees with other data items already on the database. There are three potential sources of integrity errors.

    i. Derived data. If, for example, we record the sales made individually by each member of a sales team, and also record the total sales made by the team as a whole, the total must be consistent with the individual amounts.

    ii. Foreign keys. If a data item is to become a foreign key, its value must already exist as the key of another entity. For example, if we enter order details for a customer with number 256888, this customer must already exist on the database. This type of integrity error is so important that it is given a special name, that of *referential integrity error*.

    iii. Replicated data. This should not really appear on the logical model. If, however, it does appear later, the replicated items do have to agree.

Integrity errors are usually prevented by the checking that arises out of the production of Entity Life Histories. Recall that when we developed these diagrams we asked questions about derived data to ensure that any event that affected a component item would also affect the derived one. Referential integrity errors should have been trapped by our fulsome treatment of death events.

3. Control errors. These occur when data is batched in some way and batch totals are used for checking. For example, suppose we wished to place a large number of payment receipts on the database. Before doing this we could count the number of payments made and manually calculate the total of all the payments. As the input of the batch proceeded the system would keep running totals, and at the end of the run we attempt to reconcile the figures, as a result either accepting or rejecting the batch as a whole. Such control totals would in all probability not be recorded on the database. In case it is thought that control totals only apply to batches of data, they can still be of use with single document entry. If an order is being entered, for example, we would probably use the total value of goods on the order as such a control.

4. Event sequencing errors. These are errors which arise when events do not happen in the prescribed order. As a simple example, a second reminder for a payment must only be issued after a first reminder. Any function which deals with these events must check that the ordering has been respected. To aid us in this task we will use a state transition matrix together with the appropriate Entity Life Histories (see below).

5. Business rule errors. These occur when a function attempts to do something contrary to the business rules of the organization. An example of this occurs in our Happy Camping system, if a booking were to be accepted from a Customer with a low credit rating. Ideally these situations should be part of the original definition of a function. They are the known situations where the user desires that the function does not proceed to its usual conclusion. Recognition of their existence often comes through discussions between the analyst and the user. This is why space is provided on the Function Definition form for entering details of possible errors as soon as they are recognized. In this way there is less chance of their being overlooked by the time we come to this step.

15.3 EVENT SEQUENCING ERRORS

Event sequencing errors are those in which events affect an entity in the wrong order. They are prevented by the use of a special attribute attached to an entity. This attribute is called status, status code, state variable, state indicator or something similar. Its purpose is to record the current state of an entity. In the Happy Camping system we have such an attribute for the Booking entity. Recall that the attributes of a Booking were

Booking Number
*Customer Number
*(Site Number)
(Plot Number)
*Promotion Code
Booking Date
Holiday date (start)
Holiday date (end)
Cost
Status

Status Codes
P   *Provisional Booking*
R   *Rejected Booking*
D   *Deposit received*
F   *Fully paid*
S   *Site report*
N   *Non Payment*
C   *Cancelled*

Clearly, status tells us the current state of play with respect to a particular booking. From the list of codes, it is clear that only certain changes to the status are possible. For example, if a site report is received, it must have been preceded by a payment in full (otherwise the people would not have been allowed to go on holiday). If the status of the relevant Booking occurrence had been a C an error should have been signalled.

The possible changes to the status of an entity can be explored by the use of a state transition matrix. We have produced such a matrix for the Booking status in Fig. 15.2. All the possible states are placed along both the horizontal and vertical axes of this matrix. Reading across the rows we can see immediately what might follow any particular state. Thus a provisional booking can only turn into a booking with deposit paid or a fully paid booking or a booking that hasn't been paid or a cancelled booking. Note that some states immediately follow the creation of an occurrence, while other states

	Cr	P	R	D	F	N	S	C	Del
Created		X	X						
Provisional booking (P)				X	X	X		X	
Rejected booking (R)									X
Deposit received (D)					X	X		X	
Final pay. received (F)							X	X	
Non-payment (N)									X
Site report received (S)									X
Cancelled (C)									X
Deleted									

To (column headers); From (row axis)

Fig. 15.2   State Transition Matrix for Booking

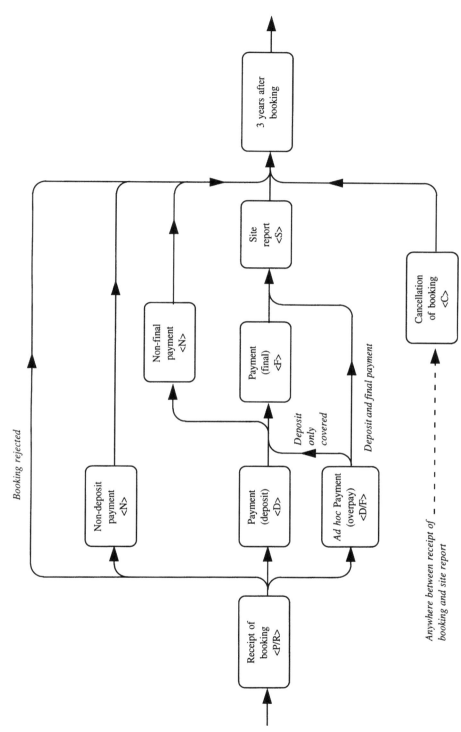

Fig. 15.3   Booking Entity Life History with States

can only be followed by its deletion. For this reason we need creation and deletion entries on the matrix. (Strictly speaking, we only need a row for creation and a column for deletion.)

The matrix can easily be cross-checked by reference to the appropriate entity life history. To help us do this we have reproduced the Entity Life History for a Booking in Fig. 15.3. On this we have also shown how each event will affect the Status. Thus the event *Cancellation of Booking* will set the Status to C, while an *Ad hoc overpayment* will set it to D or F depending on whether the payment covers the final amount due as well as the deposit.

We can then follow the flows on the Entity Life History to check any changes against those on the matrix. Note that different events on the Entity Life History can set the status to the same value. For example, we are not really interested whether the non-arrival of a payment arises from an overdue deposit or an overdue final payment. What is important is that the booking has not been paid and hence the only event that the occurrence can look forward to is deletion. (This is unlike the situation in standard SSADM where the corresponding attribute, the state indicator, would be given different values for different events on the Entity Life History).

Finally, it is quite possible for some events on an Entity Life History to leave a status attribute alone. This might occur if the Booking had an attribute like 'Number of children in party'. Then the Entity Life History would contain events like *Addition of child to party* and *Removal of child from party*. Obviously these events would appear on the Entity Life History, but there is no reason why they should change the status. Similar remarks apply to parallel lives on Entity Life Histories. If we are faced with such an Entity Life History, we have to decide which of the lives is important and use this life to keep track of the ordering of the states. The events in the other parallel life or lives might then be ignored. If, however, the ordering of events in a subsidiary life were important, we could use a second status attribute for this purpose. This second status would only be changed by events in the subsidiary life.

A second reason for using the Entity Life Histories in this step is that it enables us to decide which functions check any changes to the status attribute. From the Entity Life History we can decide which events affect the status, and then use the Event Catalogue to cross-reference these events and hence allocate the error checking to the appropriate functions. Finally, revisiting the Entity Life Histories makes us reconsider how important it is that the events do take place in an appropriate order. If for a particular life history, we do decide that we ought to check the ordering, then that entity *must* have a Status attribute. If not, we will have to provide one and update the Entity Description part of the Logical Data Model accordingly.

15.4 ALLOCATION OF ERRORS TO FUNCTIONS AND THE ERROR CATALOGUE

The first errors we allocate to functions are the event sequence errors. After doing this we visit each function in turn and list all the errors that should be trapped by the function. To do this we refer to the Function Definition form to find out which errors have already been noted. In general, these will be those that contravene the rules of the business. Next, we look at all data items input and decide what degree of checking should take place. Errors trapped by the function are noted on the Function Error List. At the same time any generated error messages are placed in the Error Catalogue. Examples taken from the Happy Camping system are given in Figs 15.4 and 15.5. Figure 15.4 shows the completion of the Function Error List for function number 41, *Make provisional booking*, while Fig. 15.5 illustrates a page taken from the Error Catalogue.

Each error in the catalogue will be graded as to its severity. The 'Re-do' grading means that the user will be given the opportunity of re-entering the data. Rather than displaying a blunt message with a blank space for re-input, we might wish to provide the user with a list of possible values, or some other form of help. We will decide on these type of measures in physical design. The 'Warning' grading means that the user is given the option of overriding the message or of re-entering the data. With both these severity grades the user always has the possibility of abandoning the function altogether. With a 'Fatal' grading, there is no choice to be made. The function abandons the user!

Error checking is usually concerned with data input. It can, however, be used when just strolling around the database. Suppose, for example, in the Happy Camping system that for a given booking we wished to display full details including the name of the site.

Function Error List

| System | Happy Camping | Func Id | 41 | Date | 14/6/93 |
| Function | Make provisional booking | | | Page | 1 of 1 |

Error	Message	Severity	Action/Comments
Invalid Customer Number	25	Re-do	For existing Customers
Credit rating not = 'A'	26	Warning	Display credit rating along with payments
Invalid Site number	27	Re-do	
Invalid date	3	Re-do	Usual check
Holiday date not Saturday	28	Re-do	Holidays must be for a whole number of weeks, starting and ending on a Saturday
Start date >= end date	29	Re-do	
Holiday > 2 weeks	30	Warning	
Site fully booked up	31	Fatal	A rejection letter will be sent, but a warning should appear on the screen

Fig. 15.4 Function Error List

Error Catalogue

System	Happy Camping		Date	31/5/93

Error Id	Error message	Functions	Severity
25	Invalid Customer number	41, 42	Re-do
26	Credit rating not acceptable	41	Warning
27	Invalid site number	41	Re-do
28	Start /End date not Saturdays	41	Re-do
29	Start date after end date	41	Re-do
30	Holiday for more than two weeks	41	Warning
31	Fully booked up on these dates	41	Fatal
32	Invalid Booking number	43, 44	Re-do
33	New Holiday costs less	44	Fatal

Fig. 15.5   Error Catalogue

In terms of the Logical Data Model, this means that we must move from the detail Booking to its masters Plot and Site. We can only do this successfully if the Booking has valid Site and Plot numbers as foreign keys. But what happens if the Site number for a particular Booking is not valid, having been corrupted in some way? Usually this means that the function crashes, informing the user of this fact in suitably opaque system-generated language. If there is any chance that this might happen, it is better public relations to inform the user in a more friendly and controlled way. Note that these errors are no more than referential integrity errors. They only arise when navigating from a detail to a master. Navigating in the opposite direction may yield an invalid set of details, but is unlikely to crash the system. To what extent one imposes navigational checks depends on whether the project team is prepared to spare time and effort in providing a robust system, or is looking for the quick and dirty solution and is willing to accept the occasional problem with the database.

As a final point, those trying to produce a system very rapidly might well argue that their target database includes a data dictionary which has very good error checking facilities, and that there is no need to worry about syntax errors and integrity errors. This argument is well and good, provided that the target database is already known and the error-trapping mechanisms are effective. Even in this case we would need to specify event sequencing and business rule types of error. Moreover, it is worth remembering that we are still in the Requirements Specification module. In theory, we do not know how we are going to physically implement the system. Certainly, if we intend going out to tender, a full specification of the error trapping process is essential. Even when developing a system in-house, thought given to errors now will mean that there is more likelihood that the functions are correctly specified.

SIXTEEN

THE END OF ANALYSIS

16.1 INTRODUCTION

The end of the Analysis phase of Rapid SSADM consists of two tasks:

- *Confirm System objectives.* This takes place in step 370, where the major task is to finalize the Function Catalogue, by ensuring that all the requirements have been covered and by confirming the Service Level Requirements.
- *Assemble Requirements Specification.* This is the usual end of module/stage task, and so involves the signing off all products produced within the stage. This step does, however, take on added importance given the fact that this is quite a common point for going out to tender. If this is to be the approach, the end of stage documentation will form the basis of the tender document.

16.2 FUNCTION CATALOGUE

The Function Catalogue, as the repository of all the required system processing, is one of the major documents produced by the end of stage 3. For each function in the catalogue, the following documentation should have been produced:

1. *Function definition.* This serves two main purposes. First, it contains overview information about the function, such as general processing details and service level requirements. Second, it includes cross-references to the documentation that follows and so really acts as the front page to the function's entry in the catalogue.

2. *Screen and report layouts.* These give some idea as to how the function will look to the user. They will normally be produced in accordance with a particular organization's standards.
3. *Access Paths.* These show possible navigation routes and volumetrics. They would probably not be produced in the case of simple enquiries.
4. *Access Path Descriptions.* These contain processing details.
5. *Error List.* This lists all possible errors that are trapped by the function and cross-references them to messages in the Error Catalogue.

In many cases, it is possible to construct the programs directly from the Function Catalogue. Indeed, if the target database is already known, is relational and comes equipped with good non-procedural programming tools such as screen painters and report generators, SSADM is all but over. In that case what remains to be done is to confirm the technical choice, convert the LDM into a database and decide how to implement the functions.

16.3 STEP 370—CONFIRM THE SYSTEM OBJECTIVES

Step 370 consists of two major tasks. The first of these is to review the Requirements Catalogue to ensure that all requirements that need meeting have indeed been met. Functional requirements should be checked directly against the Function Catalogue. As far as the non-functional requirements are concerned, some will evolve quite naturally into functional descriptions, others not. For example, if at the start of stage 1 we decide that we would like to ensure good-quality data, it is quite likely that by the end of stage 3 we would have changed this into a regular audit function, together with its associated function description, screen and report outputs and a list of users who are allowed access to the function. For other non-functional requirements, such a metamorphism is not quite so simple. As an example, suppose that we decided that all data on the database had to be encrypted. It is not something we would really consider in much detail at the logical stage, since we would normally expect mechanisms for encryption to be provided by specialist support software, rather than by home-produced programs. For this reason, we would not define any encryption functions, but ensure that this requirement is a major input to the process of selecting a technical option.

Thus all entries in the Requirements Catalogue must either be covered by appropriate functions or be highlighted to ensure they are brought forward in stage 4.

A second major task in step 370 is the confirmation of Service Level Requirements. Recall that these were established for each function in step 330. For on-line functions they would usually be quoted as response times, that is, how long the function would take in retrieving data from the database and in displaying the information. On the other hand, for off-line functions they would be defined in terms of elapsed time, that is, how long the function would take as a whole. In this step all these figures will be finalized. The figures go on to form the basis of a contract between the users of the system and the designers or providers of it. When used in this fashion, they eventually become Service Level Agreements, and, as such, form one of the key benchmarks in assessing whether the contract has succeeded or failed as a whole. The same principles apply whether the designers are in-house or are external contractors.

Unfortunately, the original Service Level Requirements we came up with in step 330 suffered from a number of drawbacks:

1. They were produced without the benefit of volumetrics. At best, such figures would be an informed guess. Now, after step 365, we have produced logical volumes for each function and so are in a much better position to see whether the figures are realistic.
2. The Service Level Requirements were produced in step 330 without due regard to practicality or cost. Given such a free gift, most users would probably insist upon the best. If some indication of the likely costs were to be provided, expectations might not be so high. One could argue that insufficient information is available at this point to make these kind of judgements, in which case the question of costs will best be left until Technical Options. If, however, we do have a feel for the likely costs, it does seem somewhat perverse to establish Service Level Requirements here, merely to dismiss them as too expensive in the next stage.
3. The original figures we came up with were far too crude. Recall that for our specimen function, we asked that each record should take no more than 3 seconds to retrieve. In practice we would be more likely to ask for a system response of something like under 2 seconds in 80 per cent of cases, of 2–5 seconds in 15 per cent of cases and accepting a system response of greater than 5 seconds in the remaining 5 per cent of cases. There is also a question as to what we mean by system response. Do we mean the time it takes to retrieve records, to validate individual data items or even to create a record and all the associated index entries?
4. In step 330 we determined Service Level Requirements on a function-by-function basis. In practice it is quite likely that such figures would be applied to a broad swathe of functions. What is likely to be an acceptable response in one on-line function is probably likely to prove acceptable in another. For this reason, we would probably divide our functions into those that are critical, those which are used frequently and those which are only used spasmodically, and apply the Service Level Requirements to these broad groupings. This might have been done before for other projects and so have evolved into generally accepted installation standards. Of course, it is still the case that special circumstances applying to specific functions may mean that Service Level Requirements have to be determined individually for that function.

16.4 ASSEMBLE REQUIREMENTS SPECIFICATION

The purpose of this task is not only to perform the usual end of stage project management activities but also to complete the Required System Specification. This consists of:

1. The Requirements Catalogue. By now all entries must be accompanied by some indications as to their solution. Most will cross-reference functions in the Function Catalogue. Requirements of a non-functional nature, which remain to be addressed as part of the technical solution, must be highlighted.
2. The Required Logical Data Model. This will consist of
    i. The Logical Data Structure

  ii. Entity/Attribute descriptions

 iii. Relationship descriptions

 iv. Volumetrics

As discussed earlier, the Entity/Attribute descriptions can be either combined or left separate, depending upon the type of computer support available.

3. The Function Catalogue. This was discussed in detail above.
4. The User Roles. A summary of the potential users of the system and of the functions available to them.
5. The Error Catalogue. The standard error messages generated by the system.

The System Specification is a large collection of documents that specify the required system in a great deal of detail. It could be passed directly to the design team, to form the starting point for the remaining SSADM activities.

Two other products are useful accompanying documentation to the Required System Specification. The first of these is the Event Catalogue. Most of the entries in this document are covered by other parts of the specification, but it does bring together information to provide a useful alternative view of the system. The second product is the selected Business System Option. This contains valuable information such as estimated costs, timescales and business impact. It is not part of the Required System Specification. The reason for this is that in a competitive tender situation these figures would not usually be passed on to prospective suppliers, but would be retained by the business to serve as a baseline against which bids could be judged.

SEVENTEEN

TECHNICAL OPTIONS

17.1 PURPOSE

A Technical System Option (TSO) describes how the selected Business System Option is to be implemented in a technical sense. In particular, decisions are to made about the hardware and software platform which will support the future system. The approach is very similar to that of Business System Options. A menu of possible technical solutions is developed in step 410 and the project board selects one of them in step 420 (Fig. 17.1).

Before any choice can be made, those involved need to be aware of what the system is being asked to do. Thus a major input will be the Required System Specification. Of particular interest are the Service Level Agreements and the Volumetrics, contained in the Function Catalogue and in the Logical Data Model respectively, as these give some indication of the performance expected of the hardware and software. Much preliminary work in regard to costs and timescales has already been done in stage 2. Although

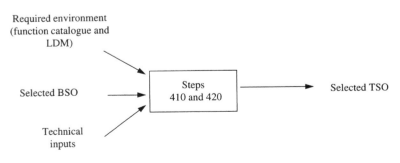

Fig. 17.1   Inputs and products

some details may have changed, work done as part of the selected Business System Option is still an important input. The final inputs are various documents which might describe the systems's likely technical environment. For example, there may be in place an organizational IS strategy which determines the hardware and the database. Over and above this, the development team might have to adhere to additional installation standards. The system might also have to fit in with existing work, which for a mainframe site might mean applying some form of capacity planning. In the case of sensitive systems, such as those in the defence sector, security considerations might be paramount. Finally, the only output from this step pertinent to later development is the Selected Technical Option. As with Business System Options, the other options together with the reasons for their rejection would be retained. Indeed, if it were the case that options were supplied by a number of external vendors, those who were unsuccessful would probably ask for feedback as to why they did not obtain the contract.

17.2 APPROACHES TO TECHNICAL OPTIONS

In SSADM Version 4.2 Technical Options is somewhat like Business System Options, but with an extra technical dimension. The user is given a choice of options, each of which is a description of how the new system might be implemented. Each option will incorporate the following details:

- *Technical Environment.* This covers such issues as hardware, software, the development method, fallback and recovery, access and security, reliability and maintenance.
- *Functionality.* Although in theory each technical option should satisfy the conditions of the selected Business System Option, in practice the Project Board may be tempted to trade some functionality for a faster, less expensive implementation.
- *Cost/benefit Analysis.* This is done according to the organization's standards.
- *Development Plans.* These are technical and resource plans describing how the rest of the development process will proceed.
- *Impact on the Business.* Consideration of business, organizational, staffing and training implications of the choice.
- *Risk.* Is the approach tried and tested or is it innovative?

Obviously the construction of any option requires a full investigation of the suppliers. The officially recommended approach is the same as for Business System Options. This is to review base constraints, to create up to six outline options, to reduce these to two or three after consultation with the users, to expand those remaining and to present them to the Project Board. All this sounds very logical, first deciding what needs to be done, then investigating how it can be achieved. In practice there are variety of problems with such an approach, and for this reason technical options *for a single project* (rather than a group of projects) are often done as follows:

- *Single Option Choice.* Often the analysts have little influence over the technical environment. There are several reasons why this might be so. Quite often there is an organizational strategy in place, which forces the team to buy certain brands of hardware and focus on a particular database product. Even if there is no formal policy, the team might be influenced by the resources available. For example, if there is a suitable machine with spare capacity, there would need to be compelling reasons for ignoring it. A second reason for the lack of choice is that of time constraints. Purchasing or procuring items of hardware often takes a considerable amount of time. If left until stage 4, it might mean that the team spending time at the end of the development cycle awaiting the arrival of the kit. This is clearly wasteful, and so technical choices are often made much earlier, for example as part of the Feasibility Study. Even where there does appear to be a genuine choice, decisions are often taken at a programme rather than a project level. Hardware and software are chosen to fulfil the needs of a whole raft of projects, rather than a single one. In all these cases, stage 4 merely involves a rubber-stamping of previously taken decisions, with different technical options involving changes only at the margin.

- *Going out to tender.* Stage 4 is quite a common place for the decision to be made to go out to tender. When this is done the remainder of the development work will be done by external contractors. As the requirements have been established by the end of stage 1, it might be argued that Business System Options are the appropriate place for this activity. While invitations to tender could be sent out at that point, it has to be said that requirements are specified in much more detail in stage 3, and so if the process is delayed the evaluation of the bids can be much more precise. The operational requirements in the tender document are based upon the required system documentation plus any strategic requirements such as the need for Open Systems. Clearly, each of the returned bids is really a technical option. After all, each will address issues such as technical environment, cost, timescales and so forth. Some might trade functionality against cost or timescales. Clearly, the Project Board might have many options to consider in this case.

- *Packages.* A package is really a technical solution to a problem and so could be considered at stage 4. However, the possibility of a package solution is usually anticipated much earlier, and much of SSADM can be ignored. If a package solution is mandatory, and if the package forms a large part of the final system, there is not a great deal of point in doing stage 3. In this case, package evaluation should take place at Business System Options. If, however, a package is only one of the available options, to be compared with bespoke software, or is to play only a minor role in the ultimate system, then the decision should be made in stage 4. Obviously, the quickness, cheapness and reliability of a package solution has to be weighed against the possibility that the package will not do exactly what the user wants. In any decision, external factors such as vendor reliability and existence of reference sites play their part.

When all the options have been gathered, the Project Board make their choice in step 420. How this is done depends upon the nature of the options. For a single-choice scenario, a paper presented to the Board is usually sufficient. In the cases of tender bids and packages, there has to be a full evaluation process. If the standard approach to Technical Options is adopted, a formal presentation is usually necessary. As with Business System Options the Board can do one of three things: choose an option, reject all options or ask for a reworking.

EIGHTEEN

PHYSICAL DESIGN

18.1 PURPOSE

The major purpose of Physical Design in SSADM is to incorporate the effects of the chosen hardware and software into the final model. This is achieved in stage 6 of SSADM (Fig. 18.1).

Broadly speaking, the major jobs in this stage are to convert the Logical Data Model into a Database Description and the Function Catalogue into Program Specifications. The other input documents play supporting roles in this drama. The Error Catalogue is used to determine how programs are to display error messages, whilst the User Roles are essential in deciding how the functions are to be bundled together in the dialogues. The Technical Option is obviously needed to determine which database product and which hardware platform are to be used for the system. The

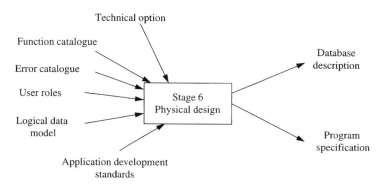

Fig. 18.1   Inputs and products

Application Development Standards contains the strategy for transforming the SSADM products into a database and programs for the chosen database. They are shown as an optional input because they may not already exist prior to stage 6. If they do not exist they will have to be created.

Physical Design in our rapid approach to SSADM will consist of the following steps:

- Step 610—*Prepare for Physical Design.* Here we produce the Application Development Standards for the chosen physical environment.
- Step 620—*Physical Data Design.* In this step we make the first attempt at a database design.
- Step 630—*Dialogue Design.* Here we design the physical dialogues.
- Step 640—*Create the Function Component Implementation Map.* The major task in this step is to allocate functions to programs.
- Step 650—*Complete Program Specifications.* This step consists of producing the appropriate documentation for the production of programs.
- Step 660—*Assemble Physical Design.* This is the usual end-of-stage step where all products are brought together and signed off.

Steps 630 and 640 are usually performed together.

It must be said that stage 6 is usually driven by the needs and requirements of the target Database Management System (DBMS). The facilities offered by competing products, especially where program design is concerned, are often radically different. For this reason, SSADM offers not much in the way of specific guidance for Physical Design but rather a number of indications as to the type of question that should be asked about a database product, and also some idea as to the range of replies that might be expected. From this it should be clearer how to perform Physical Design for that particular database. In Physical Design, SSADM is not so much a methodology, rather a meta-methodology telling you how to design a version of stage 6 for your own particular physical environment.

This all sounds pretty grim. Fortunately, things are not quite as bad as they first appear. For example, if you are using the Oracle database, the vendors have published guidance as to how the product can be used with SSADM (cf. Osborn *et al.*, 1993). When using this Database Management System, you would be best served by throwing this chapter away and using the specific Oracle guidance. At the time of writing, Oracle were the only database vendors to have produced such guidance, but by the time you come to read this they may well have been joined by others.

Second, in essence, physical design is quite simple. It's all about the task of converting the Logical Data Model into a database and the functions into programs. Anyone with sufficient expertise in the chosen database should not find this too difficult. For the majority of development teams, stage 6 then becomes a question of locating the appropriate expert. Large sites, running databases like IDMS-X, usually have such an expert on the staff. Smaller organizations usually find the database vendors more than accommodating in providing the appropriate consultancy.

The final point to make is that all relational products are broadly similar. What can be said for one can often be said for another. The further away one goes from the relational model, the more different stage 6 becomes. (A flat file structure would lead to radically different designs.) Given this remark, what we will do in this chapter is to illustrate how stage 6 might be performed for a typical relational product. If you have expertise in another Database Management System the differences should be readily apparent.

18.2 STEP 610—PREPARE FOR PHYSICAL DESIGN

The whole purpose of this step is to plan the rest of stage 6 and, in particular, prepare a Physical Design Strategy for the target Database Management System. When SSADM Version 4 was first released, CCTA hoped that each database vendor would produce something called a Product Interface Guide. These guides would demonstrate how stage 6 of SSADM could be tailored for particular products. If these wishes had come to fruition, this step would now consist of taking the appropriate volume from the shelf and using it for the rest of stage 6. As mentioned earlier, at the time of writing Oracle are the only vendors who have produced such a guide. If using another product, it might be worth telephoning the company to see if they have now released similar information.

If such a guide is unavailable, it is next worth checking whether any other projects have used the target Database Management System. If they have, they should have produced some form of Physical Design strategy as part of their work. The formal name for such a document is the 'Application Development Standards'. Note that the advice contained in this document is not specific to just one project. What usually applies to one INGRES project, for example, applies to them all. So if Application Development Standards or something similar do exist, the project team should consider using them to tailor the rest of stage 6. Clearly, they might need to be brought up to date. Database products do change quite rapidly, and the Application Development Standards might not use facilities contained in the latest release of the Database Management System.

If no guidance has been produced, the project team will have to act as pathfinders by constructing their own Application Development Standards. These contain advice for the given database product in three main areas:

1. How to design the database for the project. In other words, how can a Logical Data Model be converted into a physical database? This is needed for step 620.
2. How to design the programs. We need to know what languages are available, whether they are procedural or non-procedural and which to use in various circumstances. This is needed for steps 630 and 640.
3. What performance issues need to be considered. What are likely to be the software and backup overheads? This is needed for work with the building of the system after the end of conventional SSADM.

A more detailed description of the type of questions that might be asked is given in the Version 4 SSADM manuals. The remainder of Physical Design is guided by what is contained in the Application Development Standards. This gives us something of a problem with the rest of this chapter. For a variety of obvious reasons we cannot give product-specific guidance. What we will do, however, is to develop the rest of stage 6 with a simple relational model in mind. As we have stated earlier, most relational products are broadly similar and so the guidance for a particular Database Management System should not depart too much from what we have to say. Again it is worth restating that the guidance is only general, and nothing replaces an intimate knowledge of the target database product.

18.3 STEP 620—PHYSICAL DATA DESIGN

The major task of this step is to convert the Logical Data Model into a physical database design. This is often called the 'First Cut Database Design', being our first attempt at such a design (Fig. 18.2). We will perform the conversion according to the rules contained in the Application Development Standards. Although the precise steps we take vary from one Database Management System to another, it is probably true to say that the sort of things that are done do not vary too much between different relational products or between different hierarchical products. With this in mind we show how step 620 might be applied to a typical relational product. (Similar advice for other generic models such as CODASYL databases (e.g. IDMS, IDMS-X), Hierarchical Databases (e.g. IMS, DL/1), and Indexed Sequential Cobol Files is given in Physical Design Annex B of the SSADM Version 4 Manual (CCTA, 1990a).) For our example we will revert to the Happy Camping system.

The Logical Data Structure for the Happy Camping system is shown in Fig. 18.3 and the First Cut Database Design in Fig. 18.4. (This is merely for a reminder. The full Logical Data Model, together with entity descriptions, which we will also need, is given in Chapter 14). There is a step-by-step approach in converting one to the other:

1. Every entity becomes a table. In Fig. 18.4 the entities are denoted by square boxes.
2. Each table is given a primary index according to the following rules:
    i. If the entity has a simple key, the primary index will be based upon this attribute.
    ii. If the entity has a composite key, the primary index entries will be a concatenation of the key values. In doing this, the attributes which are uniquely defined within the system, in other words the 'major' part(s) of the key, come first. Thus the entries for the table/entity Named Person would be the concatenation

Booking Number + Person Number

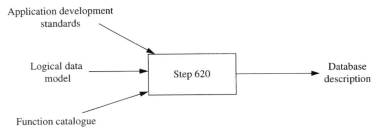

Fig. 18.2   Inputs and products for First Cut Database Design

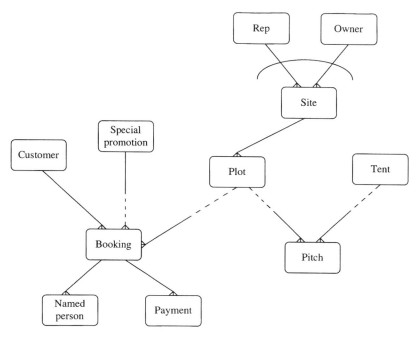

Fig. 18.3   Happy Camping required Logical Data Structure

iii. If the entity has a Compound key, the primary index entries will be a concatenation of the key values. Obviously, a decision has to be made about the ordering of the elements. For example, in the Happy Camping system, the only entity with such a key is Pitch, which has the three-way compound key (note that the composite key Site Number/Plot Number is treated as one element in the compound key):

Tent Number
(Site Number)
(Plot Number)
Date Erected

In this case each Primary Index entry will be made up from the concatenations

Tent Number + Site Number + Plot Number + Date erected

In Fig. 18.4 the primary indexes are shown by the broad arrows.

4. Minor elements of a compound key can be made into secondary indexes. Thus for the Pitch table we can always find the rows that relate to a particular tent by performing a partial search of the primary index. However, the same cannot be said of the Site and Plot. For this reason, we will construct a secondary index based upon the Site/Plot Composite key. In Fig. 18.4 all secondary indexes are shown as a soft-edged box with an arrow pointing to the table to which they refer. We could

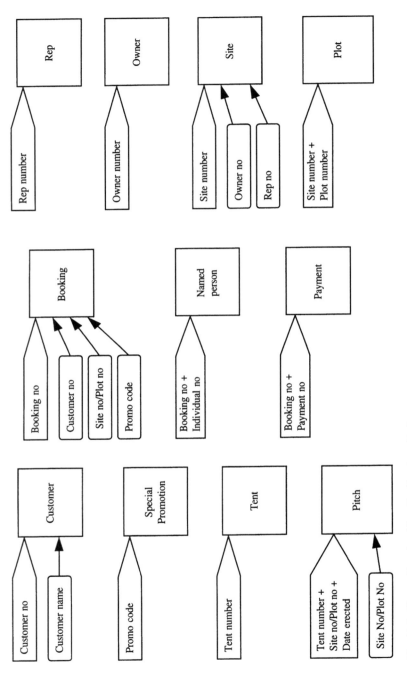

Fig. 18.4 Happy Camping First Cut Database Design

also have created a secondary index for the Erection Date, though it is not usual to do this for dates.

5. All relationships on the Logical Data Model that are not covered by primary keys should be established using foreign keys. These foreign keys then become secondary indexes. An example of this is on the Booking entity and table. The relationship between a Booking and a Customer is established by Customer Number being a foreign key in the Booking entity. On the First Cut Database Design in Fig. 18.4 one can see that this becomes a secondary index on the Booking table.

6. All Access Paths in the Function Catalogue are examined for non-key entry points. Any such are made into secondary indexes. For example, if there is a function in the Catalogue which requires that Customers be retrieved by name rather than number, the Customer Name must be the basis of a secondary index on the Customer table. This explains the secondary index on the Customer table in Fig. 18.4. In order to keep the diagram fairly simple, we have defined only one such entry point.

In essence, then, each entity on the Logical Data Structure becomes a table, and all relationship navigation is made possible by the use of indexes. Obtaining the master of a detail is done via a primary index on the master table, while obtaining the details of a master is either done by a part search of the detail's primary index or by a secondary index on the detail.

Note that in certain circumstances we would probably not use indexes. A simple example of this is when a table occupies only a few pages of disk storage. If an index were to be imposed upon such a small table, using it would probably take far longer than reading the whole of the table. Some database administrators apply this principle to every table whatever its size, and only apply indexes if the performance of the system in practice is poor. Some relational databases also use clustering indexes. This enables details to be located physically near to their masters and hence in theory can speed up some retrievals. A full discussion of the principles of clustering is given in Date (1990).

A final point concerns the implementation of sub-types. There are three ways of doing this:

1. Implement as a single super-type table. Thus in Fig. 18.5, there would be one Patient table. The columns of this table would be obtained by merging the

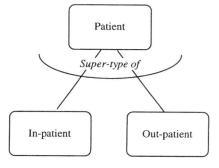

Fig. 18.5   Sub-types

attributes of all three entities. This has the advantage of simplifying any queries, but does lead to many null attributes in the table.

2. Implement as separate sub-type tables. In our example we would have an In-Patient and an Out-Patient table. This would optimize storage, but make queries difficult, there being no formal link between the two tables. It would probably mean doing everything twice and sorting the result.

3. Implement each entity separately. Thus in the example there would be three separate tables. To implement the relationships, all the tables must have the same key. This approach is a compromise, having some of the advantages of the other two, but at the cost of more complexity.

Which of these is followed depends to a large extent upon the situation and the database facilities. If, for example, two sub-types hardly differed then the first approach would be sensible.

18.4 STEP 630—DIALOGUE DESIGN

The purpose of this step is to package the on-line functions into well-designed dialogues. Obviously, the way in which dialogues are defined is very dependent upon the physical database. However, there are a number of things that need to be done whatever the physical environment. The tasks to be performed are:

1. Define super-functions
2. Define screen handling for super-functions
3. Package functions and super-functions into dialogues
4. Define error handling techniques and warning/status messages
5. Define help handling

Recall that a function was defined as a 'distinct piece of the new system's processing which can be used independently by a user'. Earlier in the book the advice given was to keep functions small. If there was a need to pass data from one function to another, then the two would be recorded as related functions. In the majority of cases this causes

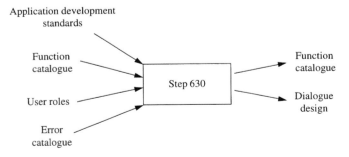

Fig. 18.6   Inputs and products for Dialogue Design

no problem, with the data transfer being effected by a database lookup or even by some form of 'cut and paste'. Sometimes, however, the data transfer can only be achieved efficiently when both functions are encapsulated within a single program or physical process. When this happens, we define a new function or *super-function* and make an extra entry in the Function Catalogue (functions and super-functions are best kept separate in the Catalogue).

Super-functions are most often required when enquiry functions are glued onto the front of update functions. As an example, consider a function that allows a user to change a Customer's name or address before making a booking. This function will need a Customer number to trigger the update process. This is all well and good if the user knows the number. However, it is quite likely that the user does not, in which case they might wish to use another function, which when given a Customer name will search for a Customer number. The resultant super-function will consist of the name search followed by the update.

A super-function obviously requires some form of screen design. As it is itself a package of existing functions, this is best done by using the techniques given in Chapter 10, perhaps using a screen flow type diagram as in Fig. 18.7. Note that the actual screens used will be documented under the individual functions.

It is worth stressing that tasks 1 and 2 might not need doing. Super-functions are only ever used to overcome the inadequacies of the physical environment. On the whole, it is preferable to avoid combining more than one function into a super-function, if that is at all possible. If we can, it is better to code or generate the functions as small independent units. This will allow us much more flexibility when designing the human–computer interface. Such an approach certainly ties in better with a Windows type of environment. If, however, this should not be the case, then each user would have available a selection of functions and super-functions. As a super-function is really no more than an overgrown kind of function, for ease of expression we will drop the distinction between functions and super-functions in the rest of the chapter.

The third task is to organize the functions from the point of view of the user. In a very basic environment, this might not be desirable. We might wish to give each program some obscure name and rely on the user typing something like 'RUN CUSTUPDT' every time he or she wishes to use the Customer Update Function. This, however, is really primitive. Nowadays with reasonable menu systems we can provide a much more user-friendly interface. This statement is even more true for modern Graphical User Interface-based interfaces.

One way of packaging the functions is illustrated in Fig. 18.8. This is a menu structure for the user role 'Customer Clerk' in the Happy Camping system. The bottom

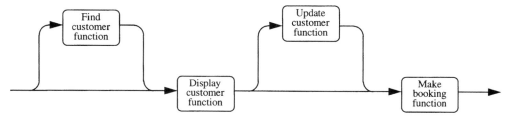

Fig. 18.7   Super-function screens

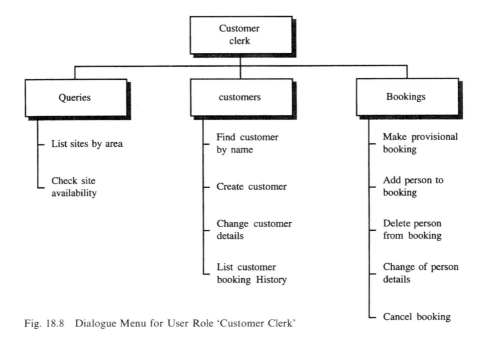

Fig. 18.8   Dialogue Menu for User Role 'Customer Clerk'

level of the menu shows all the functions available to the user. These have been divided into three broad areas or sub-menus: functions dealing with general queries, customer tasks and making bookings respectively. Thus when the user enters the queries sub-menu, he or she will have two functions to run, 'List sites by area' and 'Check site availability'. This notation is very flexible. It can easily be extended to four or more levels by placing sub-menus on separate pages. To prevent a great deal of jumping around the dialogue, we could repeat commonly used functions on different sub-menus. We could even mix functions with the sub-menus. The point to note is that the leaves or bottom elements of the structure refer to functions, while boxes which have 'descendants' are menus or sub-menus.

What we do next is to translate the menu hierarchies into some form of physical dialogue design. How we do this is very dependent upon the physical environment. We might implement the structure as character-based menus or as pull-down menus or even as pushbuttons as in Fig. 18.9. We might wish to implement each function as an icon and implement 'drag and drop' mechanisms. We might wish to specify which, if any, of the functions could be run simultaneously. We might wish to implement fast-path routes through the menus and design quick-exit routines. SSADM cannot really offer much guidance at this point. The analyst has to be guided by product-specific advice and any human–computer interface standards promulgated by the organization in which she or he works. What we do *not* do at this stage is to redesign the function outputs. This should really have been done in step 330 when defining the functions. It is useful to think of each function running in a window, independently of other functions.

The final things we have to do in this step is to design our error and warning message handling and define levels of help. The error messages generated by each function will be obtained by cross-referencing the appropriate function error messages

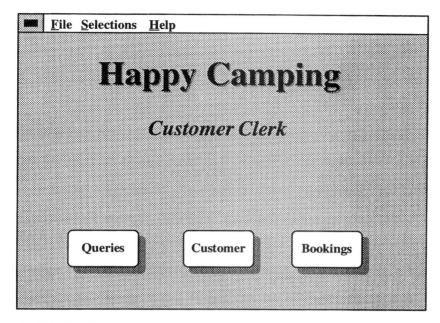

Fig. 18.9   Possible top-level menu

in the Error Catalogue. Warning and status messages are intended to keep the user informed about what is happening. They are essential during long operations where their main job is in reassuring the user that the system has not died. The way in which all these messages are displayed will depend upon facilities available in the physical environment and be influenced by any human–computer interface standards possessed by the organization. Similarly, some thought should be given to the level of help available to the users of the system. Help can be defined for individual functions and at a dialogue level. Again what is done here depends upon the physical environment and organizational standards. For example, all Windows products share a common Help interface. If designing a product for this target platform, it is obvious that one would wish to use the same interface, and employ the Microsoft Help Compiler.

18.5 STEP 640—THE FUNCTION COMPONENT IMPLEMENTATION MAP

The major purpose of this step is to map the functions onto programs. It is very difficult to give specific advice in this area as the programming facilities on offer from different database environments, even two relational products, differ considerably. However, there are a number of basic principles which can be applied to any system.

The first task of this step is the allocation of functions to programs. 'Programs' is a somewhat ambiguous term to use, as a program often means different things to different people. In some physical environments it might be called a process, a module, a procedure, a routine, or even a form. What we mean by a 'program' is the basic unit of

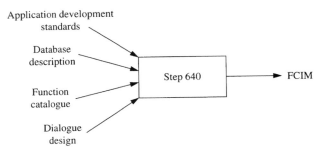

Fig. 18.10   Inputs and product for Function Component Implementation Map

physical processing or code which can be executed as a whole. In step 330 we defined a function as a job the system would do for a user. In the best of all possible worlds, each function would be implemented as a program. However, sometimes this is not possible, and we need to look at alternative strategies for implementing the functions.

The formal allocation of functions to programs is done by means of the Function Component Implementation Map. We will illustrate this in the form of a matrix as shown in Fig. 18.11. The functions are placed on the vertical axis and the programs on the horizontal one. An 'X' shows that a given function is incorporated into a particular program. As is usual with most matrices, this format can become unwieldy if the number of functions or programs grows large, but it does illustrate clearly the basic concepts involved.

One mapping is shown with regard to the functions F_1, F_2, F_3. Here the functions are in a one-to-one correspondence with the programs. This is clean and simple and certainly the situation at which one should aim.

The situation with regard to function F_7 can sometimes happen. Here the function has been implemented as a number of separate programs P_6, P_7 and P_8. This quite commonly occurs in the case of off-line functions. One could well imagine P_6 as a program that extracts data from the database, P_7 as a sort and P_8 as a reporting

	Programs							
Functions	P_1	P_2	P_3	P_4	P_5	P_6	P_7	P_8
F_1	X							
F_2		X						
F_3			X					
F_4				X	X			
F_5				X				
F_6					X			
F_7						X	X	X

Fig. 18.11   Function Component Implementation Map Structure

program. Other cases where a single function will generate more than one program is in a transaction processing type of system where each program deals with a single message pair.

The situation with regard to functions F_4, F_5 and F_6 may well be necessary. This is where a program is designed to cover many functions. This usually happens when programs are defined at the dialogue level. An example of this occurs in modern Graphical User Interface type systems where each user role is allocated a form and the functions are activated by pushbuttons. Typically, the code for the functions is 'hung' from the buttons.

If a function is implemented on client/server architecture, a decision needs to be taken as to which parts of the function are allocated to the client and which to the server. For example, consider the working of an automatic cash machine. The function 'Statement Request' would probably be implemented by means of three programs—one at the client end to handle the dialogue with the customer, one at the central bank computer to log the request and a third batch program run in the early hours of the morning to print statements.

The one thing missing from the Function Component Implementation Map is any concept of programs running programs, or in more modern parlance, forms running forms. Thus in Fig. 14.8 we might wish to design the top-level menu for the Customer Clerk as a form, which in turn can execute a separate form for each of the sub-menus. Such controlling forms must be documented on the menu hierarchies as in Fig. 18.12, *not* on the Function Component Implementation Map.

After producing the map, there are still a number of things to be done in this step:

1. We need to identify any pieces of common processing used by different functions and programs. This might be something like a common screen or a difficult piece of processing such as an allocation procedure or a common validation routine shared by several functions. To find such commonality is easier said than done. There seems to be no simple method which can be used to select these common processes. What one tends to do is to rely on the experience of the analyst concerned, and assume that in the course of their labours they have noted such processes.
2. For each program document whether it is to be written as a procedural or non-procedural process. In other words, what language will be used to write or generate the code.

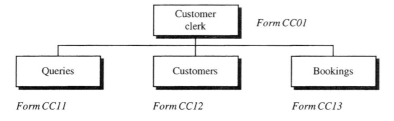

Fig. 18.12   Implementation of physical dialogues

3. For each program decide upon the physical success unit. A success unit is the amount of processing that can succeed or fail as a whole. As far as updates are concerned, it is the quantity of changes that are committed to the database 'in one go'. (For a full discussion of success units and commit operations see, for example, Date, 1990, Chapter 16. What we call a 'success unit' Date calls a '(logical) transaction'.) Usually a success unit will be equivalent to a function or program. There are, however, problems with long programs. Suppose an on-line function is used to create a record with 200 fields. If things go wrong, they will, of course, go wrong when the user is entering the 199th field. To avoid repeatedly losing substantial amounts of work, it might be worth committing data to the database every 50 fields, say. In this case the program would consist of four physical success units. Similar arguments apply to long batch programs.

Although we have considered 630 and 640 as separate steps, it is abundantly clear that they must be done in parallel. It is impossible to package the functions into dialogues without some idea as to how they might be implemented as programs, and conversely it is often the case that program design cannot commence without a knowledge of how the functions are to be combined.

18.6 STEP 650—COMPLETE PROGRAM SPECIFICATIONS

The final technical step in SSADM is to produce program specifications. These document program requirements to a level sufficient to be passed to a programmer or to generate code. There are no fixed SSADM standards as to how this should be done. A full specification of a program might include the following:

> Program description
> Detail of Inputs
> Output layouts
> Database design
> Error messages
> Help availability
> Common processes or library routines used
> Physical Success Units

Obviously much of this will be based upon entries in the Function Catalogue. The degree of detail required in a specification depends upon circumstances. The amount of documentation required for a program to be implemented as a single SQL statement would, for example, be rather different from that for a program written as 10 000 lines of C coding. In all this, one has to be guided by installation standards.

Finally, in the case of off-line functions, one might consider producing Batch Run Flows. If a function is implemented as a number of different programs, these diagrams would show how the programs interact. Batch runs are usually found in the older type of system, and for something that has been around for such a long time, there are several ways of drawing them. Figure 18.13 illustrates one such convention.

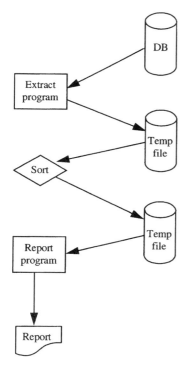

Fig. 18.13   Typical batch run flow

18.7 STEP 660—ASSEMBLE PHYSICAL DESIGN

This, the final step in SSADM, is really a management step. The final products of SSADM, that is,

> The Database Design
> Program Specifications

are checked for consistency and completeness and finally signed off. All that remains to be done is to build the system and to physically implement it.

18.8 WHAT'S MISSING FROM STAGE 6?

A number of steps and techniques in standard SSADM are missing. It might be as well to pause and consider why they have not been included in our approach.

The first thing that is missing is the Physical Data Model (sometimes known as the Universal Database Design). In standard SSADM, the Required Logical Data Model is converted in a very general way to something called the Physical Data Model before product-specific guidance is applied. What this interim model does is to divide the entities into physical groups, each group headed by a root entity. The purpose of doing this is to facilitate the exploiting of any 'place near' mechanism possessed by the Database Management System. This approach seems reasonable if the target database is IDMS-X, but is of little use elsewhere. Indeed, if a relational product is being used, the designer, when producing the database design, would not bother with the Physical Data Model but work directly from the Required Logical Data Model. Given this fact, there is no point in producing something which will not be used.

The second thing that is missing is any mechanism for tuning the database. In standard SSADM a whole step, called 'Optimization of the Physical Data Design', is devoted to this task. In it the database is sized, critical programs are identified and estimates made of how long they are liable to take. All these estimates are made on paper, no experimental models are built and no comparisons with similar existing systems are made. There are various courses of action suggested if the database appears to be too big, or if the programs appear to take too long. In my opinion, this seems the wrong place to make these kind of decisions. If there are likely to be major performance problems, stage 6 seems far too late in the design process to do anything about it. Indeed, these problems should have been identified well before we made our technical decisions in stage 4. On the other hand, if the problems appear to be a minor kind, there is probably very little that can sensibly be done about them at this stage. Given the complexities of modern Database Management System software, it is more than likely that any program timings are, at best, a guesstimate, and so we could well spend a great deal of time in attempting to solve problems that will not in any case arise! In our tailoring of the method, we suggest a two-pronged approach to performance issues. Major problems should be identified in step 370 when we work out logical volumetrics. This will be sufficient to inform our choice of technical platform. Minor problems are probably best left until the system is being built, and the designers know that they are facing a real rather than a theoretical problem.

The final thing missing is the Process Data Interface (PDI). In brief, this is a piece of software that forms an interface between the programs and the physical database. Standard SSADM suggest building this in the case where the Physical Database diverges considerably from the Logical Data Model. It is envisaged that when such an interface is used the programs will be written as if the Logical Data Model had been directly implemented, and that any calls by the programs to retrieve data from it would be intercepted by the Process Data Interface which would then work out where this data was held on the physical database. Similar remarks apply to updates. The argument made in favour of a Process Data Interface is that it would aid maintenance and portability. Thus, further changes to the database would be implemented on the 'clean' Logical Data Model rather than the 'dirty' physical database. Second, if the target Database Management System were to be changed, the Logical Data Model would remain unaltered, and so all that would require modification would be the Process Data Interface. Although these arguments sound quite persuasive, in reality the construction of a Process Data Interface is probably not going to be worth the effort required. In the first place, most database products implement the Logical Data Model fairly directly, and any conversion between the logical view of data and the underlying file structure is accomplished by the Database Management System itself. Any tuning of the system is likely to be of a minor nature, and so the imposition of yet another layer between the programs and the database is liable to complicate maintenance rather than ease it. From the point of view of most systems, the portability argument also does not stand up. Most project teams who choose to use SSADM are probably developing a fairly straightforward information system for a single organization. Having chosen the hardware and software platform, they would probably be unlikely to change either within the lifetime of the application. The portability argument is only of interest to those organizations, such as specialized software consultancies, producing fairly general-purpose packages which they wish to sell to a wide variety of customers. Building a robust Process Data Interface is a non-trivial task and they are liable to be the only type of organization with staff possessing the requisite specialized software engineering skills.

FURTHER CUSTOMIZATION

TAILORING THE METHOD

The preceding chapters gave a reasonably full version of SSADM. Apart from stage 5, not much is missing. There have been changes to some of the techniques, some differences in approach, but essentially we have covered the same sort of ground as standard SSADM. This does beg the question as to whether we need to include everything or if there is scope for further reductions.

There are essentially two approaches to further tailoring of the method. The first is to consider the scope for reducing or even omitting items of documentation. The second is to shrink the method itself by leaving out some of the steps. Obviously, whichever of these approaches is pursued it might result in having to do something in the other direction as well. If, for example, we omit an item of documentation, we cannot then perform a step for which it is an input. Bearing this in mind, it still seems sensible to consider the two approaches separately.

19.1 REDUCING THE DOCUMENTATION

There are two types of documentation, one that is long-lasting and one that is transitory. The long-lasting documents are the final products of SSADM and are documented in Appendix 1. The transitory documentation refers to working papers produced as part of performing a specific technique, and is not required beyond the confines of the step where it is produced. For example, the documents produced as part of Relational Data Analysis are obviously essential to step 340, but once the Logical Data Model is checked these working papers are of no further use. The question as to whether we need to produce such documentation is really one of whether we need to perform the step and so is best left until we consider the second of our approaches to tailoring of the method.

Let us consider therefore the final products of SSADM. Before we make radical changes to them, or even discard them, it is as well to note a number of factors that might influence the degree to which tailoring is deemed desirable on a given project. First, these documents form part of the project deliverables, and are used by the system developers for the construction and maintenance of the system. If we abandon large swathes of work we might jeopardize later development. Second, the larger the project, the more people will be involved in system development, and the greater is the need for documentation. Thus, on a small project the same person could well be responsible for steps 360 and 365. In this case, the developer probably will not need to reference the Event Catalogue when developing Access Paths. The same cannot be said where different teams are responsible for the products of steps 360 and 365. Here the Event Catalogue is an essential vehicle for communication between the two teams. Finally, if a CASE tool is being used, it is clear that this will influence the choice of what is produced and the form in which it is presented. Accepting the fact that all these factors will influence our decision, what I propose to do next is to examine each product in turn and see what scope there is for reduction.

1. *The Business Activity Model.* This is mandatory. It is the one document that shows the business context in which the system operates. A full Business Activity Model consists of:
   Statement of Business Objectives
   Context Diagram
   Functional decomposition
   Business Activity Descriptions
   The last can be omitted in the quickest of projects, but the other three are essential.

2. *The Requirements Catalogue.* This is mandatory. After all, there has to be somewhere where the wishes and desires of the business are formally recorded. Having said this, a certain amount of discretion must be in evidence when completing the requirements. For example, when studying an existing system there is little point in recording each functional requirement in great detail. If we were to do this we would be in danger of constructing some form of function catalogue before we have even chosen a Business System Option to determine the future system direction. A much better approach is to keep the requirements at a high level and record processing detail on other documents. As an example, suppose we are investigating a system which pays grants to farmers. Then it should be sufficient to record 'Automate the present grant system' as a requirement in the Catalogue. All the individual functions which form part of this, such as 'Register farmers' and 'Calculate amount of grant', would be documented on a Dataflow Model, and so would not need cataloguing individually on the Requirements Catalogue. If at the Business System Option stage we decide that we will only automate part of the grant system, this can be documented on the 'Solution' part of the Catalogue.

3. *User Catalogue.* This is easy to produce and does focus attention at an early stage upon the users of the system. It is worth while.

4. *The Current Physical Dataflow Model.* Obviously if there is no current system, there can be no current Dataflow Model. In the case of existing systems, how much effort should be expended on the current Dataflow Model depends to a large extent on how much of the present system will reappear in the new system. At one extreme,

we may be translating an existing manual or computer system on a 'one-for-one' basis. Everything that appears in the current system will look much the same in the required system, even if it is implemented a little more efficiently. Here, there is a great deal of sense in meticulously documenting the existing system. At the other extreme, we have the case where the existing system is known to be 'wrong'. In this case, there is little point in recording much about a system which is to be completely replaced. Most systems occupy a position somewhere between these two extremes, and so should be documented accordingly. Recall, however, that the sole purpose of documenting the current system is to aid understanding and to provide a firm basis for the design of the new system. In the vast majority of cases, the present system is to be replaced and so it does seem a little perverse to lavish time and effort on documenting something which is destined for the wastebin.

Bearing all this in mind, let us consider the constituent parts of the model. It consists of:

- Top-level Dataflow Diagram
- Lower-level Dataflow Diagrams
- Elementary Process Descriptions
- External Entity List
- Input/Output descriptions
- Datastore descriptions

A top level Dataflow Diagram seems well worth producing. It does, after all, illustrate the scope of the project and its interfaces with the external world.* Lower-level Dataflow Diagrams and Elementary Process Descriptions need only be developed for critical areas. The Datastore Descriptions can often be collected very easily as copies of forms (for a manual system) or photocopies of file structures (for a computer system). The external entity list is fairly trivial, and is often recorded as part of system development using a CASE tool. The Input/Output descriptions are another matter. If copies of user forms or screen dumps are available, these usually suffice as a description of any major flows. If they are not available, recording every item of data transported by every dataflow is a time-consuming task and should not be lightly undertaken. We are, after all, documenting the current system and it is doubtful whether this degree of detail is really necessary.

5. *The Logical Data Model (Current System)*. This is mandatory except for the case where there is no existing system. The model consists of:

- Logical Data Structure
- Entity descriptions
- Relationship descriptions
- Volumetrics

The Logical Data Structure is essential. Entity descriptions are also required but need not be completed to the finest detail. Keys, for example, do not yet assume the

---

*There is an argument that even these are not necessary and that the Business Activity Model in the form of a functional decomposition should be developed directly from discussions with the users. While this is a possible approach, it does entail greater risks. By not documenting in detail how tasks are performed, it is quite likely that important processing details are skated over. For this reason, unless pressures of time are considerable, I would not advocate ignoring the Current Physical Dataflow Model.

importance that they do later in the required system model. Relationship descriptions can often be involved and so this document may be modified or dropped completely. Volumetric information is vital especially at the later stages of SSADM and so should be collected whenever and wherever it becomes available.

6. *The Logical Dataflow Model (Current System)*. There is some debate as to how much of the model is required or if it is required at all. The essential processes are adequately described by means of a functional decomposition. (The only situation in which the production of Logical Dataflow Diagrams can really be justified is if the organization's standards officers deem them mandatory!)

7. *Business System Options*. These are mandatory. At the very least they must address functionality, costs, timescales, business impact and risk. The format in which they are produced depends upon the standards of the organization. To save time, they could be combined with the Technical Options.

8. *The Logical Data Model for the Required System*. This is essential and must be developed in full. Again it will consist of:
   - Logical Data Structure
   - Entity descriptions
   - Relationship descriptions
   - Volumetrics

   This time the entity descriptions will have to be completely developed, with keys identified and all attributes fully described. The easiest way of doing this is to use a data dictionary on a CASE tool. Relationship descriptions should also be described in full and as much volumetric information taken on board as possible.

9. *The Required Processing Model*. With a little foresight, there is scope for reducing the amount of work here. This model will consist of:
   - Context diagram
   - Functional Decomposition
   - Dataflow Diagrams (all levels)
   - Elementary Process Descriptions
   - External Entity List
   - Input/Output Descriptions
   - Datastore/Entity Cross-Reference

   Again the Functional Decomposition is essential. The Context Diagram should be produced as the interfaces between the system and the external world might have changed from those on the current system. As with the Current Logical Dataflow Diagram, there is some question as to whether the Dataflow Diagrams are really essential. They are not really appropriate for communicating with users and serve no useful purpose in designing the new system. Indeed, the relationship between processing and data is best shown by the Access Paths in the Function Catalogue rather than by the Input/Output descriptions on the Dataflow Model. The only items really needed are the Elementary Process Descriptions, to clarify entries in the bottom level of the hierarchy, and possibly a top-level Dataflow Diagram which serves to illustrate the interfaces between the system and the outside world.

   With even more foresight, the Functional Decomposition can be constructed so that the bottom-level entries become functions. This will enable the Function Catalogue to be read directly from the decomposition.

10. *The Function Catalogue.* This is mandatory as it is that part of the System Specification that describes the required processing in detail. For each function in the Function Catalogue the following could be recorded:
    - Function definition
    - Input and output formats (screen and print layouts)
    - Access Path
    - Access Path Description
    - Function Error List

    How much of this is produced depends to a large extent upon the complexity of the function under consideration. An Access Path and its associated description are probably not worth producing for most enquiries and simple updates. The error list might not be produced if the final programs rely on standard database messages. The minimum amount that suffices for many functions is probably the function definition together with the input and output formats.

11. *User Roles.* This document is easy to produce and is needed in order to package the user dialogues. With larger systems it is a useful reference document.

12. *Entity Life Histories.* These are really working documents whose primary purpose is to see that no functions are missed. The only time they are ever needed, outside step 360, is in step 367 where they can be used to check the State Transition Matrix. They are not, however, essential for this purpose. Therefore, the number of Entity Life Histories produced depends to a large extent upon how thoroughly step 360 is done. If the Entity Life Histories are thrown away at the end of this step, it will not matter a great deal unless evolutionary prototyping is being used (see Chapter 19).

13. *Event Catalogue.* The major purpose of this document is to cross-reference the events to the functions and to act as a starting point for the production of Access Paths for the update functions. It just acts as a convenient repository for event data. With a small team and with tight deadlines it is possible to produce Access Paths directly from a knowledge of the processing needs of the system.

14. *Error Catalogue.* Although not needed for later technical development, without it, it is quite likely that error messages will be confusing. The Error Catalogue should be viewed as a management tool, whose major purpose is to enforce a standard user interface. If time permits, this is well worth developing.

15. *Technical Option.* Rather like Business System Options, these should be developed according to the standards of the organization. In many situations there is a single option, in which case it can be ignored.

16. *Application Development Standards.* These should be developed for an organization rather than for a single project. If, for example, INGRES is being used, someone somewhere should write down formally the rules and strategies for using the product. However, if they are not available, and time is short, they need not be developed as part of a particular project (providing that the team know what they are doing!).

17. *Database design.* This is essential.

18. *Function Component Implementation Map.* This shows the correspondence between functions and programs. With sufficient foresight in the function definition step, and with the right kind of database product, one could achieve a one-to-one mapping between programs and functions, and so make this product irrelevant.

19. *Dialogue Specifications.* These merely show how the functions are packaged for each user role. A simple diagram is not difficult to produce and documents choices made in dialogue design.
20. *Program Specifications.* In a simple system, if the functions are defined in a sensible way, the function definition forms should serve as program specifications. If this is so, all that needs to be done is to name the functions in a computer-friendly fashion.

19.2 SHRINKING THE METHOD

We now turn to the actual method itself, and investigate the scope for reducing the steps in the method. Reducing the method does entail increased risk. The method as presented so far is complete in that it includes numerous techniques whose major purpose is to cross-check other techniques. Thus Relational Data Analysis only exists within SSADM to check the Logical Data Model. Omitting such a checking mechanism does increase the possibility of errors.

To help us shrink the method we will produce a number of 'routemaps' around the method. For each of the 'technique-based steps' of the method these will show what inputs are required and what outputs are produced. An alternative name for a routemap would, therefore, be a Product Flow Diagram. These are not sufficient in themselves to produce a good system. After all, we do need to ensure some form of management control and user interaction before embarking upon any project!

Our basic routemaps are shown in Figs 19.1 and 19.2. Figure 19.1 is the routemap for the Analysis phase of rapid SSADM, Fig. 19.2 is for the Design phase. These are the starting points for subsequent tailoring. Note that products which appear to 'drop off' the end of the Design diagram are those which will be passed forward to the system developers. The two steps that appear in every routemap are Business Activity Modelling and Requirements Definition. This is because any project must be driven by user requirements and the needs of the business.

Most of these routemaps can be mapped onto the System Development Template (see Chapter 2). This has not been done here in order to keep the diagrams simple. However, if any further customization is attempted, it should be borne in mind which techniques are appropriate to the Conceptual Model, which to the External Design, and so on. For a more detailed treatment of this and further customization issues see CCTA (1994).

19.3 FEASIBILITY ROUTEMAP

The most obvious tailoring is for a Feasibility Study. This is defined as steps 020 and 030 in SSADM Version 4.2 but is really no more than a high-level run through the first three stages. In Fig. 19.3, the thick boxes with italic labels denote that the step is not done in full.

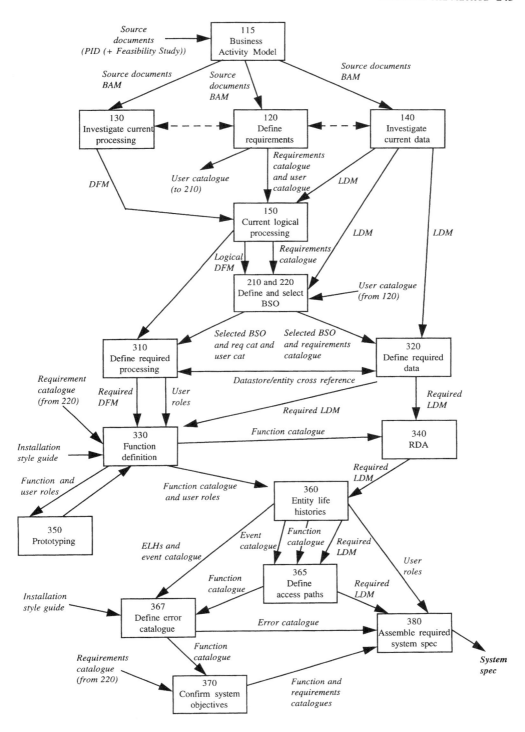

Fig. 19.1   Full Analysis

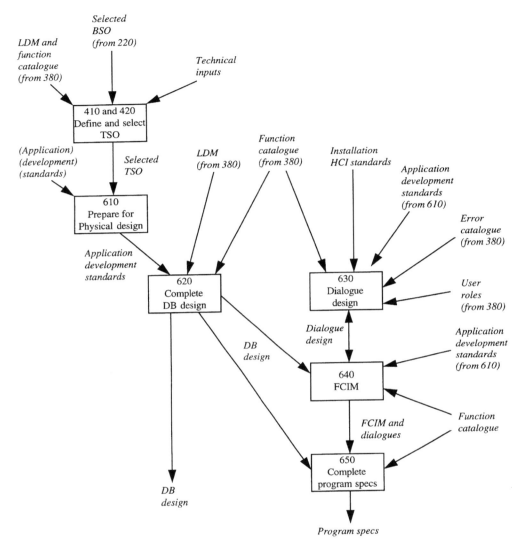

Fig. 19.2   Full design

19.4 GREENFIELD SITE ROUTEMAP

What happens if there is no existing system? Obviously a Dataflow Model and a Logical Data Model of the Current System are completely out of the question. All that can be done before producing Business System Options is to record the requirements. This is illustrated in Fig. 19.4.

For each of the Business System Options, it is important that the scope and the interfaces between the system and the external world are fully understood. For this reason it is proposed that a functional decomposition, a context diagram and an

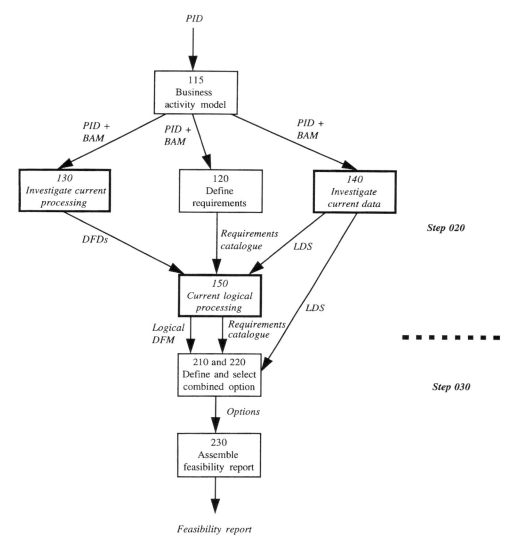

Fig. 19.3   Feasibility Study routeplan

overview Logical Data Model should be developed for each of the options. From stage 3 development should proceed as normal.

19.5 THE RAPID RAPID DEVELOPMENT ROUTEMAP

This tailoring of the method is for those who wish to use SSADM in order to develop systems as fast as possible with a minimum of documentation. In some sense, it is the minimum that a development team could do and still claim to be using SSADM!

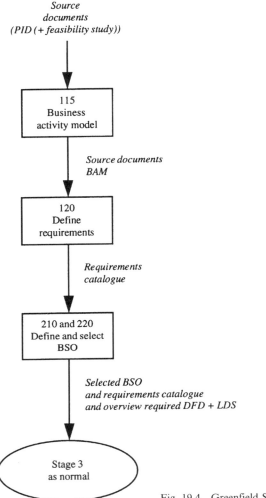

Fig. 19.4   Greenfield Site analysis routeplan

The routemap for this approach is shown in Fig. 19.5. On the diagram the boxes with thick tinted edges and italic labels indicate that the technique will be curtailed somewhat. The normal boxes indicate that the step should be performed as normal.

In this situation it is unlikely that a full Feasibility Study would have been done. The Business Activity Model, the Requirements Catalogue and the Current Logical Data Model should be developed as usual. Production of a full Dataflow Model is often quite a long, drawn-out process, and so steps 130 and 150 could well be pruned in line with the recommendations in the first part of this chapter. The Current Physical Dataflow Model should only be developed to a level sufficient to develop a full under-standing of the current system. This might just consist of a top-level Dataflow Diagram and lower levels only for the critical processes. The Logical Dataflow Model could well

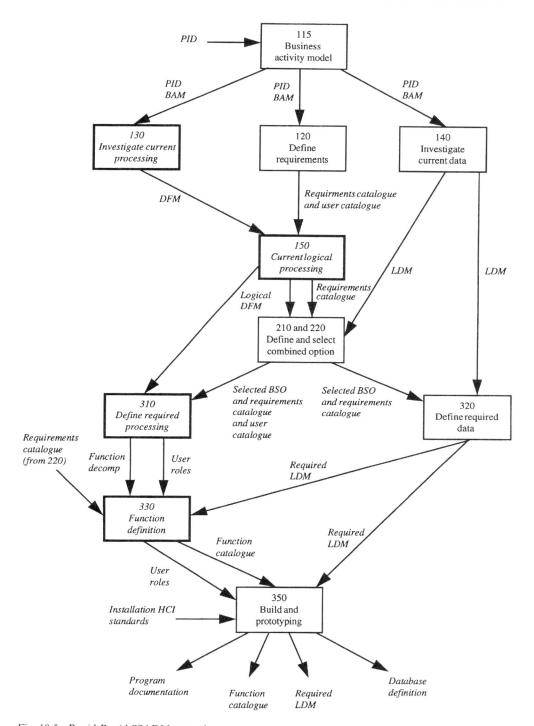

Fig. 19.5 Rapid Rapid SSADM routeplan

be replaced by a Functional Decomposition and a Context Diagram. There is probably no need to develop the full Dataflow Diagram(s).

As far as the required system is concerned, the Logical Data Model should be developed in full. After all, this is the cornerstone of the new system design. There are various shortcuts that can be applied to the processing. When we define the Required Processing in step 310, we could develop a functional decomposition, but not bother with the Dataflow Model. This does, however, suffer from the defect that any interfaces between the required system and the external world would not be clear. Therefore, a Context Diagram, or even a top-level Dataflow Diagram, might be developed from the first level of the decomposition. Moving onto Function Definition, it does not seem sensible to complete full Function Definition forms for each and every function. It is better to use the Functional Decomposition and document all the functions fully in step 350. A little forethought is useful here. If the hierarchy is developed correctly in step 310, the functions could be read directly from the lowest level of the decomposition.

There seems little point in doing Relational Data Analysis, other than in the most superficial way. Neither are full Entity Life Histories recommended. This is a little more serious as it is quite likely that some functions will be missed. For this reason the Logical Data Model is shown as an input for step 330, so that when the functions are listed, a check can be made that each and every entity is created, deleted and subject to some modification.

The crux of this approach lies in step 350, where the model is built and tested. This will be illustrated below. Suffice it to say that the final products obtained from this approach are:

- A fully documented Logical Data Model for the Required System
- A database description
- A fully documented Function Catalogue
- Program Specifications

It is unlikely that both of the last two would be required.

19.6 STEP 350 IN THE RAPID RAPID APPROACH

Step 350 is the heart of the Rapid Rapid approach. This is where the system is built, tested and modified. Obviously a Prototyping Approach could be used here.

The inputs to this step are a fully documented Logical Data Model and the Function Catalogue. At the start of step 350, the Function Catalogue will probably consist of no more than a list of putative functions. What happens next is that all or part of the system is designed, built and tested or prototyped with the user. The results are reviewed and a decision is made as to what to do next. If the results are not acceptable or if more of the system is to be built, the Logical Data Model and Function Catalogue are revisited and updated. The existing model is modified or, in extreme cases, a new model is built, and the cycle starts again.

The iteration will continue until the end result proves acceptable to the user. When this occurs the system is signed off, and the documentation completed.

19.7 MANDATORY PACKAGE ROUTEMAP

What happens in the situation where a strategic decision has been made that a package is the only acceptable solution? SSADM, with drastic modifications, can be used here (Fig. 19.7).

In this situation we would again start as normal. The Business Activity Model and the Current System Processing need a full investigation, since the project team will have to be aware of the environment in which a package is expected to work. An additional reason for doing this is that the analysis undertaken may elicit extra requirements. In theory, if a package is to be selected, there is no point in developing a data model since this may not be implemented in a package. Personally, however, I would develop a

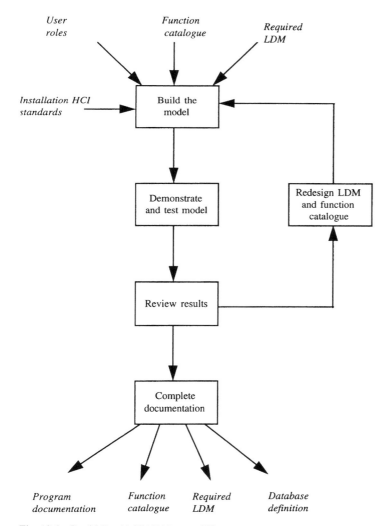

Fig. 19.6   Rapid Rapid SSADM, step 350

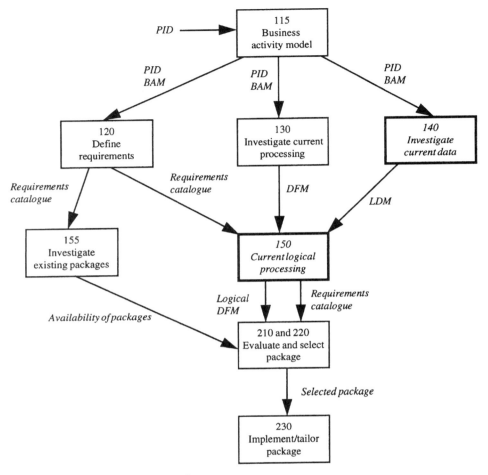

Fig. 19.7   Mandatory Package routeplan

Logical Data Structure, regarding this purely as an analysis tool whose main purpose is to engender further understanding of the system. Similarly, in step 150, the enhancement of the functional decomposition, but not the development of a full Dataflow Model, would aid all concerned in agreeing the objectives of the business.

As soon as the requirements have been recognized, the team can commence their search for relevant packages. When any have been identified, those available are reviewed and evaluated. This should lead to the selection of an outright winner as the preferred package solution. There are many proprietary methods developed by organizations to interface package selection with SSADM and procurement criteria. See, for example, the PACE method (Baker, 1994).

If it should happen that no package sufficiently measures up to the evaluation criteria, sufficient analysis has now been done to enable the team to switch to another routemap and so develop an in-house solution.

RAPID APPLICATION DEVELOPMENT

To users and systems staff alike, Rapid Application Development sounds like the ultimate in free lunches. After all, who could object to the idea of high-quality business applications being developed as quickly as possible? Given these obvious attractions, the question must arise as to why Rapid Application Development is not used universally and why other 'slower' methods persist. Before we can answer these questions and so identify which projects could benefit most from this, we must first clarify our understanding of what is actually meant by Rapid Application Development.

20.1 PRINCIPLES OF RAPID APPLICATION DEVELOPMENT

Unlike standard methodologies such as SSADM and Information Engineering, Rapid Application Development is usually not defined in terms of structure and of analysis techniques. It is not so much a prescribed list of activities, but rather a philosophical approach to system development. As such, it can be used in conjunction with any of the standard methodologies, overlaying the structure rather than replacing it. Given this widespread applicability, it is not surprising that Rapid Application Development exists under a variety of different names. (Joint Application Development, FAST techniques are some of the others. Pressman (1994) uses the term '4GL techniques' to mean much the same.) Whatever it is called, though, every Rapid Application Development approach employs some or all of the following features:

- *Timeboxing*. This is probably the one feature common to all Rapid Application Development approaches. At the start of the project, a fixed period of time, called the timebox, is allocated for all system development activities. By the end of the timebox a working system must be delivered to the customers. Typically, timeboxes range in length from two to six months. The size of the timebox will determine the scope of the requirements that can be addressed. This contrasts starkly with the traditional approach in which the number and range of requirements determines the project length. It might be thought that such an arbitrary culling of requirements could lead to a system that is unlikely to satisfy the user's needs. Experience does, however, show that this restriction forces analyst and user alike to focus upon the essential aspects of the system. Longer timescales might delay delivery to such an extent that the business and hence the requirements change. It is better to provide crucial functionality quickly than a completed perfect system too late.

- *A simple lifecycle.* Timeboxing rarely allows analysts the luxury of using the full range of techniques available in a comprehensive methodology such as SSADM. This does not mean that structured methods should be ignored completely. To do so is to embrace hacking and so court disaster. Most Rapid Application Development projects adopt a lifecycle that is a variant of that shown in Fig. 20.1. This diagram, based on Pressman's 4GL technique, is somewhat vague and needs elaboration in terms of the techniques to be employed. In the case of SSADM, Fig. 20.1 could be expanded into Rapid Rapid SSADM by defining
  — 'Investigation' as stage 1
  — 'Design' as Business System Options and steps 310–330
  — 'Implementation' and 'Testing' as step 350
  Business System Options cannot be developed in full when a timebox is in operation, since the time allocated and the resources available have already been decided. All that can be done is to choose which requirements can be satisfied within the available time. There seems little point in asking the Project Board to make the choice since the major financial decisions have already been made. Finally, it is worth noting that other lifecycles, such as those involving a package solution, could also be timeboxed.

- *User workshops.* Given the time constraints, traditional methods of communication between analysts and users prove to be difficult. The sequence of observation, interview, documentation, and user review followed by extra meetings to clear up misunderstandings is far too time consuming. Most Rapid Application Development approaches get round this difficulty by bringing users and analysts together so that decisions can be made on the spot. Typically, these joint meetings define user requirements, document existing procedures and agree proposed solutions. The meetings are usually organized as workshops, with the participants forming small groups under the direction of an independent facilitator. The workshops aim to produce concrete results and not to act as mere talking shops, and so the choice of medium for the display of results, whether it be flip charts, whiteboards or post-it stamps, is vital. Joint user/analyst workshops have proved so popular that methods such as JAD and FAST are based on the workshops alone. (For a more detailed description of a JAD or FAST workshop, see Pressman, 1994.)

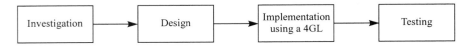

Fig. 20.1 Simple lifecycle

In terms of Rapid Rapid SSADM, the workshops can be used to produce a Requirements Catalogue and a Description of Current Services. Given that untrained users could be involved in the production of Dataflow Diagrams and Logical Data Models, it is unlikely that all products would be developed in full. In particular, the processing hierarchies would certainly replace the Logical Dataflow Diagrams. Indeed, it is quite likely that this view of current business processing would be developed directly without recourse to Physical Dataflow Diagrams. To aid the transition to design, the hierarchies might be supplemented by something like task modelling (see Chapter 21). Finally a joint user/analyst workshop would be charged with developing a solution, defined in terms of selected requirements (Business System Options), Logical Data Models and Function Decomposition.

- *Tools.* Most Rapid Application Development projects are impossible without some form of automated code generation. Hand-crafted code just takes far too long. Obviously, the more that can be automated, the better. This is why proprietary Rapid Application Development methods are usually based around a full lifecycle CASE tool.

- *Prototyping.* This is a natural extension of the user workshops into the area of system build. As there is insufficient time to perform the full range of unit, system and acceptance tests, prototyping is well-nigh essential. Prototyping can also be used as a device for eliciting requirements in the early stages of analysis.

- *Re-use.* Many Rapid Application Development methods advocate re-using previously written and tested software components. Often this is no more than an open invitation to plunder previously installed systems. With in-house Rapid Application Development this is quite sensible, for not only will the copying of chunks of code and screen layouts cut down development time, it will also engender a 'common look and feel' to the organization's products. The situation with regard to projects developed under contract is a little more problematic. One part of one customer's system cannot suddenly make an appearance in the system of another customer!

  Most Rapid Application Development projects do define re-use in terms of straightforward copying. Although this can work well for small organizations operating in stable environments, problems do arise. Similar procedures in different systems often differ slightly and so their use elsewhere can involve minor modifications. This often proves to be far more trouble than it is worth. Moreover, with a large organization, finding similar routines is often so difficult that it is often quicker just to rewrite the code. These problems are addressed directly by object orientation with its use of encapsulation and class libraries, and so the real benefits of re-use will not be evident until this method of development becomes widespread.

- *Small teams.* Most Rapid Application Development approaches assert that a development team should consist of no more than about six individuals. If the size of the team increases beyond this, internal communications and management will become more difficult. There will be less reliance on word of mouth, more and more will have to be written down, and this increasing bureaucracy will inevitably breed delay.

- *Empowerment.* Not only should the teams be small, they should also be empowered to take relevant decisions. No project has the slightest chance of being rapid if senior management have to be consulted before the smallest change can be made.

- *Management commitment.* All Rapid Application Development approaches agree that the most essential ingredient for a successful Rapid Application Development project is a commitment by senior management to support and fund this approach. In particular, the user management must make appropriate staff available for inclusion in the development team. This, however, is not sufficient. Many of the Rapid Application Development principles, for example small teams and empowerment, run counter to the prevailing culture in many large organizations. In such cases, senior management must recognize that such an approach will have political implications.

20.2 PROTOTYPING AND THE DYNAMIC SYSTEMS DEVELOPMENT METHOD

Virtually all Rapid Application Development approaches embrace prototyping as the most appropriate approach to the design and building of systems. In Chapter 12, where prototyping was discussed, it was stated that only specification prototyping plays a role in SSADM. This, of course, seems extremely wasteful to anyone involved in a Rapid Application Development project. From the perspective of the timebox, throwing anything away which has taken effort to develop can best be regarded as foolhardy. Rapid Application Development approaches therefore embrace incremental and even evolutionary prototyping.

So far, 'non-throwaway' prototyping has only been encountered in step 350 of Rapid Rapid SSADM (see Chapter 19). There, not much advice was given about the design or content of prototypes. Without such advice, there is always the danger that systems development will develop into some form of 'hacking'. Indeed, given the time constraints imposed on most projects, any system emerging from step 350 could well be badly designed and inefficient.

These problems have been recognized by a number of people and most suggest a three- or four-stage prototyping process. Typical of these is the approach of Connel and Shafer (1989) in which after initial planning, the project is divided into three cycles:

- *Cycle 1.* Rapid Analysis is followed by database creation, design of the menus and then the functions. Rapid Analysis is rather like Rapid Rapid SSADM. The database is assumed to be relational.
- *Cycle 2.* Within the design parameters of cycle 1 this consists of a number of exercisings of a prototype.
- *Cycle 3.* This consists of user approval of the final prototype, completion of design, tuning and finally operation and maintenance.

Although many of the versions of prototyping look similar, until recently there has been no standard approach. In 1994 a number of large British companies and other organizations sought to rectify the situation. They formed a consortium to develop a standard Rapid Application Development approach, and the result of their work, the Dynamic Systems Development Method (DSDM), was published in February 1995 (DSDM Consortium, 1995).

The structure of the Dynamic Systems Development Method is as indicated in Fig. 20.2. A project would go through a number of phases:

- *Feasibility.* This is a fairly standard, if reduced, approach to feasibility studies.
- *Business Study.* This is akin to standard analysis and design. The Dynamic Systems Development Method is not prescriptive about which techniques to use and draws examples from a variety of system development methods. There are descriptions of dataflow diagrams, entity relationship and state transition diagrams. There are alternatives for those wishing to employ Object Orientated techniques.
- *Functional prototype iteration.* The key objective of this phase is to establish the business functionality addressed by the system. The prototypes are not intended to be particularly user friendly. In the Dynamic Systems Development Method approach, requirements are only baselined during the Business Study, and their full detail will only emerge during this phase. Each iteration consists of four steps—identify prototype, agree schedule, create prototype, review prototype.
- *Design prototype iteration.* Here emphasis switches to the usability of the system. The prototyping steps are similar to those of the previous phase. Other prototypes, concentrating on capacity and performance, may also be developed.
- *Implementation.* This consists of four steps—obtain user approval, train users, implement system, review business. Rather like the prototyping, the implementation phase can be repeated a number of times.

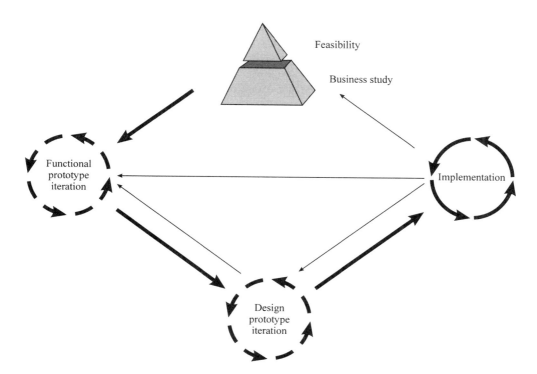

Fig. 20.2 Dynamic Systems Development Method

In most cases the Dynamic Systems Development Method follows the path indicated by the thick arrows in Fig. 20.2. The method, however, does recognize that it might be necessary to backtrack to earlier phases. This is shown by the lighter arrows.

It should not be thought that this all there is to the Dynamic Systems Development Method. The structure is but a small part of the method. Much of it is concerned with management issues such as team structures, user involvement, estimation, risk assessment, configuration management, testing, quality assurance and testing. The method even contains a draft contract for use in Rapid Application Development projects! For this reason, the Dynamic Systems Development Method does not replace SSADM. Indeed, Rapid Rapid SSADM maps very successfully onto the structure. All except step 350 are subsumed by the Business Study, while the prototyping iterations are a useful expansion of step 350.

20.3 LIMITATIONS OF RAPID APPLICATION DEVELOPMENT

Most Rapid Application Development approaches seem to be limited to small information systems projects involving small teams of people. Indeed, it is doubtful whether the user workshops could be run with a large number of people. Once the number of users and analysts cross a critical threshold, problems of communication, management and control will slow down the whole development process and make timeboxes virtually impossible. This would seem to rule out many large capital-intensive projects, especially those in which the development is contracted to a third party.

A second type of project unsuitable to Rapid Application Development methods are those in which a high degree of faith is placed in the correctness of the final product. Although no one developing a system would knowingly release incorrect software, Rapid Application Development tends to emphasize the timeliness of a system rather than its accuracy. It is thus inappropriate for safety-critical systems and those such as payroll in which accuracy is a prime consideration.

One final point to make about Rapid Application Development is that it is inevitable that not all requirements can be addressed within the limitations imposed by a timebox. At the end of the project, some things will be left undone. In the majority of cases the extra functionality will have to be added later. Thus Rapid Application Development must lead to incremental or evolutionary development, which is the subject of the next chapter.

TWENTY-ONE

EVOLUTIONARY DEVELOPMENT

21.1 THE EVOLUTIONARY SPIRAL

Whenever time constraints for a project are particularly tight, it is likely that some user requirements will not be met. The final system might lack functionality or might be difficult to use or just might be slow. Such shortcomings are usually addressed after the initial release of the system software. In effect, the project has been split into phases and the final system been delivered in a piecemeal fashion. Such an approach does not really fit with the waterfall model of system development. Indeed when this model is used, there is a danger that the developers regard the major analysis and design activities as taking place in phase one of the project, with subsequent work being relegated to the status of mere maintenance. This is fine if any subsequent modifications are minor, less so if major updates are required. What is needed is an approach which recognizes that major tasks are often left undone from the first phase of the project.

The most appropriate model for this type of development is based on a spiral and was first introduced by Boehm (1988).* It is illustrated in Fig. 21.1. On each turn through the spiral the analysts will repeat a number of activities:

- *Cycle Objectives*. Agreeing the broad objectives of the cycle with the Project Board.
- *Planning*. Planning the rest of the cycle.
- *Analysis*. Describing the current system and establishing what are the requirements for the new system.
- *Options*. Choosing which requirements are to be met in the current cycle.

---

*The model presented here is only loosely based on Boehm's work. He was mainly interested in risk, gave different names to activities on the spiral and limited it to four cycles. As we will see, the model does have far greater applicability than this.

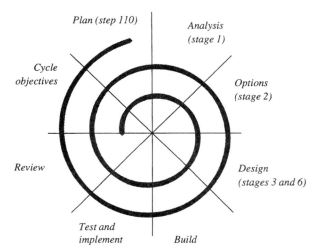

Fig. 21.1   Evolutionary spiral

- *Build.* Producing a working system.
- *Testing and Implementation.* Some combination of unit, system and acceptance tests, followed by user acceptance, data conversion and handover.
- *Review.* Evaluating the results of the cycle.

   Each cycle could be regarded as a mini-project run under the waterfall approach. The activities on each part of the cycle are not fixed, and could be done in a variety of different ways, in some situations even being omitted. For example, a first cycle might be performed as a feasibility study in which no system is built. Later cycles might be concerned just with tuning performance or improving the user interface, in which case the analysis activities would be minimal.

   Despite the seemingly unending nature of the spiral, it is clear that no project can continue indefinitely and that at some time a halt has to be called. The natural finishing place for a project is at the conclusion of a review when all agree that the vast majority of the user requirements have been satisfied. Others will be foreshortened, if it becomes clear that the project will not achieve its objectives. Here the stop point will probably occur at the end of the Cycle Objectives phase. It should be noted that this does not necessarily mean that the project has been abandoned, but rather that further development is not deemed worth while. The customers might well be left with a partially completed, but still usable, product. A final possibility for stopping the project is during the Options phase. While this might well happen during a long cycle, it is less likely if the work is timeboxed and resources are allocated at the start of the cycle.

   The spiral model for software development is the most general in that it subsumes all other linear approaches. Boehm argues that the spiral method can also be applied to parallel activities. He talks of 'parallel spirals'. One full turn around the spiral gives the waterfall approach, two turns give two-pass analysis, with a feasibility and full study, while an analysis pass followed by multiple build and test passes is a model for incremental prototyping. Despite this apparent generality, the spiral model is mainly applicable to those projects developed in an evolutionary way. Here the activities of analysis, design and system building can occur at any stage in the project. Pressman (1994) notes that with the spiral model evolving products can be represented by the radial arrows, as in Fig. 21.2. Thus the analysis phase of each cycle adds to the picture of the current system and the design phase to the logical design. Each successive build could give rise to a new release of the software, which would be formally accepted after the review part of the cycle. Finally, as more of the system is delivered, estimates will become more accurate and any risks will become more identifiable and containable.

It is this ability to respond to customer feedback and to control risk that has attracted so many to evolutionary development. However, to do this effectively each cycle has to be short and preferably timeboxed. Gilb (1988) states this succinctly by gearing development around the question 'How little development resource can we expend, and still accomplish something useful in the direction of our ultimate objectives?' Indeed, Gilb would argue that *every* project can be sub-divided into between ten and a hundred steps of useful delivery and so should be the subject of evolutionary development.

21.2 PROJECT BOARD RESPONSIBILITIES

Evolutionary development will only succeed with the full backing of senior management, for without this the project is likely to lack credibility in the eyes of the user community. In terms of PRINCE, the natural structure of an evolutionary project is to regard each cycle as a stage, and for the Project Board to appoint a Project/Stage Manager to look after the details of the individual cycles. The Project Board will only concern themselves with horizon planning and overall resource control. To be more specific, their responsibilities in an evolutionary development are:

- *Setting overall objectives.* The Board need to appreciate how the project fits in with the overall business and to decide which requirements are critical to the success of the project and which need to be addressed first. They must take the decision to use

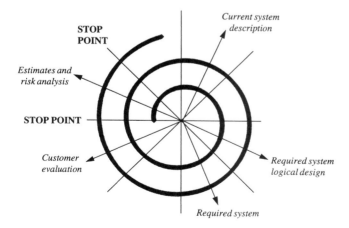

Fig. 21.2   Evolutionary products

an evolutionary approach and to agree a rough evolutionary plan. This need not be done right at the start. A standard feasibility study might indicate that an evolutionary development is best, in which case it then becomes the first cycle of the spiral.

- *Deciding on overall constraints.* How long the project must take, what resources are to be available and how the project should interface with existing systems and business practices.

- *Exercising overall management and control.* As the Project or Stage Manager could change from cycle to cycle, it is important that the Board retain overall control of the project. They will need overall estimates as to how long the entire project will take and what resources it will consume. At the end of each cycle these plans will be reviewed against the progress made.

- *Determining Open Architecture.* As the scope and size of the project will change from cycle to cycle, any method of implementation needs to be flexible. It is important therefore that the project is not limited by the choice of hardware platform or Database Management System. This might mean choosing a Database Management System that can be placed on a variety of platforms. At the very least some form of migration strategy needs to be formulated.

- *Ensuring the existence of a management infrastructure.* In most evolutionary developments, the cycles tend to be quick and the products ever-changing. For this reason it is vital that the following are addressed:
  — Configuration Management. This is needed to keep track of the numerous versions of any given product.
  — Quality Reviews. It is all too tempting on quick cycles to skimp quality/user reviews. This is a mistake. Quality procedures whether implemented by means of formal reviews, Fagin inspections or user workshops, are essential.
  — Testing and User Acceptance. In particular, what criteria are to be deployed before the software is formally released to the users?
  — Risk Management. Risk analysis attempts to measure the likelihood that the project will fail to achieve its objectives. When risks are recognized, they have to be managed. This might entail identifying critical success factors and threats, quantifying the impact of failure and measuring performance against the original analysis.* As both Gilb and Boehm have noted, the very adoption of an evolutionary approach makes risk management easier.

- *Communication with the project manager.* This generally takes place at two points in a cycle. Each cycle can only be authorized if a formal initiation document is agreed, while at the end the Project Board will review the results of the cycle. At both points the project could be stopped. Very occasionally the Board might be involved with the selection of options.

21.3 CYCLE TYPES

One of the great virtues of the spiral model is the way in which different approaches can be used on different cycles. A cycle can be of one of the following types:

---

*Risk management is the subject of a burgeoning literature. See, for example, Boehm (1989), Charette (1989) and Scarf *et al.* (1993).

- Exploratory
- Feasibility
- Rapid SSADM
- Rapid Rapid SSADM
- Package

An Exploratory Cycle is very informal, with its main objective being to explore areas of risk. It might involve building a preliminary prototype, benchmarking, visiting reference sites or simulations. If there is some doubt as to whether the business really needs a system, a soft systems approach could be used. At the end of an Exploratory Cycle it should be clearer as to whether the project is technically feasible and is really needed. A Feasibility Cycle might follow or even replace an Exploratory Cycle. This type of cycle uses the routemap appropriate to a feasibility study. Here most of the work takes place in the early part of the cycle, with combined business and technical options being presented to the Board. The design, build and test phases are not used and the review is concerned solely with assembling the Feasibility Report.

These preliminary cycles may or may not be used. Software development is accomplished by means of any of the other remaining cycle types. Quite often each cycle might focus on different areas of the business and do the analysis and design in full. Successive cycles need not, however, be of the same type. We might, for example, wish to release a 'quick and dirty' version of the software, which we would enhance later. For this, Rapid Rapid SSADM, followed by standard Rapid SSADM might be the appropriate development path. Other combinations can revolve around package solutions. The package routemap might be followed on the initial cycle, so giving the user a tried and tested system quickly. Subsequent cycles might be concerned with adding extra functionality to or around the package using Rapid SSADM in one of its formats.

21.4 THE CYCLE OBJECTIVES

This is where a formal agreement is made between the Project Board and the Project Manager as to the aims and objectives of the cycle. The agreement covers:

- *Broad objectives.* What is the major aim of the cycle and what are expected to be the major products? Initial cycle objectives are usually derived from overall project aims, but in later cycles might well be modified in the light of customer feedback to earlier work or of a changing business environment.
- *Timescales.* How long should the cycle take? It is usual for each cycle to be time-boxed and so take from two to six months.
- *Resources.* What staff, money and possibly computer facilities are available in the current cycle?
- *Priorities, constraints and limitations.* Every cycle gives the project management an opportunity to reassess these factors. They might have changed since the start of the project.
- *Cycle type.* Which routemap is to be followed by this cycle?
- *Technical platform.* If software is to be built, what is the target hardware and database?

The formal document which covers all these aspects is rather like a mini-Project Initiation Document which we will call a *Cycle Initiation Document* (CID).

As well as concentrating upon the immediate cycle the Project Manager has to consider the project as a whole, and so update overall Project Estimates and revisit Risk Analysis.

21.5 ANALYSIS

Analysis activities are usually far more detailed in earlier cycles. In later cycles, which might be devoted to refining an existing product, little more needs to be done than updating the Requirements and User Catalogues. Indeed in this case it might be sensible to split the Requirements Catalogue into

- The Requirements Catalogue proper—the original 'wish list'
- A Change Request Catalogue—changes to previous releases

One problem which does arise with incremental development is that of interim products. Do the Dataflow Diagrams and Logical Data Models describe the original base system, or do they include the products released in previous cycles?

For current Physical Dataflow Diagrams, the answer to this question depends to a large extent upon the way in which the project is structured. If the cycles look like

$$A, A, A, D + B, D + B, D + B, D + B, \ldots$$

where A stands for analysis and D + B for design and build, then analysis is confined to the first few cycles, with later cycles concentrating on adding polish and functionality to the basic product. A complete picture of the current physical system is obtained after the third cycle, and there seems little point in producing a series of Physical Dataflow Diagrams which show a partially manual, partially computerized system. On the other hand, cycles might look like

$$A + D + B, A + D + B, A + D + B, \ldots$$

This might be because the project is dealing separately with distinct business areas. It is unlikely here that the analysts could ever visualize a full Physical Dataflow Diagram of the original system since the products of earlier cycles will have become part of the working practices by the time the later analysis takes place. In this case, the Current Physical Dataflow Diagrams should reflect the interim systems.

The situation with regard to Logical Data Models and the functional decompositions is a little simpler. At each stage, the Logical Data Model represents the most complete picture of the data available at that time. Some entities may represent already computerized tables or files, others non-automated data in the system. Thus the current Logical Data Model is merely a step on the way towards the required Logical Data Model, and so must include the required model from previous cycles. In one sense we could regard a Logical Data Model from previous cycles as a type of corporate database that has to be included in the data model of the current cycle. The situation with regard to processing hierarchies is similar. In any cycle, a hierarchy consists of two parts, the computerized processes and those which are to be added to the system.

21.6 OPTIONS

If a cycle is long enough to merit a formal consideration of options, then a Combined Business and Technical Option is most appropriate. In most cases, however, the cycle is timeboxed and the technical platform, development costs, resources and timescales have already been decided and indeed form part of the Cycle Initiation Document. Thus, Options consists only of identifying those requirements to be addressed in the current cycle given the imposed constraints. These requirements should be chosen on basis of picking the low-cost, high-value ones first. The high-value ones are those of greatest importance to the users, the low-cost ones those that can be developed at smallest cost to the IS team. Any requirement which scores high on both counts is a prime candidate for inclusion in the system build. (In the words of Gilb, 1988, we choose the 'juiciest bits first'.)

   If the choice of options is limited in this way, there is usually no need to delay matters by submitting the options to the Project Board for approval.

21.7 DESIGN, BUILD, TEST AND IMPLEMENT

If full Rapid SSADM is used on a cycle these three phases would be kept separate, but if Rapid Rapid SSADM were to be used they would be combined. In the latter case, the interim software would itself be prototyped, leading to a model that appears to be a spiral within a spiral! Thus depending on the routemap chosen, testing can range from something that is included in prototyping to the full range of unit, system and acceptance testing. A major advantage of the evolutionary approach is that the consequences of incomplete or faulty testing are not quite so threatening as in the waterfall approach. If bugs do appear in a release of the software, they can be brought to the attention of the developers at a review, and addressed quite naturally as part of a later cycle. The principle of an open architecture underlying evolutionary development ensures that the product should be flexible enough to encompass any subsequent modifications.

   During these phases other non-SSADM products may be produced. In particular, user manuals need to be written and user training programmes designed. Finally, this phase might include the taking on of data. This might be done by porting information from one platform to another, or just by keying in data as part of user acceptance testing. (If, however, a lot of data needs to be captured for the first time, it would normally be done in parallel almost as if it were another project.)

21.8 REVIEW

The purpose of this phase is to evaluate the work done in the cycle and to report back to the Board. For an Exploratory Cycle this just consists of provisional findings and recommendations as to future action. In a Feasibility Cycle the findings are documented more formally by means of the Feasibility Report. If, however, a product has been built during the cycle, the report will cover:

- *Requirements addressed.* This details which requirements have been incorporated into the software and which are still outstanding.
- *Technical review.* This covers the efficiency of the system in terms of utilization of hardware and responsiveness.
- *Financial review.* This should compare the actual development and operating costs against the original estimates.
- *Customer evaluation.* This addresses the effectiveness of the system and its ease of use. It might involve a formal evaluation of the system against the non-functional usability requirements such as productivity, learnability, user satisfaction, memorability and error rates. The customer evaluation can also include problems that have arisen with earlier releases of the software in the course of time. Any issues cited by the customer could be brought forward as requirements for the next cycle.
- *Release decision.* A decision as to whether any software produced in this cycle is to be formally released or whether it will need further modifications.
- *Progress against plans.* A re-evaluation of the overall project estimates and plans in the light of progress within the cycle.
- *Recommendation.* This will examine if further cycles are necessary, and if they are, what should be their aims?

The review document will go to the Project Board who then decide either to stop the project or to proceed with further cycles.

21.9 ADVANTAGES OF AN EVOLUTIONARY APPROACH

1. *Ability to deal with 'problem requirements'.* In the introduction to this book it was argued that the waterfall approach was best suited to those projects, such as payroll, where the requirements are well known and stable. Unfortunately, projects of this type have mostly been done already, only surfacing from time to time as a legacy system in need of first aid. Modern projects are often characterized by fuzzy requirements which frequently change. An evolutionary approach is well suited to such cases. Many users are unsure as to what they really need until such time as they use a system for real. Early cycles of the spiral can be used as a low-cost mechanism to clarify requirements. Often it is then a case of users realizing what they do *not* want, but, even so, the chance to work with low-cost prototypes is valuable. Similarly, the evolutionary model is better able to cope with changing business requirements. The short timescales of the cycles and the resultant customer feedback will give ample warnings of any new requirements, and the flexibility implicit in a commitment to an open architecture makes a change in direction less difficult. Changing direction in the waterfall approach is rather like attempting to turn an oil tanker.

2. *Ability to deal with usability requirements.* All non-functional requirements such as user satisfaction are measured against a sliding scale. It is unlikely that such a requirement could be totally satisfied at the first attempt. Customer feedback,

however belated, is essential and opportunities have to be provided for making improvements to the system.

3. *User satisfaction.* The major way in which an evolutionary development aids user satisfaction is in the fast delivery of key aspects of the system. Half of a system within three months, with the rest following later, is usually far more preferable to the whole of the project in two years. Gilb (1988) describes a Swedish map-making project where the customers were so pleased with the early delivery of parts of the system that they were unconcerned about the late delivery of the rest. The in-built feedback mechanism also adds to user satisfaction. Not only can the development team react quickly to changing needs, but less satisfactory models can also be reworked.

4. *Reduction of risk.* Evolutionary projects are inherently less risky than waterfall projects. Any technical implementation difficulties are identified early in the project and can be addressed. Each cycle has a short timescale, expenditure is incremental and products are delivered earlier. At the end of each cycle the project management can measure progress against estimates and so obtain a more complete picture of the risk to the project. In the final analysis this means that the project can be cancelled early at minimum cost!

21.10 DISADVANTAGES OF AN EVOLUTIONARY APPROACH

1. *Change control.* In any evolutionary development many different versions of the same product will be produced. Without a strict and effective configuration management system, there is always the danger that the team works with out-of-date products.

2. *Painting oneself into a corner.* One of the prime requirements of an evolutionary approach is the adoption of an open architecture. This, however, is easier said than done. Even with sufficient care and foresight there is always the danger that hardware or database products appropriate to the more limited functionality or smaller scope of the earlier cycles might not be able to cope with the demands of later cycles.

3. *Managing contracts.* Evolutionary development is most appropriate to those systems that are built in-house or in conjunction with a stable partner. To make the whole of an evolutionary project the subject of a fixed contract poses problems. If the requirements are not expressed in full at the start of the project, there are no fixed criteria against which to judge the work should disagreements arise with a third party. On the other hand, making each cycle the subject of separate bids is little better. The very philosophy of evolutionary developments means that products evolve rather than being created afresh each cycle. Thus each new team on the project would have to accept the work of their predecessors, something that might prove difficult in a competitive situation.

4. *Never-ending project.* Unless managed carefully, an evolutionary project can go on forever. This is unlikely to happen in those situations where a customer is charged separately for each cycle, but is a real danger if in-house projects are developed under some form of general funding umbrella.

5. *Rewriting*. Evolutionary products do get recast and rewritten. Although this should lead to a better product, it is expensive.

21.11 THE FUTURE

Evolutionary development is not fully accepted at the moment. In the opinion of the author this is something that will inevitably have to change in the next few years. The major reason for this is to do with the changing business environment. The days of the two-year project, let alone the five-year one, are long gone. Business requirements change month by month, and the systems we build must be flexible enough to accommodate these changes. The standard waterfall approach really requires the requirements set in concrete at the start of the project and this is no longer feasible. In adopting an evolutionary approach we are at least attempting to confront reality.

Current technical changes provide us with a second reason for the adoption of evolutionary methods of development. In the past few years powerful 4GLs have become more and more common. These tools provide us with the power to generate systems quickly, and make an open architecture much more achievable. At worst, migration from one product to another does not have the dire consequences it once had in the days of proprietary operating systems and hand-crafted code. At the time of writing a major issue concerns the development of Graphical User Interfaces. Allied to this is the increasing concentration on non-functional requirements such as usability. Users often want more than a standard IS solution from their systems, for they are increasingly aware of Graphical User Interfaces and multimedia. In the author's opinion, a truly usable system will usually evolve from customer feedback to working systems, rather than be designed from paper requirements. A waterfall approach is really best suited to satisfying functional requirements, those that are done or not done. An evolutionary approach does, moreover, give the development team an opportunity to explore innovative technical solutions. Finally, appearing from over the horizon are Object Orientated methods. Although many attempts have been made to overlay standard methodologies with object orientated principles, the waterfall approach seems contrary to the Object Orientated paradigm.

TWENTY-TWO

GRAPHICAL USER INTERFACES AND OBJECT ORIENTATION

22.1 INTRODUCTION

In the past few years two major themes running through systems development work have been the rise of the Graphical User Interface and the approach of Object Orientation. It is impossible to give a full description of these topics within the confines of this book, but what we can do is to indicate the impact each might have on Rapid SSADM.

22.2 GRAPHICAL USER INTERFACES

The term 'Graphical User Interface' is used to describe a particular type of screen handling which supports communication between a user and the system. These screens are typically designed around a number of components, referred to collectively by the acronym WIMP (Windows, Icons, Menus and Pointing devices). A window is a re-sizable area of the screen within which a function can run. At any one time several windows can occupy the screen, although only one is usually active. An icon is a small image of an object, which might be a document, record, or even a process, such as a spreadsheet. The use of icons enables 'drag and drop' actions. The best known of these is probably on the Apple Macintosh, where a document is deleted by dragging its icon and dropping it onto the wastebin icon. Menus usually present the user with lists via a 'pull-down' or 'pop-up' mechanism. Finally, the pointing device is something which can be used to select objects on the screen, and in most systems consists of a mouse. Its use leads to the use of pushbuttons, radio buttons and check boxes in the dialogues.

Until comparatively recently, the user interface on many systems was implemented on dumb terminals, which were character-based and monochrome. This was especially true for those systems intended to run on large mainframes. Nowadays, more and more systems are being designed on client/server architecture with a Graphical User Interface specified as part of the requirements. The increasing popularity of these interfaces has in part been supplier driven with developers eager to use the new tools, but on the whole has been demand led with customers insisting that their bespoke systems are as easy to use as their Windows-based wordprocessors and spreadsheets.

In spite of a superficial surface attractiveness, there is no guarantee that a Graphical User Interface is inherently easier to use than a character-based interface. Graphical User Interfaces do present the system designer with a large number of facilities and allow her or him a great deal of freedom. Unfortunately, this merely increases the possibility of producing a bad, if not thoroughly unusable, interface. It seems that few people have the right combination of technical ability and artistic flair needed to create an effective Graphical User Interface on their own. The rest of us need guidance. Fortunately, there is a good deal of advice on how to design Graphical User Interfaces and on how to support the work of users with one. What is less common are guidelines as to how this advice can be incorporated into SSADM. At present, there appear to be just two approaches advocated:

1. System-centred approach. Here the major analysis and design activities are done as usual, and the Graphical User Interface advice merely consists of guidelines on how screens should be designed in a Windows type of environment.
2. User-centred approach. This is more radical. The required system is viewed not so much as something that is important in itself but as something that enables and supports the work of users. Much of the initial analysis of SSADM is changed to reflect these principles.

Whichever approach is used, there is agreement that standards are vital. Graphical User Interfaces allow so much freedom, that without agreed standards users might be confronted with a variety of conflicting Graphical User Interface screens and so end up being thoroughly confused. Both approaches advocate the creation of an Installation Style Guide, a document which establishes guidelines so that all an organization's systems are given a common 'look and feel'. Such a guide will probably be based upon recognized industry-wide standards contained in the advice issued by the major vendors (cf. Apple Computer Inc., 1992 and Microsoft, 1992).

22.3 SYSTEM-CENTRED APPROACH

The main advocates of the system-centred approach are Robinson and Berrisford (1994). This approach requires little change to the structure of SSADM, with windows being defined around events and enquiries. The authors define windows as being one of a number of types:

- *System Entry Menus.* A window used to control entry to the system.
- *Entity Reference Lists.* How to display a collection of entity occurrences. This could be done as a table or as a scrollable list.

- *Entity Reference Window*. How the details of an entity are to be displayed. Typically this would be realized as some kind of form.
- *Data Entry Windows*. These are used to obtain the data necessary to trigger an event or enquiry.
- *Response Windows*. These are used to display the results of an event or, more particularly, an enquiry.
- *Message Boxes*. These are used for confirmation, error and success messages.

The authors also define a number of 'mini-dialogue' templates to show how these windows can be combined to deal with simple enquiries and events. More complicated windows are constructed to deal with 'multi-event' functions, such as those where a master and all its accompanying details are dealt with together. Finally, dialogue navigation is illustrated by means of a flowchart type of mechanism.

This approach to Graphical User Interface design does not impact greatly upon the structure of Rapid SSADM as presented so far. The major difference is the way that Robinson and Berrisford define update processing in terms of events rather than functions. This, however, is no great problem provided that functions are kept small. When this is done there will usually be a one-to-one correspondence between events and functions, and so the Graphical User Interface design principles can be applied equally as well to a function as to an event. Those instances in which a function incorporates many events are covered by their multi-event window. The mini-dialogue templates show a marked similarity to the syntax diagrams we used for dialogue navigation. Much of this design activity would take place in step 330 of Rapid SSADM, with the remaining advice about dialogue navigation being more applicable to the work of step 630.

Robinson and Berrisford admit that the system-centred approach to Graphical User Interface design does tend to generate a fairly crude interface. On the other hand, it can be produced rapidly and caters for all the functionality of the required system. One interesting problem highlighted by this approach is that of windows in a multi-user environment. What happens to inactive windows if their data is changed by another user? This problem is rarely addressed by user-centred approaches, which by their very nature tend to focus on the needs of the individual.

Robinson and Berrisford are concerned with Graphical User Interface design that is applicable to any windowing type of system. The advice they give has to be general, since it has to apply to any suitable technical option. In practice, the target database is usually known, and if speed is of the essence, a 'quick and dirty' approach of modifying some of the automatically generated screens may be of value. Microsoft Access, for example, contains a number of in-built 'wizards' to make such a task even easier. Finally, many products come bundled with sample databases, which can themselves prove to be a fruitful source of ideas.

22.4 USER-CENTRED APPROACH

This approach to Graphical User Interface design is more fundamental in the sense that much of the philosophy and many of the techniques embodied in such an approach underlie the very design of the desktop metaphor incorporated into a windowing type of interface. It is very broadly based, calling upon elements of psychology and other behavioural sciences. As such, it is a more radical departure from traditional SSADM in that in that its major objective is not to automate an existing *system* but to support the work of an *individual* user. In order to bridge this gap, the SSADM User Group established a working party to produce some definitive guidance. This they did and published the results in the book *SSADM and GUI Design: A Project Manager's Guide*. It is not a complete guide in that it does not document or recommend specific techniques for practitioners, but rather points them in the direction of the appropriate literature. In line with its title, it gives project managers advice on what new products will be required, what additional activities should take place and where in the method this all should happen. The activities recommended by the working party for inclusion in SSADM are as follows:

- *User Analysis.* The purpose here is to provide a much more detailed description of the users of the proposed system than that traditionally provided by the SSADM User Catalogue. Frequency of use, existing Information Technology experience, languages and other computer systems used are only a few of the factors to be considered. The main product of this activity are User Class Descriptions which are added to the end of the User Catalogue.
- *Usability Analysis.* The working party argued that usability requirements are essential for any Graphical User Interface development. These are referred to collectively by the acronym PLUME (Productivity, Learnability, User Satisfaction, Error Rates and Memorability). We have already argued that these criteria should be applied to any system, not just those incorporating Graphical User Interfaces, and so have included usability criteria as non-functional requirements.
- *Task Modelling.* This technique can be used to document user tasks. It emphasizes the sequencing of tasks and indicates those that can be done in parallel. The official guide is not specific about how the task model should be documented. Flowcharts or syntax diagrams are possibilities. Browne (1994) uses Jackson structures. This is probably best if a top-down approach, decomposing tasks into sub-tasks, is appropriate to the situation being analysed. Browne also recommends a number of additional techniques—Knowledge Representation Grammars, Task Allocation Charts and Dichotomy Scoping Charts—to complete a full picture of user activity.
- *Task Scenario Definition.* This activity is carried on in parallel with task modelling. Its purpose is to provide specific concrete examples of user tasks. It can be used to initiate the task modelling process and also to provide test cases for validation of the final task model. Hix and Hartson (1993) use a technique called User Action Notation for this purpose. Use Cases, invented by Jacobson *et al.* (1992), do a similar job from an Object Orientated perspective.
- *Style Guide Definition.* The purpose of this is to ensure that all an organization's applications have a common look and feel. There is a great deal of advice on this topic, including some from CCTA (CCTA, 1991a, b). Probably most influential is that produced by the manufacturers (see, for example Apple Computer Inc., 1992, and Microsoft, 1992). All this advice needs to be adapted to the specific organization and included in the Installation Style Guide.
- *User Conceptual Modelling.* The purpose of this technique is to identify user objects. These are the things that the user believes makes up the system and they could vary

between individual users. User objects can have attributes, behaviour and relationships with other objects. As well as business objects, such as Customers, they might also include interface objects, such as printers. User Objects seem little different from objects as defined in Object Orientated Analysis methods. They can be used to identify functions in a similar manner to the way in which we used groupings on the Logical Data Model.

- *Graphical User Interface Design.* The main objective here is to list the windows and other Graphical User Interface components needed to support the processing, to design the individual windows and to specify the navigation between windows. The approach suggested in SSUG (1994) is to base windows upon User Objects and to use Task Scenarios to validate the design. An alternative approach, suggested by Browne (1994), is to base the design more directly on the task model, and use a number of heuristics, such as the need to make a decision, for the identification of windows.

- *User Interface Prototyping.* This is essential when a Graphical User Interface is employed. A full description of this activity is given in CCTA (1993) and Browne (1994).

- *Graphical User Interface Evaluation.* As we have noted, most of the usability requirements have to be tested. Doing this against the prototype will indicate how successful the system is likely to be. Impact tables, as defined in Gilb (1988), can be used for this purpose.

22.5 CHANGES TO THE STRUCTURAL MODEL

The SSADM User Group Working party did consider what changes to the structure of SSADM Version 4 would result from the adoption of these user-centred Graphical User Interface techniques. In a similar way we will need to see how they affect Rapid SSADM.

Only minimal changes have to made to stages 1 and 2. As we have already included usability criteria in our basic model, all that needs adding to step 120 is an extended User Catalogue. The Dataflow Model in step 130 will probably be augmented by Task Scenarios and Task Models for the current system. If this is done, the bottom-level processes on the Current Physical Dataflow Model will often be named after tasks, in which case it is clear that Task Models will then replace Elementary Process Descriptions. Given this emphasis on current procedures, there seems little point in developing the Logical Dataflow Model beyond a functional decomposition. As far as stage 2 is concerned, the working party also suggested that Business System Options should include the selection of an appropriate Graphical User Interface standard. This is unlikely to be a major issue as such a standard will probably have already been adopted by the organization as a whole.

It is in stage 3 that the major changes take place. Figure 22.1 shows a Graphical User Interface routemap with the additional steps highlighted. The first of these is step 305 in which a Task Model is developed for the required system. The tasks that have been identified together with any work that is less user centred, such as housekeeping, go to make up the Required Dataflow Model. As so much of the processing is incorporated into the task models, there seems little point in developing a full Dataflow

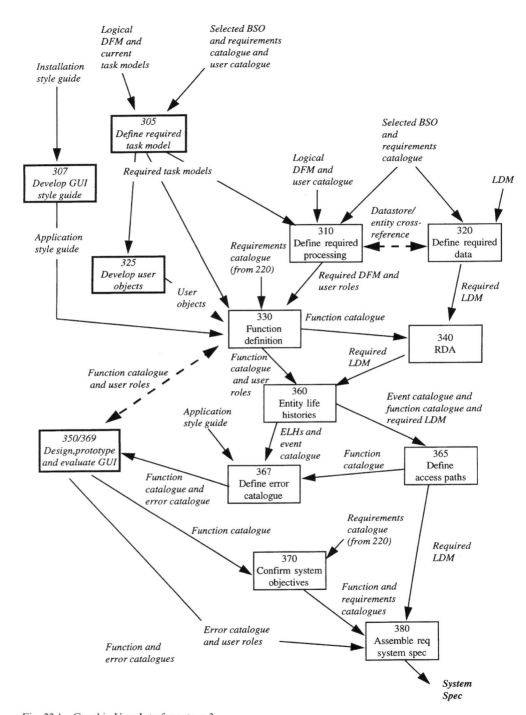

Fig. 22.1 Graphic User Interface stage 3

Model; a functional decomposition and context diagram would probably suffice. The task models can also be used as an input to the development of User Objects in step 325. Browne (1994) shows how Knowledge Representation Grammars, which he generates in conjunction with task models, can generate Object Lists. The User Objects, the User Tasks and the required processes all represent functions from subtly different perspectives, and so all serve as inputs to function definition. Function definition is also concerned with the definition of input and output. In their guide, the working party suggested abandoning I/O structures and using annotated I/O descriptions. Rapid SSADM suggests going a stage further than this and producing initial window designs. These will be very much a first cut and may be modified considerably by the process of Graphical User Interface design. However, this does mean that the Application Style Guide must be completed before Function Definition. For this reason it has been given the step number of 307, not 335 as in SSUG (1994). This is unlikely to be a major problem, since any Installation Standards are conceived as providing a common interface for a whole raft of projects and so would in all probability already exist. Finally, in SSUG (1994) Graphical User Interface design, Prototyping and Graphical User Interface Evaluation take place after Entity Life Histories, in step 365. Unfortunately, we already use this step for Access Path Analysis, and so have had to call it step 369. As the first cut windows are produced as part of Function Definition in Rapid SSADM, Specification Prototyping could well be pulled forward to its usual place, that is, step 350.

The rest of Rapid SSADM is not greatly affected by Graphical User Interface issues. Obviously, the Technical Option will have to support the chosen Graphical User Interface. The majority of the Graphical User Interface design issues will be documented in the Function Catalogue that emerges from the prototyping step. In Dialogue Design, step 630, the packaging of the functions and the navigation between the functions will be finalized.

As far as Rapid Rapid SSADM is concerned, the changes are quite minimal. Task modelling can be regarded as an additional way of describing the current system, User Objects another way of teasing out functions and GUI design and prototyping as something to be included in step 350, the rapid prototype and build step.

22.6 OBJECT ORIENTATION

A second area of concern to systems analysts is Object Orientation. Advocates of Object Orientated (OO) methods claim that its emphasis on re-usable components, or 'objects', leads to a simpler, fast and more cost-effective design process. There is some debate as to whether these claims are real or are just hype.* If, however, Object Orientation does realize a fraction of what is promised, it is something that cannot be ignored by any systems development methodology.

---

*The author believes that re-use as a justification for Object Orientation is vastly over-rated outside a few specialist areas such as Graphical User Interface design. There appear to be very few libraries of business objects commercially available. In the author's opinion encapsulation and message passing are where the true benefits of Object Orientation lie. Both lead to a simpler design especially in situations characterized by distributed processing including client/server.

One common misconception about Object Orientation is that it is another term for Graphical User Interface construction. Although most modern Graphical User Interfaces are built from predefined components using Object Orientation principles, it is perfectly possible, if more tedious, to do this using conventional programming methods. Conversely, Graphical User Interface design is only one area addressed by Object Orientation methods. The principles of object orientation can be applied to analysis, design and programming of any system. These systems can range from standard business to process control systems.

Object orientated methods are characterized by the following concepts:

- *Objects.* An object is the basic building block of the system. It represents something of interest to the system and about which the system wishes to keep information. Like an entity, an object will have properties or attributes, but it will also have behaviour, usually called methods or operations. Generally speaking, an object should represent something in the real world, for example 'John Smith' or 'The New Grants project'.
- *Abstraction.* Objects which have the same structure and behaviour are grouped into classes. Thus a class may be regarded as a template out of which new objects can be created. One often says that an object is an instance of a class. In analysis we normally deal with classes rather than particular objects. Figure 22.2 shows a popular graphical representation of a class (due to Coad and Yourdon, 1990).
- *Encapsulation.* This is sometimes known as 'information hiding'. The data structures and the internal workings of the methods of a particular object are hidden from all other objects in the system. An object presents a public interface to other objects and can only be addressed by calling its methods. This principle should also apply to its attributes. Thus for a *Bank Account* object it should not be possible to access the Balance directly, but only via a method called 'Get Balance', say.
- *Inheritance.* A class can be a sub-class of another class and inherit attributes and methods from the superclass. Thus in Fig. 22.3, the classes *Cheque A/C* and *Savings A/C* are really types of Bank Accounts. Each of the two sub-classes inherits the attributes 'Customer' and 'Balance' and the methods 'Make Deposit' and 'Make withdrawal' from the Bank Account class. Each also adds attributes and methods of its own.
- *Message passing.* Objects communicate by passing messages. The message activates a method in the receiving object which usually sends a response.
- *Polymorphism.* This is the ability to use the same name to denote different methods.

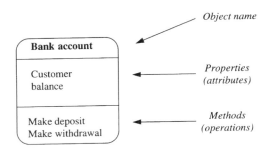

Fig. 22.2   Encapsulation

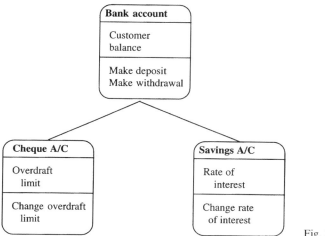

Fig. 22.3   Inheritance

Different objects might react to the same message in different ways. Thus an object representing a *Cash Machine* might understand the message 'Make withdrawal' but respond in a different way to a *Safe* object.

- *Re-use*. This is achieved by declaring a new sub-class of an existing class. The new class inherits all the tried and tested attributes and methods of the old class, but can also be equipped with newly created attributes and methods and have undesirable ones overridden.

Object orientated ideas were first used in the programming field. Since the 1980s a number of Object Orientation programming languages have been successfully employed. The chief among these are C++ and Smalltalk. The success of these languages led to an interest in Object Orientation System Design which itself triggered the search for an Object Orientation System Analysis method. Good surveys of the work done in this field are Graham (1994) and Henderson-Sellers (1992).

As far as Analysis and Design is concerned, Graham documents nearly fifty competing methods. These he divides into two types, those that rely solely on an Object Model and those that draw on the experience of structured methods by having three views of the required system. These views are:

- An Object Model. This usually looks a little like a Logical Data Model, but with extra types of relationship and with the addition of methods.
- A Dynamic Model. This attempts to model the changes that can occur to an object. We will refer to this as an Object Life History, though technically it really is a Class Life History. The favoured representation tends to be State Transition Diagrams rather than Jackson diagrams.
- A Functional Model. This usually describes the required system in terms of Dataflow Diagrams or of a functional decomposition.

The best known of the 'three-view' approaches is OMT (Rumbaugh *et al.*, 1991) and at present looks to be the most favoured method for those attempting to migrate from

SSADM. This might not be the case in the future, as day by day new methods are being invented and older ones tend to coalesce. What is not in doubt is the increasing awareness of the Object Orientation community to the importance of structured methods, and to the need to produce an easy migration path from them to an Object Orientation method.

Figure 22.4 shows what SSADM analysis *might* look like if we attempt to incorporate elements of something similar to OMT into the method. Many of the Object Orientation techniques have their parallels in SSADM. For this reason, I have tried to keep in line with the structure of Rapid SSADM, mapping similar techniques onto the same step number. This has given rise to a number of anomalies, not least of which is that step 360 appears to precede step 330. Indeed, it could well be argued that the three-schema architecture would be a much better representation of the method, since an Object Model embodies many business rules, and so is almost a complete SSADM Conceptual Model.

Stage 1 of SSADM looks fairly familiar. An investigation of the current processing could involve the production of Dataflow Diagrams, task scenarios or task models. An overall picture of what the system does is best done by means of a processing hierarchy in step 150. The establishment of the Requirement and User Catalogues in step 120 is again the same as in standard SSADM. An alternate approach to process documentation and requirements elicitation is that of the Use Case (Jacobson *et al.*, 1992).

Producing the Object Model must be the heart of any Object Orientation analysis method. At first, this is very similar to producing a Logical Data Model. Indeed, the Object Model of OMT looks just like a Logical Data Structure with additional types of relationship denoting inheritance and aggregation. The weak link in most Object Orientation approaches seems to be the identification of methods. Many of these approaches leave this task to the Dynamic and Functional models, only adding methods to the Object Model when the three approaches are reconciled. While this is a good way of checking that the appropriate methods exist, using it as the sole way of generating them seems to be far too application dependent and would mitigate against future re-use. As Henderson-Sellers (1992) notes, after identifying a *Bank Account* object, we need to take a step backwards and ask ourselves what sort of thing would or could we want to do with this object. One approach which might offer something here is that of CRC cards (see Wirfs-Brock *et al.*, 1990).

Stage 2 of SSADM looks the same. If users are to be provided with some form of choice, Business System Options are essential. In step 310 processing is defined for the new system. Again this can be done by means of Dataflow Diagrams, task models or a functional decomposition. The required Object Model is developed in step 320, with Object Life Histories documented soon after. Although most Object Orientation methods tend to use State Transition diagrams, there is no reason why Object Life Histories should not be developed in the same way as Entity Life Histories, that is, using eventflows or Jackson diagrams.* The major purpose of any form of life history analysis is to ensure that system processing exists to cope with all the identified events.

---

*Graham (1994) has argued that the reason most Object Orientation methods use State Transition diagrams is to do with their roots in real-time systems, where the state of an object (e.g. 'idle', 'in use') is important. There is no reason to think that this should be so in IS applications.

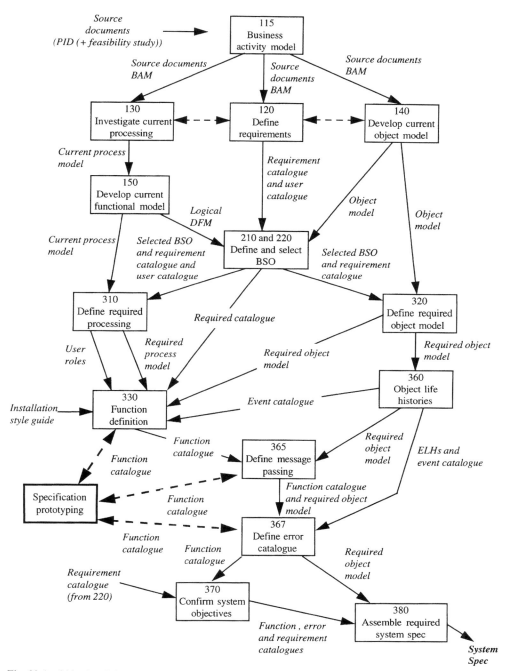

Fig. 22.4   Objective Orientation Analysis

Thus the life histories can be cross-checked immediately against the methods on the Object Model and the entries on the functional decomposition. Functions would be defined in the usual SSADM way as user-defined processing tasks. If there is difficulty in constructing functions, as with the Graphical User Interface approach the objects themselves might prove to be useful starting points. First cut screen/window and report layouts are also produced as part of function definition.

Step 365 assumes a greater importance in Object Orientation analysis than it does in standard SSADM. The Access Path notation can be extended to deal with message passing and with method invocation. One 'Message Diagram' will be produced per function and can be used to validate the object model, ensuring not only that the methods exist but also that the attributes required for generation of the output are present. An example is illustrated in Fig. 22.5. This shows the message passing that takes place when all transactions during the previous month are displayed on screen. The soft-edged boxes denote the objects and the arrows the messages together with accompanying parameters. The methods invoked are shown in the bottom section of the object nodes. Class methods, as distinct from instance methods, are shown by a 'double-edged' box. Finally, note that the interface objects, such as keyboard and screen, are also required. The Message Diagrams are also useful in revisiting the allocation of responsibilities between objects. If, for example, Object A often calls upon method X in Object B, the question should be raised as to whether method X could be transferred to A.

Specification processing has been included without a step number. It can be used during Function Definition to test the User Interface and later to evaluate the full design. One technique that is missing from Fig. 22.4 is RDA. This is quite intentional, since many of the objects might not be normalized. The classic example of this is an *Order*. Using Relational Data Analysis this would be split into two entities *Order (Head)* and *Order Line*. As far as objects are concerned, there is no reason for this split. Each line is an intrinsic part of an order and would be perceived as such by a user.

Our routemap stops at the end of stage 3, without addressing the detailed design, build and testing of the system. At present, there is no agreed standard way of proceeding. Object Orientation analysis could lead on to Object Orientation design with Object Orientation languages or it could lead to conventional programming. Object Databases are still in their infancy, and a number of techniques exist for mapping objects onto relational databases. Finally, there is the question of how to search existing class libraries in pursuit of the Holy Grail of re-use! Thus for the present, there seems no easy way of extending Fig. 22.4 to incorporate physical design. In practice, an analyst would have to rely on a number of strategies that could be applied in different situations.

A final point needs to be made about prototyping. Both Graphical User Interface Design and Object Orientation have been presented as straight-through, waterfall type models. In practice, neither would be used like this, but would be subject to an evolutionary form of development. Thus the routemaps presented in this chapter can best be thought of as being one cycle around the evolutionary spiral.

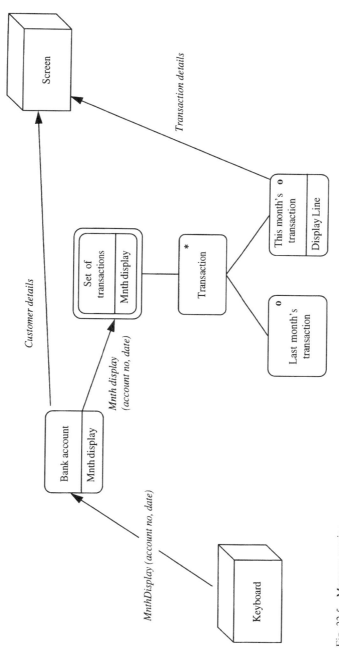

Fig. 22.5 Message passing

REFERENCES

Apple Computer Inc. (1992): *Macintosh Human Interface Guidelines*, Addison-Wesley, Reading, MA, USA.

Ashworth, C. and Slater, L. (1993): *An Introduction to SSADM Version 4*, McGraw-Hill Book Company Europe, Maidenhead, UK.

Bachman, C. W. (1969): 'Data structure diagrams', *Data Base*, **1**, No 2, Summer.

Baker, K. (1994): 'Setting the pace in IT purchasing', *Government Computing*, February.

Berard, E. V. (1990): 'Life-cycle approaches', *Hotline on Object-Oriented Technology*, **1** (6), p. 364.

Boehm, B. W. (1988): 'A spiral model of development and enhancement', *IEEE Computer*, **21** No. 5, May, pp. 61–72.

Boehm, B. W. (1989): *Software Risk Management*, IEEE Computer Society Press, New York, USA.

Browne, D. (1994): S*TUDIO: STructured User-interface Design for Interaction Optimisation*, Prentice Hall, Englewood Cliffs, NJ, USA.

CCTA (1990a): *SSADM Version 4 Reference Manual*, NCC/Blackwell, Oxford, UK.

CCTA (1990b): *PRINCE: Structured Project Management*, NCC/Blackwell, Oxford, UK.

CCTA (1990c): *PRINCE in Small IT Projects*, NCC/Blackwell, Oxford, UK.

CCTA (1991a): *User Interface: Style Guide Issues*, HMSO, London, UK.

CCTA (1991b): *User Interface: Style Migration Issues*, HMSO, London, UK.

CCTA (1993): *Prototyping in an SSADM Environment*, HMSO, London, UK.

CCTA (1994): *Customising SSADM*, HMSO, London, UK.

CCTA (1995): *SSADM Version 4.2 Reference Manual*, NCC/Blackwell, Oxford, UK.

Chen, P. P. (1976): 'The entity-relationship model — towards a unified view of data', *ACM TODS*, **1**, No. 1.

Charete, R. N. (1989): *Software Engineering Risk Analysis and Management*, McGraw-Hill Book Company Europe, Maidenhead, UK.

Checkland, P. B. (1981): *Systems Thinking, Systems Practice*, Wiley, New York, USA.

Clifton, H. D. (1990): *Business Data Systems*, 4th edition, Prentice Hall, Englewood Cliffs, NJ, USA.

Coad, P. and Yourdon, E. (1990): *Object-Orientated Analysis*, Prentice-Hall, Englewood Cliffs, NJ, USA.

Codd, E. F. (1970): 'A relational model of data for large shared data banks', *CACM*, **13**, No. 6, June, 1970.

Codd, E. F. (1972): *Further Normalisation of the Data Base Relational Model*, Data Base Systems, Courant Computer Science Symposia Series, Vol. 6, Prentice Hall, Englewood Cliffs, NJ, USA.

Connel, J. L. and Shafer L. B. (1989): *Structured Rapid Prototyping: An Evolutionary Approach to Software Development*, Yourdon Press/Prentice-Hall, New York.

Date, C. J. (1978): *Structured Analysis and System Specification*, Prentice Hall, Englewood Cliffs, NJ, USA.

De Marco, T. (1978): *Structured Analysis and System Specification*, Yourdon Press/Prentice Hall, New York.

DSDM Consortium (1995): *Dynamic Systems Development Method*, Tesserat Publishing, Farnham, Surrey, UK.

Eva, M. (1992): *SSADM Version 4: A User's Guide*, McGraw-Hill Book Company Europe, Maidenhead, UK.

Gane, C. and Sarson T. (1977): *Structured Systems Analysis: tools and techniques*, Improved System Technologies Inc., USA

Gardner, M. (1970): *The Annotated Alice* (revised edition), Penguin Books, Harmondsworth, Middlesex, UK.

Gilb, T. (1988): *Principles of Software Engineering Management*, Addison-Wesley, Reading, MA, USA.

Goodland, M. and Slater, C. (1995): *SSADM: A Practical Approach*, 2nd edition, McGraw-Hill, Maidenhead, UK.

Graham, I. (1994): *Object Orientated Methods*, 2nd edition, Addison-Wesley, Reading, MA, USA.

Hargrave, D. (1995): *The Limitations of Jackson Representations*, ISUG Technical Journal, 1995.

Henderson-Sellers, B. (1992): *A Book of Object-Orientated Knowledge*, Prentice Hall, Englewood Cliffs, NJ, USA.

Hix, D. and Hartson, H. R. (1993): *Developing User Interfaces: Ensuring Usability through Product and Process*, Wiley, New York, USA.

Hopcroft, J. E. and Ullman, J. D. (1979): *Introduction to Automata Theory, Languages and Computation*, Addison-Wesley, Reading, MA, USA.

Jacobson, I., Christerson, M., Jonsson, P. and Overgaard, G. (1992): *Object Orientated Software Engineering: A Use Case Driven Approach*, Addison-Wesley, Reading, MA, USA.

Love, T. (1995): *Seven Deadly Sins of Object-Orientated Development*, Information Systems Management, vol. 12, No. 3, Summer 1995.

Microsoft (1992): *The Windows Interface, an Application Design Guide*, USA.

Osborn, A., McFadyen, A. and Holdship, S. (1993): *SSADM Oracle Interface Guide*, Oracle, USA.

Pressman, R. S. (1994): *Software Engineering: A Practitioner's Approach*, McGraw-Hill Book Company Europe, Maidenhead, UK.

Rayward-Smith, V. J. (1983): *A First Course in Formal Language Theory*, Blackwell, Oxford, UK.

Robinson, K. and Berrisford, G. (1994): *Object-Orientated SSADM*, Prentice Hall, Englewood Cliffs, NJ, USA.

Rumbaugh, J., Blaha, M., Premerlani, W., Eddy, F. and Lorensen, W. (1991): *Object-Orientated Modelling and Design*, Prentice Hall, Englewood Cliffs, NJ, USA.

Scarff, F., Carty, A. and Charette, R. (1993): *Introduction to the Management of Risk*, CCTA/HMSO, London, UK.

Skidmore, S., Farmer, R. and Mills, G. (1992): *SSADM Version 4 Models and Methods*, NCC/Blackwell, Oxford, UK.

SSUG (International SSADM User Group) (1994): *SSADM and GUI Design: A Project Manager's Guide*, London, UK.

Weaver, P. L. (1993): *Practical SSADM Version 4*, Pitman, London, UK.

Williams, M. (1994): 'Managing project risks systematically', *Project Manager Today*, **VII**(6).

Wilson, B. (1992): *Systems: Concepts, Methodologies and Applications*, (2nd ed.), Wiley, New York, USA.

Wirfs-Brock, R., Wilkerson, B. and Wiener, L. (1990): *Designing Object Orientated Software*, Prentice Hall, Englewood Cliffs, NJ, USA.

ONE

PRODUCT DESCRIPTIONS

This appendix consists of two parts:

1. A complete list of all the final products produced by the full version of Rapid SSADM. Note that it does not contain transient products that are internal to a particular step (e.g. Entity Access Matrix). *These products can be tailored (reduced or omitted) for even faster versions of SSADM!*
2. A Products Usage matrix showing the steps at which these products are created, updated and just used without change. Not only does this give an idea of the importance of products, it is also useful in Version Control.

Application Development Standards   This documents the Physical Design Strategy for the proposed database product. It will show how the Logical Data Model can be converted into a physical database and the functions into programs.

Business Activity Model (BAM)   Used to establish the business context in which the system is to operate. It consists of:
Statement of Business Objectives
Context Diagram
Functional decomposition
Business Activity Descriptions

Business System Option (BSO)   The selected Business System Option is produced in stage 2 and basically shows which requirements are to be satisfied by the proposed system. This list is accompanied by estimated costs and benefits, proposed development timescales, some indication as to the impact on the business and the option's risk. Note that the non-selected options, although forming part of the project management documentation, are not really final products as far as SSADM is concerned.

Database design   Developed according to the Application Development Standards.

Dataflow Model (DFM)   Two versions of this are produced, one for the Current Physical System and one for the Current Logical System. It consists of:

Dataflow diagrams (all levels)
Elementary Process Descriptions
External Entity List
Input/Output Descriptions
Datastore descriptions

Dialogue Specifications   Show how the programs are packaged together for each User Role. Developed according to the Application Development Standards.

Entity Life Histories (ELHs)   For each entity these show what can create, change and delete an occurrence of the entity. They are produced in step 360, and are only used in one other step (367), where they cross-check any state transition matrices that are produced. For this reason they are not really final products in the same sense as others listed here.

Error Catalogue   Documents all the error messages produced by the functions.

Event Catalogue   Lists all the events in the system that trigger updates and cross-references events to functions.

Function Catalogue   Describes the processing requirements of the Required System. Contains for each function:

Function Definition
Input and Output formats
Access Path
Access Path Description
Function Error List

Function Component Implementation Map (FCIM)   This is a matrix which cross-references functions to programs.

Logical Data Model (LDM)   Describes the data used in the system. Two versions of the model produced, one for the current system and one for the required system. It consists of:

Logical Data Structure
Entity descriptions
Relationship descriptions
Volumetrics

Program Specifications   Developed according to the Application Development Standards.

Required Processing Model   Used to model the processing in the Required System. A full model consists of:

Context Diagram
Functional Decomposition
Dataflow Diagrams (all levels)
Elementary Process Descriptions
External Entity List
Input/Output Descriptions
Datastore entity cross-reference

Requirements Catalogue   A much-used document which itemizes all the requirements for the required system. Modified later at Business System Option stage.

Technical System Option (TSO)   The selected Technical System Option basically shows how the requirements of the proposed system are to be technically implemented. The option consists of technical environment description, the functionality of the proposed system, estimated costs and benefits, proposed development timescales, some indication as to the impact on the business and the option's risk. Note that the non-selected options, although forming part of the project management documentation, are not really final products as far as SSADM is concerned.

User Catalogue   List of prospective users of the new system.

User Roles Catalogue   Users of the new system cross-referenced against the required functions.

Product Usage

Technical products	Step 115	Step 120	Step 130	Step 140	Step 150	Step 210/20	Step 310	Step 320	Step 330	Step 340	Step 350	Step 360	Step 365	Step 367	Step 370	Step 410/20	Step 610	Step 620	Step 630	Step 640	Step 650
Business Activity Model	C																				
Requirements Catalogue		C	U	U	U	I	I	I	I		I*	I				I					
User Catalogue		C	U	U	U	I	U				I*	I								I	
Current Physical DFM			C	I	I	U															
Current LDM				C	I	I															
Current Logical DFM					C	I															
Business System Option					C	C															
Required Processing Model						I	C														
Required LDM						I	C	C	C	U	U	U	U	U	U						
Function Catalogue							I	I	C	I	I*	C	C	C	I	I	I	I	I	I	I
User Roles									C	I*					I	I	I	I	I	I	I
ELHs									C	I	C										
Event Catalogue										I	I*	C	U	U							
Error Catalogue										I	I*	C	U	C							
Technical Option											U	C	C		C	I	I	I			
Application Development Standards																C	C/I				
DB design																C	C/I	C	C	C	
FCIM																I	I	I	I	I	
Dialogue Specifications																			C	C	I
Program Specifications																					C
Non-SSADM products																					
PID	I	I				I										I					
Feasibility Report	I	I				I										I					
Installation HCI Standards														I						I	

C = Product created
U = Product updated
I = Product used as input

* In step 350 all products might change

285

TWO

ALTERNATIVE REPRESENTATIONS OF ENTITY LIFE HISTORIES

In SSADM Entity Life Histories are depicted by the use of Jackson diagrams. There are, however, many different notations that can be used to represent an Entity Life History. For example:

1. Regular Expressions
2. Jackson diagrams
3. Event Flow Diagrams
4. State Transition Diagrams
5. Finite state automata

Indeed, it is possible to prove mathematically that the notations are equivalent. For a proof of this see, for example, Hopcroft and Ullmann (1979). The purpose of this appendix is to take a simple example and see how it might be represented using each of the notations.

Let us start off with Jackson. Figure A2.1 depicts a simple example of an Entity Life History using this notation This is the standard representation of an Entity Life History in SSADM. It states that in the life of the (unnamed) entity, either events a or b will happen first, followed by event c, followed by zero or more occurrences of event d, with event e rounding things off. Any Jackson diagram can be represented as a regular expression. The regular expression corresponding to Figure A2.1 is given in equation (A2.1).

$$(a + b)cd^*e \qquad \text{(A2.1)}$$

Figure A2.2 shows the corresponding Event Flow Diagram.

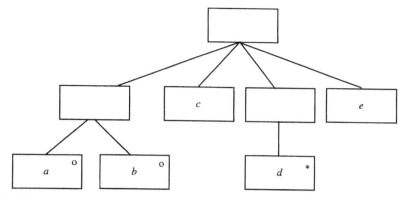

Fig. A2.1   Jackson structure

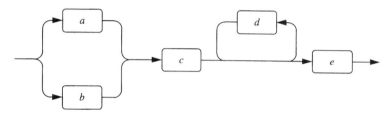

Fig. A2.2   Event Flow Diagram

State Transition Diagrams and finite state automata take a slightly different approach. In both of these we concentrate upon the state of an entity after an event has occurred. Thus we can write S_1 as the state of the entity after event a, S_2 as the state after event b, etc.

Writing S_0 as the initial state of the entity, the state transition diagram looks as in Fig. A2.3. It is fairly self-evident what this is saying. If the entity is in state S_3, event d and event d only will move it to state S_4. The extra circle around S_5 indicates that it is a final state. Those fully conversant with standard SSADM will recognize these states as the values that can be taken by the state indicators following the various events.

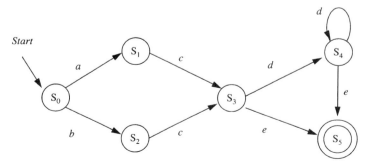

Fig. A2.3   State Transition Diagram

Finally, note that there is not a unique state transition diagram equivalent to a given regular expression, but that there is a minimal diagram. Figure A2.4 shows the minimal solution for our example. It is equivalent to the previous state transition diagram. Obviously, the meaning of the states has now changed. S_1 now denotes the state of the entity after event a or b. (Interestingly, this approach bears some resemblance to the concept of 'optimized state indicators' as introduced as an option in SSADM Version 4.2.)

Finally, a finite state automaton is merely the mathematical formalization of a State Transition Diagram. It is defined as a 5-tuple $(Q, q_0, \sum, \delta, F)$ where Q is a set of states, $q_0 \in Q$ is a start state, $\sum$ is a set called the alphabet, $\delta : Q \times \sum \to Q$ is a mapping and $F \subseteq Q$ is a set of final states. The finite state automaton corresponding to our initial example is shown in equation (A2.2).

The 5-tuple $(Q, q_0, \sum, \delta, F)$ where

$$Q = \{S_0, \ldots, S_5\} \qquad q_0 = S_0$$

$$\sum = \{a, b, c, d, e\} \qquad F = \{S_5\}$$

and $\delta : \sum \times Q \to Q$ is defined by

$$\begin{aligned} \delta(a, S_0) &= S_1 & \delta(d, S_3) &= S_4 \\ \delta(b, S_0) &= S_2 & \delta(d, S_4) &= S_4 \\ \delta(c, S_1) &= S_3 & \delta(e, S_3) &= S_5 \\ \delta(c, S_2) &= S_3 & \delta(e, S_4) &= S_5 \end{aligned}$$

$$(A2.2)$$

As far as the practical use of these notations is concerned, we can obviously rule out regular expressions and finite state automata. State Transition Diagrams are useful if we are interested in the state of an entity between events. If, however, we wish to concentrate on events and the possible ordering of events, it becomes a choice between Jackson diagrams and Event Flow Diagrams. Each of these approaches has advantages and disadvantages.

Event Flow Diagrams are easy to produce and I believe are more likely to be intelligible to users. There is an economy of symbols in the notation, in that on each diagram there is only the one box for each event. Also the diagrams are more intuitive than Jackson diagrams. The flows are reminiscent of railway tracks and following the diagrams is like predicting where the train will go. On the negative side, solutions appear to be non-unique. Different analysts looking at the same problem can often come up with diagrams which, although topologically equivalent, might look radically

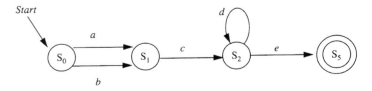

Fig. A2.4   Minimal State Transition Diagram

different. Also, without care and without a certain amount of redrafting the diagrams can look somewhat messy.

Analysts using Jackson diagrams, however, tend to produce apparently similar solutions to the same problem. Jackson structures are also used for program design and many people believe that it is only a small step from a Jackson Entity Life History to a program. So small is this step that they believe it should be possible for programs to be automatically generated by a CASE tool, many of which support the technique. I have yet to hear anyone make similar claims for Event Flow Diagrams. On the other hand, it has to be said that many analysts find Jackson diagrams extremely difficult to produce. Learning to draw legal Jackson structures can take considerable time and proficiency only comes with practice and experience. Indeed, such is the apprehension that this technique engenders in some practitioners that quite a few projects have been known to omit Entity Life Histories altogether. A second problem is that a Jackson diagram may contain many extra structure boxes. These are in addition to the boxes depicting the events and the entity. Such a situation does not make for easy reading. A third problem is that a small change in the logic of the problem often leads to a complete restructuring of the diagrams. Finally Jackson diagrams have been used in SSADM for over a decade and there is little evidence that they are easily understood by users.

Rather than placing all one's faith in any one of these techniques, it is as well to be aware that they are all tackling the same problem, and employ the one which proves to be the most useful in any particular situation.

INDEX